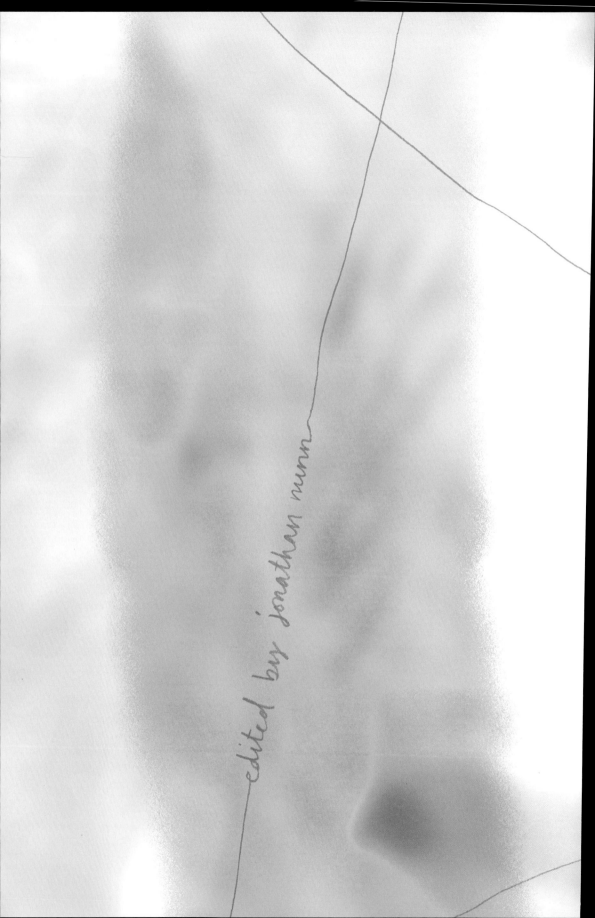

edited by jonathan nunn

london feeds itself

open cities

A few months ago, I arrived at a vegetarian Gujarati restaurant a fortnight early for a lunch date with a friend. I had written the date down wrong, scheduling our catch up optimistically. I am fond of this friend and love their company. We meet regularly to discuss everything except the thing we both do, which is write. Instead, we talk about things that interest us, from food to music to skateboarding to the expanse of the sea, leading out to the point where the line between the water and the sky becomes undefined. When we were discussing when to meet, they had given me dates so far in the future, I felt a bit of despondency at having to wait so long to see them.

Which is how I ended up at this restaurant two weeks early. It was empty, both inside and out, so I sat outside, reading a comic, checking my phone as the hour approached. Eventually, I moved inside, as the shade of the courtyard I was in had created a cold through-draft. I'm not so acclimatised to the ways of the English that I sat outside at every opportunity: when it wasn't raining; sometimes when it actually was raining.

When I moved inside, I gave my friend's name – he had made the reservation. It was needless. There was no one else here. I couldn't tell if the confusion was because of my insistence on the reservation, given that it was a Tuesday, or because they couldn't find it. I remembered that my friend had sent me a screengrab of the reservation and when I brought it up on my phone, to see if there was a reference number, I noticed the date.

I smiled at the confused manager and said, Oh, I'm early. She asked how early. Two weeks, I said, and she laughed efficiently. A joke had been made but she had a restaurant to run. Expecting me to leave out of embarrassment, she started looking down at her tablet, scrolling through various screens.

Can I have a table, please? I asked.

Eating by yourself gives an opportunity to take in where you are. The places we eat at represent more than a meal. Whether it's a kitchen table, a community space or a restaurant that has been well reviewed in your favourite food column, a food space can tell you so much about a city. And London revels in having many of these spaces.

I slowly made my way through a series of small dishes and ended by ordering gobi 65 (I'm not a dessert guy – I like to finish savoury). I watched the rhythms of the staff, the various photos that threw back to the owner's heritage, the strange mix of sporting equipment and medals that took up corner shelves. In the forty or so minutes I was in that restaurant, a fortnight early for a friend date I was excited about, I realised that each meal gives a sense of home, that each restaurant or food space has some semblance of how the owners grew up, however small it was. As a still moment, where I existed only for my own company, thoughts and expectations, I realised I rarely do this. As writers, so much of our job is to notice, to curate, to omit and to spotlight and slow down time. That is what the writers of the essays in this collection do, and by doing so, they give you glimpses into the worlds, lives, heritages and, most importantly, *people* who make up this fine city and eat in it.

After the meal, I thanked my hosts, paid, and said I would see them in a few weeks. The manager asked whether I'd be ordering anything again. I said I would see, and apologised again, even though I had nothing to worry about. I noticed, above the bar, a small mandap, a homespun one, and I knew, in that moment, who these people were and how this place was, for them, a home of sorts.

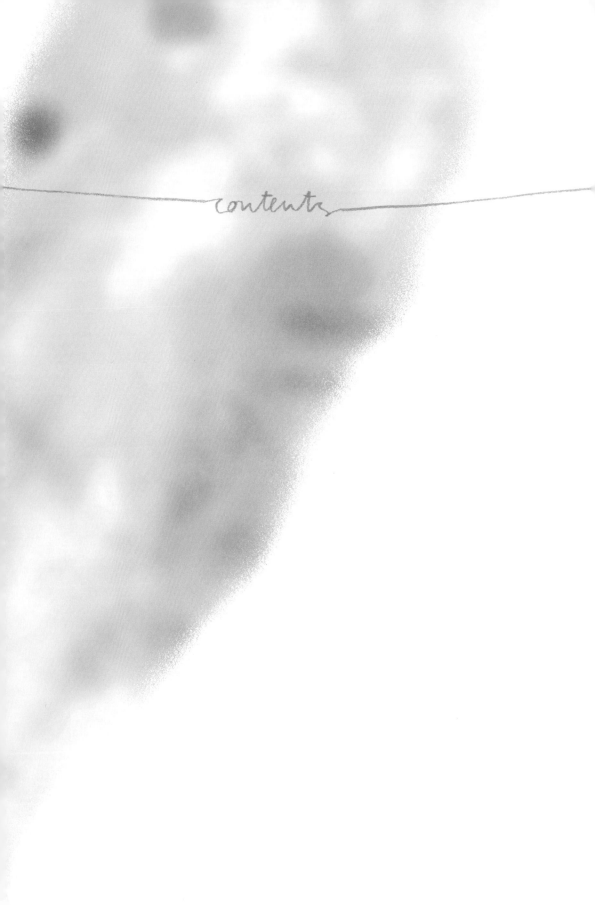

contents

introduction

london eats itself

Is it possible to write a food book through architecture? Or, rather, an architecture book through food?

The two are not natural bedfellows at first glance. My initial thoughts on what a 'food and architecture' book might look like, in order of when they came to me, were: 1) a kind of urban food systems book, already done so well by writer-architects like Carolyn Steel; 2) something about grand dining rooms, art deco cafes and listed pie and mash shops that would please precisely no one; and 3) whatever it is that Jonathan Meades does. Yet ten Owen Hatherley books and a quick glance at the Wikipedia entry on architecture later, I realised that everything about London and food that interests me fits into this seemingly niche intersection, and I sketched out the bare-bones framing for the book you have in your hands: 25 chapters about 25 different buildings, structures and public amenities in which various aspects of London's vernacular food culture can be found, seen through the eyes of food writers, architecture writers, journalists, activists, and even one MP. Each chapter has some lateral relationship to the chapters that surround it, although you can read them in any order you like, choosing to enter or exit the city via The Port or The Airport.

There are no purely historical pieces in this book and, apart from in the very first essay on The Port, there is no talk of ghosts (unless it is to exorcise them) or psychogeography (in fact, the word 'liminal' has been banned). I am, as are all of the writers in this book, interested in London as it is now, how we eat and live today; when history is invoked it is done so to find out where the city is going and how quickly, to track London's velocity as it spreads outwards in radial pulses, seeing where kinetic energy has been transformed and stored as potential energy, and vice versa. Institutional food – hospitals, schools, prisons – has for the most part been avoided; these essays are about places where good food exists *because of*, not in spite of, the urban conditions that surround it.

But what type of urban conditions? The architecture writer Ian Nairn once remarked of Sacred Heart Secondary School (just round the corner from where I live in Camberwell), that 'you can get along from day to day without masterpieces, but you can't get along without this kind of quiet humanity'. The chapters of this book are about the spaces and food that get us through the day-to-day; they are about the quiet humanity, not the masterpieces. And yet, London is a city seemingly obsessed with masterpieces. It is intent on getting more grand, more beautiful, more expensive, more masterful, more, more, more. London consumes the rest of the country, but it is also an autophagic city – self consuming. 'London: the city that ate itself' was the headline to a perceptive 2015 *Observer* article by the paper's architecture critic Rowan Moore – a city where 'anything distinctive is converted into property value', where working-class markets are shut, replaced with cookie-cutter street food placed on pseudo-public property; where food production is being shunted to its peripheries or out of the city altogether; where community centres are shutting and food banks are rising; where new restaurants open just to be a notch on the landlord's bedpost. If Orwell's vision of the future was a boot stamping on a human face forever, then I have an even more chilling one: a Franco Manca opening in your neighbourhood, soon.

The title of this book, *London Feeds Itself*, is not intended to suggest that London is self-sufficient, or that it is a Singaporean city state (in fact, the idea that London is somehow innately different and disconnected from the country that surrounds it is the source of so much that is wrong with the city), but to offer an opposing vision of the capital to the vertigos of finance, house prices and property portfolios that are symptoms of its autophagy. It is also a simple statement of fact. London feeds itself, and it does so in its own unusual ways – in its warehouses, parks, church halls, mosques, community centres, and even its baths: spaces where monetary transaction is peripheral or even completely absent.

london plays itself

Originally, this book wasn't going to cover restaurants at all. Imagine it: a whole book about London food culture without once mentioning the R word! It would be a statement, at least. Alas, I lost my nerve in the end, but will attempt to explain why.

What is the most-read urbanist writing in Britain today? Outside of the few hundred weirdos (me included) who keep buying Iain Sinclair books and who walk round the North Circular for fun, the answer for most people is restaurant criticism. Unlike almost every other branch of criticism – except, notably, architecture – restaurant writing is impossible to extract from place: whether it's El Bulli perched on the coast of the Balearic Sea or a cafe on an industrial estate, the review starts with the journey there: where it is, who lives there, and how its location might be surprising (a small plates restaurant run by a white chef opening in Peckham in 2011) or typical (a small plates restaurant run by a white chef opening in Peckham in 2022). This makes restaurant criticism far more important than a list of things that went into someone's mouth: it is writing that, by its very nature – in the decisions its authors make on where to write about, and how to write about it – is political.

In Thom Andersen's 2003 essay documentary, *Los Angeles Plays Itself*, the director interrogates the use of Los Angeles as a backdrop to films. Los Angeles, Andersen argues, is cinema's hidden protagonist, its buildings, streets and monuments reconfigured, spat out and often disrespected into forms that resemble a version of the city unrecognisable to those who live there. Andersen reserves much of his ire for Hollywood location scouts, who lazily use the wealth of modernist architecture scattered across the surrounding hills and valleys as the lairs of villains and gangsters, subverting the buildings' utopian intentions and usage. Yes, Los Angeles might be a character in a film, but it is just that – a character. It is unwittingly playing a version of itself that does not exist.

I think of Andersen's film when I read restaurant criticism in British broadsheet papers because London is usually the hidden protagonist of the review. Prior to March 2020, when restaurants temporarily shut, I looked at the last hundred reviews from eight national broadsheets: 68% were for London restaurants, with 20% of them in Mayfair and Chelsea and another 20% in Soho and Fitzrovia. That's 40% of the entire country's restaurant reviews taken up by a few square miles of the most expensive real estate in central London. Given that the readership of these papers lives largely outside of London, the reviews function much like Hollywood's depictions of Los Angeles: a kind of light entertainment; a satire for those who have no intention of going. The object of the satire may vary: oligarchs, idiotic tourists, rich Arabs, East London hipsters, whatever nonsensical idea some chef has concocted to appeal to insufferable London foodies. But the upshot of this is that the London depicted in reviews – neophilic, absurd, infinitely affluent – bears little resemblance to the city as a whole.

Yet when restaurant critics do eventually venture outside of the city centre, the effect is even more ruinous. The satire, having no obvious target to latch on to, moves to focus on the neighbourhoods themselves: South London is described as 'stabby', Elephant and Castle where you 'might pick up a nasty skin condition' – whole areas written off as 'shitholes' while Britain's food critics pretend they deserve the George Cross for getting on the Thameslink. These reviews have a genuinely pernicious effect: they become handmaidens of developer-led gentrification and displacement. Brixton and Peckham – two significantly Black neighbourhoods – have taken the brunt of this; here, restaurants and street food ventures are written up as new, exciting phenomena that did not exist there beforehand, with what was already flourishing there completely ignored. House prices go up and these restaurants – mainly with PR, mainly on property in the process of being developed – proliferate. The review can be as powerful an advertisement that an area has *changed* as anything in an estate agent's window.

Restaurants, for good or for ill, are integral to London's food ecosystem, as well as its financial markets and sense of civic pride, but I am interested in what restaurant writing looks like when it is not allied to PR, profit and property, or anchored to hierarchies of taste forged by colonialism. So for each essay, I have written an accompanying guide to restaurants which share the theme of that chapter. Some of these categorisations are obvious and geographical (restaurants in Chinatowns, restaurants on the Old Kent Road) although others (restaurants by bodies of water, restaurants to go to after a sauna) are less intuitive. Together they amount to a patchwork of London's peripheries, of neighbourhoods where restaurants serve working-class and diaspora communities sculpted by the city's role as a former imperial capital, where restaurants fulfil a function of remembrance and transform the city into other cities, or meld with the city to create something that is uniquely its own. I hope that London appears once again as a character – although this time, one with an agency of its own.

london feeds itself

In the 1966 *Time* article 'Great Britain: You Can Walk Across It On the Grass', writer Piri Halasz introduced the theory that every city has its ten-year epoch, and that the 1960s were being defined by London's resurgence as a countercultural capital. 'More important than all the other changes is the fact that the center, the heart of London, has gravitated slowly westward to the haunts of the city's new elite, just as it did in centuries gone by', she says. Tracking the shift from the City to Westminster, she placed London's new centre 'somewhere in Mayfair, between the green fields and orators of Hyde Park and the impish statue of Eros in Piccadilly Circus.'

Where is London's centre today? Some might place it back east, in a taqueria in Shoreditch, but it's truer to say that London is now a city without a cultural centre; it is polyvalent, with multiple centres located in ever-expanding concentric circles emanating out from its geographic centre point. What was once the centre is being pushed out to the peripheries. In an inversion of Paris (where Paris is always the arrondissements, and everything outside of the arrondissements is not-Paris), what is in the London suburbs increasingly feels more like London than what is in its core.

It is no coincidence, then, that many of the places in this book are located outside the city centre, nor that the buildings and structures discussed have been traditionally viewed as marginal. Yes, there are more exciting culinary things going on in Ilford, Wembley and Hounslow than Soho and Mayfair, but there are also libraries and baths serving food on industrial estates, fiestas in suburban parks and in church halls, meals cooked in community centres and gurdware, food produced in railway arches and viaducts. In a city where every inch of land is monetisable, squeezed like a near-empty toothpaste tube, these are creative, inspired uses of space, with each community becoming their own Thomas Müller – a raumdeuter – a space interpreter.

If this is a book about space, it is also about time. There are multiple villains in this book – international developers, the City of London Corporation, landlords, the British Library cafe, the pandemic and, in the case of Jeremy Corbyn's allotment, Barnet council – but the final boss is time. It is time that turns the city we recognise into one we don't: the Peckham of lost time remembered in The Arcades (p104), or the tabula rasa vandalism wrought at Elephant and Castle in The Housing Estate (p86). These spaces sometimes force time to continually repeat itself: the second lives of Kurdish warehouses, the spinning water wheel of history powered by the River Kilburn (p194), the cycle of immigration that takes place in a Hampstead Garden Suburb synagogue (p56). Often these spaces reverse time, taking those who have lost spaces back to their past: a lost Damascus (p122), a lost Hong Kong (p14), a lost moment in time in pre-partition India (p138).

To write about the city is to be in a constant state of grief for the spaces we lose to time: Elephant and Castle's bingo hall, Chinatown, Edmonton Green (p96), the arepa stand that became a Sports Direct, the Kurdish community centre that became a Beyond Retro. But the best spaces seem to exist outside time itself, defying the financialisation of time that measures out leisure in thimble-sized portions: the atemporality of the New Docklands sauna (p64), a plot of land for growing food, a community centre cafe, the way both a park and a viaduct can shield a space from the usual sense of London-time encroaching on it, spaces that constantly regenerate to house new flow, new communities – sticking points, as writer Rebecca May Johnson calls them – in the endless river of capital that courses through the city. It is not a surprise that all these spaces are, in their own ways, precarious, besieged by time and in constant need of protection.

Velocity is, of course, space over time plus direction, and everything in London is expanding outwards and upwards at a pace that seems almost unstoppable. London *is* eating itself, but this is neither irreversible or inevitable. Italo Calvino warned us about cities being 'the inferno of the living' in his 1972 book *Invisible Cities*. London is a city as infernal as any other, but Calvino also gave us the cheat codes: to 'seek and learn to recognize who and what, in the midst of inferno, are not inferno, then make them endure, give them space'. London is feeding itself too. This book hopes to recognise the places that feed us and, with your help, to make them endure: to give them space.

My son asked, 'Grandfather, where is Hong Kong's Chinatown?' My father replied, 'The entire city is its Chinatown, and no other Chinatown in the world is comparable.'

William Poon, owner of Poon's Restaurant, formerly of Chinatown

It starts, as things often do, with a cup of tea.

During the first half of the 19th century the British Empire crept further east under the cloak of an unregulated corporation called the East India Company which controlled an entire subcontinent from a single anonymous office on Leadenhall Street. As tea became the stimulant of empire, the ignominy of having a trade deficit with China provoked the company to resort to drug-pushing, initiating the first of two Opium Wars. The result was the beginning of China's century of humiliation, the cession of the Island of Hong Kong to the UK, and the establishment of five treaty ports – Xiamen, Guangzhou, Fuzhou, Ningbo and, most importantly, Shanghai – where foreign trade could be enforced at gunpoint on terms amenable to the British. To facilitate trade, particularly of opium – which vacillated between the British Raj and China, funnelled through the ports of Hong Kong and Shanghai – the British set up a bank: The Hongkong and Shanghai Banking Corporation.

While the defeated Qing Dynasty attempted to crack down on widespread emigration, it was through these ports, now swelling with wealth, that its ban could be flouted. Chinese seamen escaped, borne through the sea on ships, and made new lives at new ports.

In this moment the germs of two powerful ideas were born: the modern conception of Hong Kong, and the existence of Chinatowns.

jonathan nunn

For the last 150 years, the cities of London, Hong Kong and Shanghai have formed three corners of an unbreakable triangle, where the fates and fortunes at one point necessarily affect the fates and fortunes of the others, forming unequal shapes – isosceles, scalene – but always connected. These cities are linked by their relationship to water – indeed, their very names refer to their status as ports: 'fragrant harbour' and 'on the sea' respectively. London was built on still and flowing water: if the Thames kept the city fed, the port made it fat, spreading the rump of its wealth horizontally over Rotherhithe, Limehouse and Millwall, shifting the entire gravity of the city eastwards. Docks were cut across the river where it spiralled in great loop-de-loops, acting as the biggest ingredient-storage cupboards the world had ever seen – East India Docks for tea, West India for sugar, Tobacco for tobacco. It was here in the Port of London, enriched and swollen through Chinese tea, that many of the first Chinese sailors decided to jump ship.

Chinatown turns the triangle into a tetrahedron, forming a central fourth point that can only be understood in relation to the other three – for all Chinatowns that exist in this world are reflections of reflections of Hong Kong and the treaty ports. They are reconstructions of a city's memory, made visible through signs and architecture: mazes of traditional and simplified characters, statues, street names and interventions in the landscape. If the original Chinatown was Hong Kong itself, one of its first mirror images was at Limehouse, near the West India Docks.

In the title cards to D. W. Griffith's 1919 film *Broken Blossoms*, Limehouse is introduced as 'where the Orient squats at the portals of the West', while an eerie stone pyramid by the Church of St Anne's was fictionalised by the novelist Sax Rohmer as the secret portal to his character Fu Manchu's hideout, with Rohmer tapping into feverish conspiracy theories of a Chinese Moriarty who controlled crime in the docks (the extremely unsalacious truth was that the pyramid was designed by Nicholas Hawksmoor). Meanwhile, in a foreshadowing of what restaurant critics would do to Peckham in 100 years' time, journalists visited Limehouse and printed ever more outlandish stories about Chinese sailors pushing opium on Londoners: a sure sign of a guilty conscience.

In reality, the Limehouse Chinatown, even at its zenith, was only two disjointed streets of houses and small businesses, a tiny conurbation divided by language, port and, ultimately, West India Dock Road: the sailors from Shanghai located on Pennyfields, and those from Hong Kong and Guangzhou on Limehouse Causeway. In 1932, there were around 20–30 Chinese-owned businesses, with very few of them based around food: tobacconists, launderettes, bookmakers, a workers' club, a three-tiered restaurant called Dai Ting Lao, two grocers. The grocers sold imported goods and homemade lap cheong – Hong Kong-style cured sausage that could be made on-site – and doubled up as herbalists, selling medicine and remedies to those who distrusted Western doctors. The only visual cues that indicated you might be in a Chinatown were names on doors; characters on archways that ran counter-clockwise; inscriptions on walls; and a handful of street names: Canton (Guangzhou) Street, Nankin Street and Amoy (Xiamen) Place.

By the time King Street was renamed Ming Street in 1938, Limehouse was already in decline – the damage wrought during the Blitz, slum clearances, and the movement of the major docks to Tilbury had all suffocated it. Chinatown was dead, and had to be reborn elsewhere.

East & West Chinese restaurant, Limehouse, 1955
© Henry Grant Collection / Museum of London

In 1951, the decline of Chinese restaurants in London was unexpectedly arrested by Herbert Morrison's Festival of Britain, a celebration of British art, science and technology which was meant to coincide with the 100-year anniversary of the Great Exhibition, but which also happened to mark both the start of Britain's geopolitical twilight and the end of China's century of humiliation. The cookery writer Deh-Ta Hsiung remembers how the festival brought a huge wave of visitors into central London, and that the handful of centrally-located Chinese restaurants were revitalised by a new crowd who, in the festival's spirit, embraced the modernity of Chinese food.

The Soho 'Chinatown' we see in central London today almost never was one; in another universe it could have been an Indiatown. Like Limehouse, it centred around two distinct streets – Wardour and Lisle – with Indian restaurants and grocers on the former, and Chinese on the latter. The names of the treaty ports were not found on street names, but on restaurants and grocers: the Canton in Newport Place, the Hong Kong Emporium on Rupert Street, the Nanking on Charlotte Street. The Bombay Emporium in Leicester Place started the Rajah brand, but also popularised the Amoy brand, catering for the new market. This Chinatown, unlike Limehouse, was centred around food, which had the effect of bringing outsiders and tourists in. By 1970, Gerrard Street was being talked up in the *New York Times* as a new Chinatown, with another article counting seven restaurants (and two hairdressers, a beauty salon, a travel agency, a supermarket and two car-hire firms) on the street alone.

When a city names something and makes it official, its purpose is always to monetise it, to make coherent something which was never meant to be resolved. In this sense, the media and government approved creation of Chinatown was somewhat cynical; only two years before, the Commonwealth Immigrants Act had put restrictions on the right of Hongkongers to reside in the UK, while those who were already here and worked in Chinatown were met with racism from diners who often refused to pay, and from police who denied them protection. Despite the tourists, the main purpose of Chinatown was a defensive: to bring in all the amenities a community needed in a city where Cantonese culture was seen as marginal.

By the time the city discovered what it had, the internet had replaced the need for most of Chinatown's book and film shops, while once-vital grocery stores could be found in the suburbs, such as Barnet, where many of the old wave of Cantonese immigrants now lived. Once the streets were renamed, this time in Chinese characters, and a stone lion put on Gerrard Street to canonise it, the reason for Chinatown's existence no longer made sense. What was once alive became heritage, a retail opportunity zone; a portfolio to be traded by property developers.

Yet Chinatown is the city's most effective meme because it never quite replicates itself when it moves across ports; there is always a mutation, giving it an unstable definition. The movement of Chinatown from Limehouse to the centre of London didn't just change Chinatown, it also marked a shift in what Chinatown could *mean*. If Limehouse was a Chinatown of the imaginary, spoken in a language meant to be understood by few, the Soho Chinatown was a Chinatown of commerce, speaking to insiders and outsiders alike. Limehouse was a place where Chinese people lived; Soho was where they worked. Both were predicated on a relationship between London, Hong Kong and Shanghai which has *fundamentally* changed. The Chinatowns of the future will be based on a reformulation of the triangle, but they won't look like the Chinatowns of the past.

As the 20th century unscrolled, the Port of Hong Kong overtook the Port of London to become the biggest port in the world, which was then swiftly overtaken by the Port of Shanghai. The city of Hong Kong switched from British rule to Chinese. In his landmark book *Why the West Rules – For Now*, historian Ian Morris argues that it was the moment when Britain assumed the sovereignty of Hong Kong Island which decisively swung the finely tuned balance of global power between the East and the West to the East End of London. It has now started to swing back: future historians with a sense of humour might look at the development of Haidilao, China's biggest hotpot chain, which started in Jianyang in Sichuan in 1994, opened in Shanghai in 2008, Hong Kong in 2017, and in 2019 created its first European outlet, in London's Chinatown.

Haidilao reveals the shape of Chinatowns to come. China is no longer exporting labour or people; it is exporting its own chains. Therefore, Chinatowns are no longer reflections of a past Hong Kong or Canton but of the freshly created state-level new areas, and the

most advanced cities in the world: Shanghai and the city-state
of Chongqing. Walk through Soho and you will find more bubble
tea shops and dessert parlours than dim sum restaurants, while
Bloomsbury and Spitalfields have been reshaped to accommodate
the on-trend tastes of mainland Chinese students. Walk through
Limehouse today and you will find little sign of Chinatown, although
you can still walk down Canton Street, Nankin Street and Amoy
Place – now filled with council housing built for the Festival of
Britain, courtyards, and walkways that feel like a municipal take on
an Oxbridge quad. You may search for the only two names missing –
Hong Kong and Shanghai – until you look up, towards the metallic
skyline of Canary Wharf, and there they are, adorning the Norman
Foster-designed HSBC building.

The wealth of the Docklands now imposes itself vertically, in glass
towers and spires grown from the scorched earth of London's former
port at the Isle of Dogs. It is here, according to the 2011 census, that
the biggest proportion of people in London who identify as Chinese
now reside – around 15 times the city average. It has become a kind
of proto-Chinatown, not an enclave or ghetto, but diffused throughout the entire docks in an area where Chinese people now live and
work: Dongbei hotpots in Canary Wharf, Sichuan barbecue at All
Saints, a Chinese grocers that delivers meals via Deliveroo in Millwall,
a warehouse that sells fresh tofu in Greenwich, a Sichuan restaurant
in a North Greenwich retail park. You might have bet good money
on this being the Chinatown of the future: in 2013, then-mayor Boris
Johnson announced that the Royal Albert Dock development would
once again become 'arteries of trade and commerce', funded by
the Chinese-owned ABP to the tune of £1.7 billion in order to turn
it into a commercial and financial hub to rival Canary Wharf, an
investment deal presided over by Xi Jinping on his visit to London
in 2015. In return, the Canary Wharf Group has invested in Xiong'An,
one of the latest state-level new areas in Hebei province.

Yet history is never thrown away; it is always recycled. Not all of
the old Cantonese population of the Docklands left: in the middle
of this proto-Chinatown of capital, there is an older, vestigial
Chinatown, of takeaways that still serve jar jow, a uniquely Limehouse
take on sweet-and-sour pork; dim sum restaurants in Holiday Inns,
on floating docks, in storage warehouses in the shadow of the ExCeL
Centre, overlooking London City Airport, in dining rooms the size

of aircraft hangers. Their numbers are being swelled by the biggest planned migration Britain has seen since Windrush, caused by China trying to turn Hong Kong into another Shanghai – Hongkongers on British National Overseas passports, affluent and middle-aged, who crave the security of suburbia and watch YouTube videos by British-Cantonese influencers titled 'TOP PLACE TO LIVE IN THE UK – healthiest town, Wokingham'.

It may well be that the Chinatowns of the future will look like Britain's own state-led new areas, like Milton Keynes, or Sutton – one of London's blandest suburbs, where many Hongkongers are currently choosing to settle, opening nostalgic Western-influenced bakeries and cha chaan tengs unique to Hong Kong in memory of a city that has been lost to them. Meanwhile, the Royal Albert Dock development is a ghost town, dormant if not dead, with threats made by the Greater London Authority to remove ABP from the project. Instead of a boom in 'trade and commerce', the mainland Chinese restaurants of the Docklands may well see a decline from a sudden vacuum of Chinese students and professions.

The triangle is now finely poised, a perfect equilateral for the first time since 1839. Whatever route history takes, there will once again be a Chinatown formed by London, Hong Kong and Shanghai, built over the roads and waterways that still bear the names of the cities' ghosts.

De-Ta Hsiung interviewed by Anna Chen and Mukti Jain Campion, Chinese in Britain Interviews

Seed, John, 'Limehouse Blues: Looking for Chinatown in the London Docks, 1900-1940', *History Workshop Journal, Issue 62*, 2006

Interview with William Poon, China Exchange, *The Making of Chinatown*, 2019

THE SIX CHINATOWNS

Until the late 20th century, the precondition of a Chinatown was artifice; a Chineseness signified through ornamental architectural interventions like pagodas, stone lions, curled eaves, patterned tiles and pi-shaped gateways. This did not start in Hong Kong or any Chinese city, but in San Francisco, when the earthquake of 1906 decimated the 24 blocks that made up its nascent Chinatown. To stop the whole district from being relocated by the municipal government (who resented its central position but also relied on the Chinese traders), the community hired a group of white American architects who rebuilt Chinatown as a theme park, not to be unseen as another working-class, immigrant enclave, but to be claimed as part of the city's visible warp and weft: somewhere to be visited. The new Chinatown was such a success that it not only secured the location of San Francisco's Chinatown, but its signs and aesthetic proliferated into Vancouver, New York, Melbourne, Toronto, Washington and London.

There was a need for a new Chinatown before the destruction of Limehouse in the Blitz, but this did expedite its move to Soho in the 1950s and 60s, when papers noted Gerrard Street as Chinatown's ground zero. This was a Chinatown as we commonly understand it – an area of Chinese commerce that is at once separate from and a part of the city; made official and then finally accepted onto the map as 'Chinatown'. It is a phenomenon that depends on the creative and defensive use of space by a community with few resources.

That era of Chinatown is over; you could pin-point its death with the handover in 1997, or with the economic rise of China, or with the move of all non-restaurant businesses away from Chinatown. With the advent of the internet, which means Chinese culture can be accessed elsewhere, Chinatown has become what it always threatened to be: a theme park of restaurants. Meanwhile, other forms of Chinatowns are springing up elsewhere, in places where Chinese people actually live. You might be able to argue that there are, including Soho and the Docklands, six Chinatowns in London – a restaurant Chinatown, a suburban Chinatown, a student Chinatown, a housing Chinatown – all containing different groups and classes of people, and therefore a different type of restaurant. (Six, that is, if you want to call them Chinatowns; either we need a new definition, or we might have to accept that soon, Chinatown won't exist at all.)

SOHO
THE TIKTOK CHINATOWN

The Soho Chinatown was canonised as late as the 1980s, when the pavilion was added to Newport Court, along with bilingual street names – a sure sign of a community whose heyday is over (see Brick Lane). Since the neighbourhood's takeover by Shaftesbury PLC, one of the most powerful landlords in central London, the pavilion has gone, and in its place is a proliferation of eating options: no longer just Cantonese food but bubble tea shops, dessert parlours, Korean hot dogs, Filipino ice cream. These cater to two new key demographics: teenagers from the Home Counties, who crawl from place to place following viral TikTok videos, and Chinese students from the mainland. If the best of old Chinatown is located in the chaise-longue luxury comfort dishes at CAFE TPT (especially the Macau pork chop rice) then the one place that epitomises the new Chinatown it's FOOD HOUSE, a restaurant specialising in cuisines from central China where everyone inside, including the waiters, seem to have just emerged from Dover Street Market dressed head to toe in Comme.

QUEENSWAY
THE RESTAURANT CHINATOWN

The Chinatown of Queensway has historically been the alternative Chinatown in the west – smaller, but with higher quality restaurants and a character of its own. Lotus House, which was opened in Bayswater in 1958, may have been the first Chinese takeaway in London: so large were its Dishoom-like queues that someone clever reasoned that people might just like to take home their food instead. Queensway has preserved its Cantonese character better than Soho Chinatown has, but it has also long been in stasis, with no markers of being a Chinatown except for restaurants, and only a few remaining at that (the last was New Fortune Cookie in 2011, bringing the total up to six). The best of these is probably still MANDARIN KITCHEN, a former Italian disco turned-Cantonese seafood restaurant that introduced the city to lobster noodles. The decor (which now has the look of a luxe aquarium) has changed, but the noodles haven't: they still emerge from the kitchen and are portioned out with the same theatricality as a canard à la presse from an old-school French bistro.

BLOOMSBURY
THE STUDENT CHINATOWN

From 2009–2019, the number of Chinese students in the UK doubled, with its London contingent representing an economy on par with a small European principality. LSE, UCL, Kings College and SOAS all have campuses located in or abutting Bloomsbury, which has slowly become London's tertiary dining destination for East Asian students, with around a dozen regional Chinese restaurants on New Oxford Street, Red Lion Street and Southampton Row alone, and just as many Japanese and Korean restaurants again. A more casual type of restaurant dominates here – communal hotpot cafes, skewer joints, do-it-yourself noodles – with Sichuan, Hunan, Jiangnan, Henan, Dongbei and Shaanxi cuisines all represented at restaurants like CHANG'S NOODLE and MASTER WEI. The restaurant that epitomises the Bloomsbury scene most is JINCHENG ALLEY, a restaurant decked out in gold and white like a chilli-scented Louis Vuitton store where you can order Sichuan-style suckling pig from a menu shaped like a fan.

BARNET
THE SUBURBAN CHINATOWN

In his 2008 book *Chinatown in Britain*, academic Wai-ki E. Luk describes the phenomenon of satellite Chinatowns 'driven by forces of enclave decentralisation'. As workers get pushed out of the centre, they move into affluent neighbourhoods, transforming the demography of the area and opening new businesses. The area of London this has happened in, Luk argues, is the borough of Barnet, where the first wave of Cantonese immigrants moved, and where Oriental City and Wing Yip marked its western borders. Further north and east, into Barnet proper, you'll now find CHU CHIN CHOW, a neighbourhood Chinese restaurant hiding one of the best Malaysian-Cantonese banquet menus in Zone 5 London: a whole poached chicken, pink flesh and yellow skin like a Battenberg; poon choi; goose feet and abalone; curry buns as big as a WWE wrestler's thigh; and fried chicken with perfectly caramelised wands of lemongrass. That is, of course, if you order in advance, preferably in Cantonese.

SPITALFIELDS
THE HOUSING CHINATOWN

A kind of midway point between the very student-y Bloomsbury Chinatown and the workers' Chinatown of the Docklands, Spitalfields is where the students go if they have a bit of money, or the Canary Wharf set go if they want to escape cabin fever on the Isle of Dogs. The development around the market is driven by the abundance of student housing in the area – after the Soho Chinatown, it probably has the highest concentration of Chinese restaurants in London. NOODLE & BEER on Bell Lane feels like it's been plucked straight out of Chongqing: tian-shui mian – thick udon noodles that look like intertwining serpents strangling Laocoön – are plainly seasoned with a sweet, nutty sauce that focuses the mind on the chewy texture of the noodles. It completely upends the myth that Sichuan cuisine is about aggression and chilli heat – here every dish is harmonious with itself and with the dishes around it.

the church

On a crisp October Sunday in North London, I go for lunch at
Our Lady of Muswell's church hall. The place is packed with a mix of
diners reflecting Muswell Hill's congregation: Goan, Italian, Ugandan,
Brazilian and Portuguese, but the biggest contingent is made up of
Filipinos. They're hard to miss: they staff the doors selling raffle tick-
ets, they're at the buffet table and in the kitchen serving up a spread
of spring rolls, pancit and chicken adobo – traditional fare at Filipino
parties. They're also on stage, DJing and taking turns at the karaoke.
An emcee calls out winning numbers to whoops from the tables.
It's a raucous, celebratory affair, more bingo hall than church hall.

Where the church itself is for solemn rituals, the church *hall* –
usually a one-storey building tucked at the back – is a social space
equipped with a kitchen. These religious spaces, for communal
meals or social gatherings, don't even exist in the Philippines.
Priests' residences and convents are not designed to host village
feasts, instead these are held in civic spaces like the village hall
and the town plaza, or in the homes of the wealthy, who have the

room and resources to host large groups. My father used to drag us, his Manila-born kids, to his home town fiesta in the north of the Philippines in the late 1980s. The annual celebration of St Joseph's feast day was my only experience of a Catholic social – there were performances, a beauty pageant, speeches from politicians and local dignitaries, and dancing to a live band. Paying guests bought tickets to eat catered meals, the highlight being chunks of lechon (hog roast). Meanwhile, townsfolk rubbernecked over the fence to watch the revels of the great and the good.

I saw the fiesta as a living tableau of feudal society – and my family's gnarly history straight out of a telenovela plot line. My paternal grandfather was from a landowning clan with a distinguished ascendant: the town's Spanish parish priest from 1849 until his death in 1878. The priest's partner, Fruta Montemayor, was from the local gentry. I now bear her surname because their children could not take their priest-father's one. On the other side, my paternal grandmother was the daughter of a tenant farmer advocating for a more equitable share of the harvest from the lands they had tilled for centuries. My father grew up in a hut behind the Montemayor ancestral home because his parents defied the social divide in the 1930s. It disturbed me that, in the late 20th century, some of my relatives were feasting inside a plaza while others remained outside.

Catholicism outside of Europe is inextricable from race-class hierarchies imposed by occupying powers, all of which find expression in food and cuisine. *Noli Me Tángere*, the foundational novel of Philippine nationalism written by patriot and Freemason José Rizal, details staple Filipino dishes such as chicken tinola, and the etiquette involved in apportioning it according to social rank: the fleshiest bits were reserved for the friar, who was always served first. Some churches in the Philippines which were built during the Spanish era even used egg whites to bind the masonry – food is literally baked into the foundations of the church. The more I learned about Philippine colonial history and my family's roots, the more conflicted my relationship with the Catholic faith became.

In diasporas, the impulse to find compatriots in a foreign land transcends painful histories and centuries-old divisions. In the Diocese of Westminster, to which I belong by virtue of where I live, there are 212 parishes and 208 schools located north of the Thames and west of the River Lea, counting Irish, Italians, Spanish, Polish, Portuguese, Goans, Filipinos, Latin Americans, and West and South-East Africans as well as old and new immigrants from Hong Kong among its congregations. The mix reflects the flows of migrants to London from European colonies over centuries: first British ones, such as Ireland, Nigeria and the Caribbean; then Spanish and Portuguese, like Brazil, Goa and the Philippines. Filipinos are a relatively recent addition from the 1990s, and many of them are, or were, employed in the health, care and domestic work sectors. Ate Betty, who coordinates Sunday lunch, has been involved in the parish's charity works for about a decade.

Before Filipinos, Goans were the most prominent cluster of migrants in Muswell Hill parish. Many Goans arrived in Britain during the 1960s and 70s from former British colonies in East Africa and, most recently (before Brexit) through Portugal. The extended family of this book's editor, Jonathan Nunn, used to run church hall lunches in Muswell Hill back in the 1990s. He remembers then that the congregation were mainly older Irish and British Catholics, and had to be convinced to eat foods completely new to them, like xacuti and sorpotel (they were eventually converted). Today, many of these family members, now elderly themselves, are the ones eating new cuisines at the lunches, although they're easier to convince; the Filipino-Goan connection is evident not only through their shared religion but also in their food: Sorpotel and dinuguan, for example, Goan and Filipino dishes respectively, both contain pork and offal stewed in blood and vinegar. Some of these links antedate the Spanish and Portuguese imperial projects and were forged in the maritime and trading routes of pre-colonial South-East Asia.

Our Lady of Muswell's Sunday lunches are part of this global and colonial current; like other London churches, the gatherings attract a unique mixture of migrants based on where they have settled. St Ignatius Church (run by Jesuits) in Stamford Hill hosts breakfast mornings, mostly for Polish and Eastern European people needing legal assistance in the wake of Brexit. There is a weekly mass for Spanish speakers, mirroring the demand from a large community that campaigned for 15 years to preserve the Latin Village hub of markets and food establishments up the road in Seven Sisters Market. Our Lady of Good Counsel in Stoke Newington hosts the Zimbabwean chaplaincy, and along with St Joseph's in Kingsland, runs a food bank in the Hackney area. According to 2020 figures from the Caritas Westminster Food Collective, Catholic churches run around 250 food relief projects in the Westminster Diocese alone. In many communities, these churches – and the church halls attached to them – were the only places that offered food and social interaction during the cruellest stretches of the pandemic.

There is an alternative history of the church in the Philippines, one that shows its potential as a tool for solidarity as well as political struggle. When I was growing up, the Archdiocese of Manila was run by Jaime Cardinal Sin, who was Archbishop of Manila from 1974 to 2003. He was my mother's catechism teacher in Aklan, in the central island cluster of the Philippines. When we went to have my cousins baptised by him at the Archbishop's Palace in the 1980s he welcomed us with his signature greeting: 'Welcome to the House of Sin'.

By broadcasting an appeal for civilians to protect the leaders of a coup attempt, Sin played a critical role in the uprising against the dictator Ferdinand Marcos in 1986, when hundreds of thousands of people converged around the military camps to form a human barrier in what is now known as the EDSA revolution. I started university in the same year and met fellow activists moulded in the tradition of liberation theology. One of my early political mentors was the former priest, Father Edicio de la Torre, founder of Christians for National Liberation, which was an organisation formed of priests and nuns in the anti-Marcos resistance. I had stopped attending church by this time, but my attitude towards religion and politics had broadened into a pluralist, ecumenical tendency – largely under Father Ed's influence.

With this in mind, on a Monday evening in spring, six months after Our Lady of Muswell's Filipino lunch, I venture into Shoreditch to catch the twice-weekly dinner at St Monica's in Hoxton Square. It is a small church squeezed in among the sleek blocks of flats surrounding the green, many of which are fronted by upmarket cafes and bars. The meals are prepared by volunteers of Idia's Community Kitchen, founded by chef Aina Omo-Bare. Aina started on her own in 2017, cooking hot meals and offering them in front of the post office on Hoxton Street, before gaining support among locals, charities and businesses. Three years ago, they started serving food at the weekly drop-in centre coordinated by St Monica's.

The food, the diners and the volunteers are markedly different from those of Muswell Hill's. The menu depends on donations from shops and individuals and is not centred around a particular cuisine. On the two occasions I visit, the spread consists of baked chicken, sausages, pasta, salad, and bread donated by an artisan bakery. Some of the diners are regulars and are greeted by name by the volunteers. These tend to be a mix of older white, Black and Turkish locals; the other noticeable cohort is Polish men. The rest are a mix of schoolchildren and people on their way home from work, plus a couple of international students.

One of the volunteers calls out to a passerby: 'Brother! Come eat!' M is Muslim and is fasting over Ramadan. He used to come for the food and stayed to volunteer; this is the case for many members of the team. 'Understand the power of food to build trust and community,' says Tayo, who works with his sister Aina to run what is now an expanding grass roots organisation. They grew up in Nigeria, today the biggest source of priests for Western countries suffering a clergy shortage in what is known as the 'reverse missionary' phenomenon. 'We don't impose anything on people. St Monica's is heavily involved but religion is not a factor for us; everyone is welcome.' Idia's Community Kitchen now also serves meals in public locations such as Ridley Road market and the West End. Some of the visitors take the food parcels and leave; others stay to eat and chat. 'I have osteoarthritis,' the volunteer cook confides, showing me her fingers. 'I am alone in this country', M says.

At Our Lady of Muswell, I had asked the lady sitting next to me why she comes to this particular church hall – she is originally from Uganda and is not even from this parish. 'For the company,' she responded. When Covid struck, she felt compelled to seek out community gatherings where she could feel connected to others again. None of us are untouched by years of loss and grief, nor by savage cuts that have further impoverished the most vulnerable. These community meals are so far removed from the fiestas of my childhood, and much closer to the spirit of commensality that forms the basis of the Eucharist. 'Take this, all of you, and eat it ... Do this in memory of Me.' The organising principle of Christian worship is a shared meal.

Perhaps this is the lens through which I should now view the faith I was raised in: not as a set of inequalities encased in a colonial shell, or a reminder of bitter divides in my own family's past, but as a flourishing community transformed and animated by the actions of its believers. Communion, after all, is the sharing of bread and presence. For an hour or so, we're all just Londoners eating together.

TAKE THIS AND EAT IT

If you want to get a measure of the distance between Catholicism and Protestantism, just look at their food and buildings. Comparing the architecture of their respective holy seats in his 1966 book *Nairn's London*, writer Ian Nairn described St. Paul's as floating above London, 'serene but not detached – the best kind of night-nurse', while Michelangelo's St Peter's is, he wrote, 'wound around with human passions'. While London's Classical Anglican churches feel unified by the minds of Christopher Wren, John Soane and Nicholas Hawksmoor, all sober spires and transepts, its Catholic ones are a jumble of things. As a child I attended midnight mass at neo-Byzantine Westminster Cathedral (which always seemed an absurd building when compared with the Abbey, even before I read Nairn's assessment of it: 'the difference between actually being and trying-very-hard-to-be'), the imposing brown slab of St Ignatius' twin towers in Stamford Hill (Nairn: 'this building means business'), and other churches that seemed to me to be very un-church-like: Burles, Newton and Partners' St Thomas More in Manor House, for example. This church was hidden in the fabric of a quiet suburban street, but, every Sunday, held inside a torrent of emotion, as the liturgy incorporated the call and response of the predominantly West African congregation.

If the food – like the buildings – is disparate, unresolvable as one thing, it is united by something ineffable. Can you really talk about Catholic food in the same way one might about Jewish or Muslim food? I think you can. Catholic food may be Italian, Spanish, Polish, Filipino, Goan, Congolese, Colombian, and anywhere that the church has colonised – all with different climates, ingredients and food-ways – but there's something of what usually gets locked into the confessional booth that comes out in the food: an exuberance, a barely restrained focus on pleasure; a fleshiness. Catholics understand that pleasure must necessitate some pain, some fasting, but they would never go as far as to cut out any food groups. No one would ever describe a Filipino church hall spread as 'serene'. Indeed, these are all cuisines wound with human passions.

Of course, all the best Catholic food in London is found at the church halls after mass, made by aunties who channel all that Catholic guilt away from their cooking. But outside of this, you can find it at the restaurants owned by the youngest children of Catholicism, who look after their mother while the eldest children have flown the coop. If you want to find them, just look at where the church bases its ethnic chaplaincies and masses: Goans in Wembley and Hounslow, Malayalis in East Ham, Brazilians in Kilburn and Willesden Green, Congolese in Tottenham, Sri Lankan in Earlsfield. In Catholic food you can read history's grand sweep – of blood, conversion and pork curries – in its restaurants you can read the city's future, and the church's, too.

THATTUKADA

'A Christian, a Muslim and a Hindu open a restaurant' sounds like the start of a joke, but this is the origin story of Thattukada, a Malayali restaurant in East Ham which doubles up as the community's hub. If you need a job, you go to Thattukada. If you need a room to rent, Thattukada. A whole chicken fry? Thattukada. The cuisine here is not so much Catholic as it is omnivorous, reflecting the lower rate of sectarianism in Kerala and its food. The Malayali love of fried things could adorn any modern bar menu in the city – this is food designed to pair with beers in the lazy heat of a coastal city, after all. The whole chicken fry is more exuberant than all of London's new-wave chicken joints, the netholi (anchovy) fry more delicious than any gastropub whitebait, while the kaka (mussel) dish would be called 'popcorn mussels' if it was anywhere else and priced at £15 a portion.

JACQUES CAFE

You may have been to restaurants which feel like someone's living room, but Jacques Cafe appears to literally be someone's living room: a house in a residential neighbourhood, decorated like an American diner's idea of France, that serves English breakfasts and Goan lunches. It is entirely Hounslow. It is also very much in tune with most Goan restaurants in London, which are 1) nothing of the sort, more like snack shops and waiting rooms, and 2) Catholic Goan, serving a very traditional Portuguese-influenced repertoire of chops, fries, rissois and both sorpotel and xacuti, the two pillars of Goan curries. A good xacuti should always look slightly grey, like the colour on a TV has been turned down, and the xacuti here is as it should be: not just another chicken or beef curry but fragrant with heavily roasted spices and grainy with coconut. This is good xacuti.

KAIPIRAS BY BARRACO

If you didn't realise Kilburn was Little Rio from the Portuguese language masses of its residents, then you will do after a night of dancing and eating at Kaipiras by Barraco, a Brazilian boteco bar tucked away on a backstreet below a block of flats, anonymous except for the 'Casa Latinoamericana' which embedded on the side of the building. If you're a fan of the small-plate explosion because you think the starter/main course/dessert paradigm is clapped, and what you want from a menu is a succession of snacks, then this is the place for you. All the best things are in the starter section: mandioca frita – fat chips of cassava that make a mockery of every fried potato; torresmo, undersold on the menu as pork scratchings but in reality huge crispy bollards of fried pork belly. This is perfect drinking food, to be eaten with one of the three Cs, the cornerstones of Brazilian cuisine: ice-cold Chopp, caipirinhas and cachaça.

THE BASH

Masses in Lingala take place at St Joan of Arc Parish in Highbury, a short drive south from the Congolese community in south Tottenham, where you will find a handful of restaurants serving some of the best barbecue in the city. The Bash is the highlight on this stretch of West Green Road –

most of the dishes are off-menu and have to be requested, so just ask for ntaba – smoky mutton paired with a scalp-sweating hot sauce – or pondu: stewed cassava leaf chock-full of chlorophyll and lifted by pieces of smoked fish. But it's the go-big-or-go-home fish here that is worth the journey: a whole malangwa (pangasius) full of meaty flesh without any dryness, with gingery radiance piercing through an onion-and-tomato sauce like a beam of sunshine..

EVEREST CURRY KING

The Sri Lankan community is so important to the church in London that it operates two Sri Lankan chaplaincies, one for Sinhalese speakers and one for Tamil – the latter of which runs masses in Earlsfield, Wembley, Southall and Lewisham, which explains the unexpected location of Everest Curry King on an otherwise characterless section of Lewisham A-road. Everest is barely a restaurant, more a Tamil canteen where curries are arrayed behind glass and heated up authentically, in the microwave. The move here is get a selection of vegetarian and/or fish and meat curries, the best of which is an outstanding aubergine and chickpea number: the aubergine cooked beyond the point of Maillard reaction until the skin has the bitter chew of liquorice and the texture of Japanese lacquerware.

the community centre

jenny lau

At 12.29pm on a Wednesday, Jabez Lam shouts 'Last game!' with more than a touch of exasperation. He is inside a shabby bungalow on a residential road by the railway arches at London Fields, where the average house is currently estimated to be worth upwards of £1 million. Blink and you could miss it, but the rumbling, clacking sound of melamine tiles and aroma of freshly steamed rice will stop you in your tracks. A hand-painted sign on the door indicates its occupants: 克尼華人中心 – Hackney Chinese Community Services (HCCS).

One minute later, inside a clinically-lit dining room, food is served: plates of white rice heaped with a variety of stir-fried vegetables, fried fish and stuffed tofu, along with bowls of pork-bone broth, start to appear. The elderly Chinese members of HCCS reluctantly leave their square mahjong tables and shuffle a few steps over to the round dining tables.

Lunch club commences.

I have come on this particular day to quench a nostalgic thirst for some homey comfort food, and to catch up with Lam, the centre manager. He quips of the mahjong players, 'They would have the perfect work ethic: they can't wait for lunch to be over with so they can get back to their game.'

Like the building itself, you'll only know about lunch club if you seek it out. It's a long-running institution that provides affordable hot meals for the elderly and isolated; at HCCS, lunch club operates three times a week. A hot meal costs £4, though it's not exclusively for centre members – anyone can drop in, and on this visit I find myself sitting on a table with a British-Indonesian poet, an Extinction Rebellion activist and a farmer. To keep prices low, menus are planned around weekly donations of fresh vegetables from a local wholesaler. That the food is actually very tasty is no surprise when you learn that the cooks are retired Chinese takeaway chefs who have spent half a century behind a wok station. 'Back in the day, if you asked an old Chinese lady what was inside her wallet, she would show you her membership cards to all the different centres. She would know which one had the best menu,' jokes Lam. I make a mental note to attempt a lunch-club tour.

Scan a list of community centre lunch clubs in your neighbourhood and the menus will tell a story of London's migrants. In Tower Hamlets they serve Bangladeshi, Somali and Chinese communities; further into Hackney it's Chinese, Vietnamese, Turkish and Kurdish, Cypriot and Afro-Caribbean. Most importantly, the meals on offer are culturally appropriate, taking into account halal or kosher requirements and cultural definitions of comfort; at HCCS, for instance, the sharing dishes are eaten family-style, and the non-negotiable traditional Chinese labour of love – clear pork broth, cooked for hours – is something the members especially crave.

Chinese community centres in East London form a rough trail around the historic settlement of ethnic Chinese migrants, most notably flanking the 'Pho Mile' stretch of Kingsland Road

photos by sirui ma

in Hoxton, and around Limehouse and Poplar – echoes of the original Chinatown, and where the first Chinese seamen disembarked from East India Company ships in the 1800s. To outsiders, these centres appear to serve one and the same community, but listen to the polyphony of Sinitic dialects at any one of the lunch clubs, and you will hear an aural map of the diasporic elders' individual migration journeys. In the Soho Chinatown LCCC (the UK's oldest Chinese community centre, wedged implausibly above the Hippodrome Casino), you are likely to hear Hokkien and Hakka mixing with Cantonese and Mandarin, where a diverse mix of Malaysian Chinese mingle with Hongkongers, Taiwanese and mainlanders. These elders used to work, even live in Chinatown – hard to believe, but the formerly seedy, no-go zone of Soho was once the only place working-class immigrants could afford and were welcome in. Now almost all of them have moved outwards, clustering in suburbs like Barnet, but still commute in for daily activities.

Further east, at HCCS, as well as at the Community of Refugees from Vietnam (CRV) East London and the Chinese Association of Tower Hamlets, you might pick up on the Cantonese-speaking overlap between the Hong Kong Chinese and Vietnamese Hoa. South of the river, these dialectic breadcrumbs continue, with Lambeth Chinese Community Association and the Vietnamese Family Partnership in Lewisham, as well as with the two stalwarts of the 'N' postcodes: Camden Chinese Community Centre and Islington Chinese Association. At Centre 151's Phở Club in Haggerston you may even hear Cambodian and Laotian.

Community centres are not a recent invention. Toynbee Hall, just a stone's throw from Brick Lane, was one of the first proto-community centres, a university settlement founded in 1884. In the post-World War public housing boom, as Britain tried to reconstruct its damaged housing stock, new council estates and housing associations came attached with their own communal halls and facilities – like the Skinner Bailey and Lubetkin-designed Cranbrook Estate, a high-rise model village plastered over former Victorian slums and concrete panacea for the 3,000 Bethnal Green homes destroyed during the Blitz.

But it was in the aftermath of the 1981 Brixton riot – itself a result of years of increasing tension between the institutionally racist Metropolitan Police and the young Black community – and on the recommendation of the subsequent *Scarman Report*, that centres sprang

up in London's most socially-deprived neighbourhoods. Often, these centres were dedicated to a particular ethnic group. Social reforms were to pay particular attention to improving leisure and social activities for Black and South Asian communities, whose lack of integration Leslie Scarman deemed a failure of state and police.

Much like their South Asian counterparts, Chinese community leaders recognised a need to support the successive waves of immigrants who had been arriving since the 1950s. There are parallels between the groups: both were typically made up of male labourers, either displaced from post-Partition India, or from Hong Kong's New Territories. By the 1980s, this now-ageing diasporic group lacked the intergenerational family care they would have received in their home countries. Many still spoke minimal English.

Another pressing issue was added to the mix. Between the end of the Vietnam War in 1975, the UK resettled roughly 19,000 Vietnamese refugees, mostly ethnic Chinese Hoa from the north. Many settled in Hackney, Lewisham and Southwark and faced the same social exclusions as the earlier waves of Chinese migrants. This was the catalyst for the founding of the now-defunct An Viet Foundation, which ran a legendary restaurant throughout the 1990s – technically the first Vietnamese restaurant in Hackney.

The case for the community centre was clear. It would help immigrants with cultural integration by providing language lessons and training. It could step in to help with daily mundanities, like booking doctor's appointments. A programme of activities would combat social isolation and cultural disconnect. Most importantly, it was a physical home from home, allowing ethnic minorities to feel safe in a city of increasing racial tension.

HCCS was founded in 1985, the year I was born, yet a whole generation of British-born Chinese like myself have grown up unaware of the existence of Chinese community centres. And why should we be? Redundancy is sometimes the best outcome of immigrant aspirations. The second and third generations have fulfilled the hopes and dreams of their ancestors, achieving remarkable upwards social mobility and integration. Yet new challenges arise: racism, identity struggles, cultural dissonance.

A generation's worth of introspection and retrospection has resulted in various movements within identity politics, all jostling for inclusive forms of self-labelling. Until recently, 'British Chinese' encompassed everyone else who doesn't have a box to tick (literally, because the alternative to 'Chinese' on the UK census is 'other Asian'). Into the 'other Asian' net fall the forgotten British ethnicities: the Japanese, Filipino, South Korean, Timorese and mixed-race kids, and anyone else who has endured homogeneity. While 'other Asian' is a self-deprecating in-joke reclaimed by some, it has also spurred a grass roots pivot towards adopting a more inclusive term: ESEA, or 'East and South East Asian'.

It was a few years back, when I went to my first lunch club, that I became aware of the minutiae of ESEA language and cultural differences among the seniors. Of course there is always rice – the *lingua franca* – but just because you and I eat rice does not mean we automatically get along. Lam tells me of how, when he started working at HCCS, there were incidents when the Cantonese elders would not share a table with the mainland Chinese guests. The indelible phrase 'You can't sit with us!' from *Mean Girls* springs to mind, for we never grow out of petty high school tribalism, regardless of age. Determined not to perpetuate the same patterns, I set about building a programme of food events at HCCS, which brings a younger generation of people together to celebrate diverse ESEA heritages. Since then, the centre has welcomed food lovers from across the generations – all from different backgrounds – to join in with pot lucks, fundraising supper clubs and tea parties. Even more recently, HCCS has become a safe haven for Hongkongers resettling in the UK amidst political uncertainty back home. The new members have wasted no time in creating their own network of support groups and cultural activities – including a weekly pop-up serving a taste of Hong Kong's cha chaan tengs – heralding fresh iterations of Cantonese influence in the multilayered make-up of the British Chinese diaspora.

Meanwhile, the lunch clubs have suffered the repercussions of both the pandemic and public spending cuts. Some have been suspended; others, like the LCCC, used to feed up to 40 members a day, but now welcome a quarter of that. The lunch club network in Hackney, which has historically received healthy financial backing, is currently down to its last year of council funding, with uncertainty as to whether the contract will be renewed. Local councils are missing the point if they deem lunch clubs to be non-essential services – addressing food poverty is the work of community kitchens and food banks, but the commensality of community centres provides vital socialisation and cultural connection that can't be found elsewhere.

In 2022, I and a motley crew of volunteers will help HCCS in transforming the defunct An Viet Foundation into the UK's first centre for East and South East Asian communities. In dropping the word 'Chinese' during its rebrand – a gesture of solidarity – HCCS deliberately seeks to start anew. At the heart of this centre will be a self-sustaining community kitchen that is not so much concerned with feeding its own as by giving back to society. The principle of lunch club will remain: to create a physical home from home that facilitates social harmony – one where we all still eat rice, and we *do* sit with each other.

The vagaries of urban immigration patterns can sometimes be explained by an easily understandable grand narrative. Why was the first Chinatown in Limehouse? Of course it made sense for it to be near the docks where so many Chinese sailors disembarked. Why are Southall and Hounslow predominantly Indian and Pakistani areas? Because so many jobs were available in the environs of Heathrow Airport. But for other (smaller and less visible) groups, there is often no convincing explanation. One day New Malden was a bland, office-worker suburb on the outskirts of Surrey; the next, it was a bland, office-worker suburb on the outskirts of Surrey with the biggest Korean population in Europe.

For anyone who has to tick the 'other Asian' box – Koreans, Vietnamese, Filipinos – this lack of attention often contributes to a flattening of a complex narrative, or sometimes a complete loss of it. There will always be a half explanation somewhere in the family history: a roulette of housing allocation, a family member it was more convenient to move near to, a church, an embassy, a rumour. Was the community centre there first, or did the centre bring the people? Very soon this becomes immaterial, because suddenly there is everything a community needs: a market, restaurants, hairdressers. An area becomes 'known for' being the place to go to; it thrives, becomes found, and then, in an eternal parabolic curve, declines, and springs up somewhere else, for equally unknown reasons. The city continues.

PHỞ THÚY TÂY

The Vietnamese community in London is formed of a patchwork of identities: north and south, student and settled, ethnic Chinese and Vietnamese. In the US, where the wave of Vietnamese immigration was predominantly from the capitalist south, stronger networks lent the community increased visibility, yet in London, many of the old rivalries die hard. Deptford was the epicentre of everything a few years ago, but rents, immigration raids and displacement have pushed things further afield –

to Greenwich one way, and Peckham another. At Phở Thúy Tây on the Old Kent Road, owner Thuy Nguyen mainly caters towards the new student population, recreating popular street food dishes from the country's north, particularly the capital, Hanoi. The weekend blackboard brings in a young, rowdy crowd anticipating deep cuts of offal (mainly intestines and blood sausage) all served with mam tom, a bureaucratic grey shrimp paste hiding a corrupt flavour – like the funk of a thousand prawn heads reduced down and down, atomised to the density of a neutron star.

SINGBURI

In a strange way, the linear trajectory of Singburi in Leytonstone marks the slow acceptance of Thai food in the city; it started as a fish and chip shop run by head chef Sirichai Kularbwong's parents, before turning into a local Thai restaurant serving a community of mainly British diners who were more into spag bol than laab. The blackboard menu added a decade ago served as a space to trial more 'authentic' southern dishes that reflected the specificity of Kularbwong's background; yet as it has increasingly become a destination restaurant rather than a local one, the cooking has become more ambitious, now reflecting the specificity of the London experience. On any given day you might be lucky to find a duck pastrami ho fun; a curry made out of blushing liver; a Thai salad inspired by Turkish ezme; or a herbal, refreshing soup made from pickled lime, winter melon and an offal meatball, playing on a 40 Maltby Street soup. Singburi has gone from a chippy, to Thai restaurant to something else entirely: a restaurant as intrinsic to London as St John, Rules or any pie and mash shop.

NORMAH'S

The concentration of great central London Malaysian restaurants (see: Dapur, Melur, Putera Puteri, Roti King) is somewhat mysterious, although it surely has much to do with the presence of the Malaysian High Commission in Bayswater and its canteen, where many of the city's best Malaysian chefs have trained. Around the corner from the Commission, in an anachronism of a mini-mall made up of money exchangers, juice-sellers, mobile phone shops, fake Apple stores, an Uzbek restaurant, an Indonesian cafe and a shop specialising in Russian films, you will find Normah's, a Malaysian restaurant run by Normah Abd Hamid. Stick to specialities from Normah's home state of Johor, particularly assam pedas, a scarlet bloodbath of whole fish and tamarind – as sour as tangy wine gums and lifted by a prickling chilli heat.

IMONE

The earliest explanation for New Malden's Korean community is convoluted, involving a joint venture between a British record company and a Korean conglomerate based in the area during the 1950s. It could have also been that the Ambassador to South Korea lived in nearby Wimbledon and everyone chose the closest location with affordable housing, or, more likely, that Samsung had their UK headquarters here. Either way, around 20,000 Koreans now live here, including a small community of North Korean defectors. Imone, on New Malden's hangul-inflected high street, is probably the best restaurant in the area. The name translates as 'auntie' due to the home-style nature of the food: highlights are the carefully modulated banchan, made from seasonal vegetables served at various temperatures with different levels of fermentation, and ssaeungsun jjim: whiting in spicy sauce which is lifted by the bitter herbaceousness of chrysanthemum greens. If you can read hangul, make sure to check the menu on the wall for specials (or cheat, and log into their online menu with a QR code.)

PANADERA

The Filipino community in London is huge (and well represented in the city's hospitals, where Filipino nurses have long been the bedrock of the NHS) but its lack of a settling point has

perhaps contributed to a sense of invisibility, especially in dining rooms. Earl's Court was once an important hub; it is still where many of the most traditional Filipino restaurants are (including the first UK branch of the beloved fast-food chain Jollibee), and you can also find individual restaurants in Brixton, Tooting, Peckham and Finchley Road. But strangely the most concentrated stretch is on Kentish Town Road – primarily because here you can find five restaurants all owned by one person, Omar Shah: the unofficial King of Kentish Town. Shah refuses to open a straight Filipino restaurant for fear of offending his aunties, but Panadera, a bakery and coffee shop opened with his partner Florence Mae Maglanoc, is not too wonky, combining the litany you would expect at a TikTok-savvy London cafe with Filipino exuberance. The ube tarts, calamansi meringue and a sandwich of sweet, fluffy pandesal bread stuffed with a corned beef croquette are particularly joyous.

the settlement

mike wilson

It's a truism that London is made up of many villages – a constantly remade and expanding muddle of neighbourhoods that are woven together to create the city. In an easily overlooked corner of Walworth is an unlikely village hall: a 'settlement' called Pembroke House. An awkward building, the product of changing financial fortunes and fashions over its thirteen decades, it resembles a red monopoly hotel that can't quite decide if it's a church or a community centre.

When I first came to Pembroke House, I was struggling to find a foothold in the city. I was raised in a rural market town and had never really found a place that felt like home in the jumble of the capital. Even Chicago, where I spent two years, felt more easily navigable, with its distinct neighbourhoods and patchwork of welcoming bars that promised new friends and experiences. But walking up the stairs and into the grand hall of the settlement – out of place in this part of Walworth – I entered a more familiar and homely scene. Simple food of sausage and mash was being served, followed by vanilla sponge disappearing in folds of custard. In the kitchen, the chef was shouting at the temperamental ovens, raising the temperature through stress alone and providing an odd backdrop to the conversations in play at the tables.

At my table, I was soon talking to Robert, a young photography assistant who was helping serve the lunch in return for a cheap room in the residency next door, and a pair of long-time Walworth residents, Val and Joan. 'Ah, widow's memories!' Joan cried as her plate of fat sausages was set in front of her, delighting in the obvious embarrassment on the bright red face of David, the local Vicar and Warden of Pembroke House.

An hour later I was rolling on the floor in an overly ambitious warm-up for a contemporary dance class for young adults with learning difficulties. A year later I joined the team. Six years after that, as Pembroke House's Executive Director, I locked up the building for the pandemic. As we turned for home, we pinned a defiant note on the settlement's door:

You can shut a building, but you can't close a community.

The settlements of London are relics of a previous time. In the late-19th Century, Charles Booth and his band of students and bemused police officers had begun to map the growing inequality of a post-industrial London, painting a picture in vivid colours and even more vivid language – from 'Upper-middle and upper classes. Wealthy' to 'Lowest class. Vicious, semi-criminal' – of a city where residents were within walking distance but worlds apart.

This inequality stalked the consciences of reformers at a time when the traditional responses of state, market or Victorian philanthropy were seen as woefully inadequate. The settlement founders – often but not always students – developed a radically simple but profound alternative: to live in the midst of neighbourhoods marked by this inequality and seek solutions from the inside.

The first of the new breed of settlement houses was Toynbee Hall, founded in Aldgate in 1884 by Reverend Samuel Barnett and his (in many ways more impressive) wife Henrietta, who was founder of the Whitechapel Gallery and later Hampstead Garden Suburb. Toynbee Hall offered housing for its founders in the form of a residency adjacent to generous spaces for social activities, clubs and educational classes. Similar settlements soon sprung up across London, adapting to both the circumstances of distinct neighbour-hoods and the particular interests of their founders.

There was no doubt a generous dose of Victorian patronage at play here, and many of the founders appear to have arrived thinking they might be able to solve inequality by teaching classics to the poor. But settlements have had a profound and often unrecognised impact on the country: the old-age pension, free legal advice and the profession of social work can all trace their roots to experiments in London's settlement houses. And some of their widest-reaching legacies can be found in the work of former residents whose hubris was turned to humility as they built new friendships in these neigh-bourhoods. Many took the lessons of settlement life into later careers, including William Beveridge (whose post-war report was in some ways an attempt to make the sporadic welfare provision of settlement houses more systematic) or Clement Atlee, the Prime Minister who brought the recommendations of that report into statute, giving birth to the modern welfare state.

The residents who have lodged at Pembroke House over the years have also witnessed Walworth undergo waves of cosmetic surgery.

Glance out of the windows today and you can view nearly 200 years' worth of contradictory housing policy: traditional squat Victorian terraces that once lined the streets in the foreground, flanked on one side by the sturdy red-brick of post-war council blocks and on the other by the grey concrete of the vast but diminishing Aylesbury estate, with the new-build high rises that are rapidly taking its place peeping into view behind. And yet, in many ways, things have stayed remarkably similar. Propped up against a wall in our office is a copy of Charles Booth's original map of inequality, an unsettling reminder that the structural patterns of inequality in Walworth remain largely unchanged nearly 140 years on. Despite the urban changes and the local achievements of Pembroke House, or those of settlements more broadly, the areas which were painted blue and black with poverty in the 1890s are still those facing the greatest challenges today.

Pembroke House, Walworth, c. 1900

At their heart, settlements have never been traditional community centres but instead *homes* into which the wider community is welcomed. As the seriousness of the pandemic became clear, our first challenge was to work out how to bring this sense of welcome to people's doors. Within days of pinning that note to the door in 2020, commercial fridges and freezers were being wheeled into Pembroke House, boxes of fruit and vegetables unpacked on office tables, and dried and canned goods arranged on repurposed library shelves. Organising alongside a network of newly formed mutual-aid groups, as well as the local authority and neighbourhood partners, the Walworth Community Food Hub came to life. Over the next 18 months, an army of cycling volunteers would go on to deliver 340 tonnes of food across Walworth in 40,000 individual packages to residents shielding or thrown into crisis by lockdown.

Food has always played a central role in settlement life, often as a pretext to bring together unlikely combinations of people, even in moments of crisis. In the Second World War, Pembroke House's lower hall was used as a makeshift bomb shelter, partly due to superstitious locals seeking the protection of the chapel above, but possibly also because of the presence of a bar in a corner of the dark room. Further down the road, All Saints Hall, an Arts and Crafts building that became part of the settlement in 2019, was put to wartime use as a British Restaurant, providing meals for families who had lost homes during the bombing.

And in 2020, even this reasonably traditional food bank model – where the danger is always in dividing neighbours into *helpers* and *helped* – the social world of the settlement shone through. Lasting relationships were formed over the socially distanced stations in the distribution centre, and the act of handing over food parcels at doorsteps provided excuses for new conversations between neighbours who may otherwise never have met. Although some of these interactions were swift, they were significant and they were encouraged. In fact, to be efficient would be to miss the point entirely.

Still, cycling food around Walworth was never going to be part of the settlement's future; the inequalities of the neighbourhood weren't going to be solved by a food bank on wheels. Our challenge was to find a way of turning the energy of the emergency response into action that could have a lasting impact in Walworth – harnessing the power of food to mobilise and connect neighbours.

It started with a hasty sketch in the depths of the third national lockdown: a dream of a food bank giving birth to a range of complementary spaces, including a community cafe, a social enterprise restaurant and a shared community kitchen, all sourcing produce from the local markets and generating wealth in Walworth – a city condensed down into a village once again. We clumsily named it the Walworth Neighbourhood Food Model, a 'whole neighbourhood' approach to tackling inequalities, where the focus would shift away from the silver bullet of a single project or building and instead to a network of related activities and spaces.

Across the world, food is being used as the catalyst for fresh approaches to neighbourhood development, whether that's in the community kitchens of La Cocina in San Francisco and Kitchen Connect in Detroit; food cooperatives like Park Slope in Brooklyn or the collective farms of the Tamil Nadu Women's Collective; or community-owned pubs like the Ivy House in Nunhead and The Bevy in Brighton. We've been inspired by all of these, but the particular opportunity we have in Walworth is to explore how similar initiatives might benefit from neighbourhood proximity. Drawing on frameworks including the Nordic Council of Ministers' *Cookbook for systems change*, we now see food as an entry point to tackling unsustainable patterns of production and consumption, fragile livelihoods and environmental decline at the neighbourhood level.

In other words: we wanted a connected set of places to eat in a neighbourhood, one where everyone has enough money to buy the food they need or want.

Almost 18 months from the day that we closed the door of Pembroke House, I'm opening up the building again and Tatum Street is disorientingly busy. Beer kegs from nearby Orbit Brewery are being heaved into position and gingham cloths rolled out on wooden tables in front of a large red bed sheet that has 'Community Pub' stitched into it in white letters. Two four-litre bottles contain the vibrant red of fruit punch and deep gold of Guyanese ginger beer, homemade gifts from 'Auntie' Faye at Kaieteur Kitchen. An upright piano and microphone hint at the entertainment soon to begin.

Beyond the makeshift stage, a homemade sign points the way to the 'Market'. I'm soon in front of a table overflowing with aubergines, peppers and green beans. In the corner are the transparent bowls that will hold produce of varying quantity and weight depending on the time of day or current demand – a signal that Harem of Adam's Fresh Fruit and Veg has brought the dynamic pricing of East Street Market to Tatum Street for the day. Further along, sofas and chairs are being positioned at angles which will encourage conversation. All Saints Hall has been transformed into the 'Walworth Living Room', a new social space and community cafe for the neighbourhood, and today it is represented by soft furnishings, silver urns of tea and plates of biscuits ready to help bridge any awkward silences.

Sandwiched between all of this, a food stall is laid out: freshly baked Bolivian salteñas and steamed humitas are being released from the foil wrapping that has protected them on the short walk from Jenecheru on the Old Kent Road, while a quinoa salad from nearby Fooditude is being constructed from constituent parts which have been transported in large white plastic tubs. The corners of the table are dotted with freshly baked carrot-and-ginger and lemon-and-thyme cakes, while surrounding stations heave with produce from local food projects: the Walworth Garden and Edible Rotherhithe, Melanin Food Co-ops (with a table covered in yams and plantains) and a display of jams from the Alberta Fruit Commons. There's a laugh from behind as Andy drops his lighter attempting to fire up his barrel BBQ, and soon the thick, sweet smell of smoke and jerk marinade fill the air.

A pub, a market, a community cafe, a food hall. A whole village laid out in miniature.

It's just a shame about the rain.

IMAGES

p47, Pembroke House Archive; p48, Adiam Yemane; p51, 52, Simon Williams

WHAT IS THE BRITISH RESTAURANT?

The British Restaurant was never really a restaurant, which is in keeping with a country where, up until the last twenty or thirty years or so, there was never really a restaurant culture. In actual fact, the British Restaurant was something akin to a canteen or a caff, the communal flip side to the ration book, an egalitarian space in which workers were guaranteed a partially state-provided hot meal. The bulldoggish name was chosen by Churchill himself, who objected to the whiff of socialism 'Communal Feeding Centres' conjured up, and the fare they served was resolutely British: despite regional variations, which were encouraged, the options mainly consisted of basic meat and veg, with soups and puddings (a healthier, Norwegian-style approach, where every meal was scientifically designed to give everyone a nutritionally balanced diet, withered in response to British tastes). The British Restaurants were a success, a proto-National Food Service, but unlike the NHS they did not carry over long after the war ended; some turned into civic restaurants, but they died off with the second Churchill government, who didn't much see the point of them.

The British restaurant as we know it today may be closer to a restaurant, but it's not so British. Take the 'Modern British' phenomenon, an epoch whose start can be traced fairly precisely to 1986 – a year when an architecture firm, Richard Rogers Partnership's canteen called The River Cafe was conceived; when another architect called Fergus Henderson started cooking in a borrowed Covent Garden restaurant each weekend (in an early version of what would later be called a 'pop-up'); when Alastair Little started moving through the gears at his eponymous Soho establishment (the culinary version of Velvet Underground's first album in that it never quite got the fame the others did, but everyone who went there seemed to open their own restaurant). This was a revolution in British cuisine, but completely inspired by the continent – French country cuisine and Italian *cucina povera* repackaged by middle-class chefs for a middle-class audience.

London's working-class food was influenced by Europe in an even more direct way. Those indisputably British institutions – the caff, the chippy, the pie and mash shop – were all being stewarded by Italians, Greeks, Cypriots: people who either didn't want to cook their own country's cuisine, or didn't have the audience for it, who repurposed native frying and grilling skills and improved the British culinary repertoire. London's fish and chip style owes much to the frying techniques of Cypriots and the Jewish tradition of using matzo meal, while every good caff in London has a pasta menu alongside its fry-ups. And pie and mash? That was Italian from its inception. Perhaps, then, the British restaurant doesn't really exist, or maybe it's up to each generation to redefine it for themselves.

KNIGHT'S FISH BAR

Most guidebooks would tell you to go to The Fryer's Delight in Holborn, an institution whose reputation is better than the experience of eating there. But this is not most guidebooks. Knight's in West Norwood is the *other* chippy in London that fries in beef dripping, due to the Cypriot owner's insistence that tallow is the only thing worth cooking chips in because of its high smoke point. Tasting them, it's difficult to argue with him: that beefy tang is better than anything Diptyque has ever been able to conjure up and bottle in a candle. These are the only fish and chips in London that could cure northern homesickness – right down to the unfeasibly low price of a daily cod and chips deal. But perhaps even better than that is the spam fritter fried in dripping – a greasy puck the texture of an infant's cheek that is one of the most uncomplicatedly blissful things available at any takeaway in the city.

ST JOHN BREAD AND WINE

St John is an unusual restaurant in the sense that every restaurant it has influenced undeniably now serves better food than the mother ship; not only does ROCHELLE CANTEEN (run by Fergus

Henderson's wife Margot) refine the formula, adding the uplit sun of Italy (and even the Levant) to St John's austere cuisine, but many of the newer generation of chefs have more fun with it, whether it's the robust cooking at QUALITY CHOP HOUSE, the Turkish fusion of (Formerly Known as) BLACK AXE MANGAL, or the new-wave CAFES (CECILIA, DECO). If you really want the St John experience, you should either sit at the bar for snacks, come after a meal for dessert, or go to Bread and Wine in Spitalfields, where head chef Farokh Talati has license to stretch the limits of the rigid St John ethos as far as it will go before breaking point (one recent menu even had bulgar on it).

QUO VADIS

Quo, as most people abbreviate it to, builds the strongest case for a building having a soul: through many decades and iterations, 26–29 Dean Street has housed a brothel, an ill-fated restaurant helmed by Marco Pierre White and Damien Hirst, the sculptor Joseph Nollekens, and, improbably, Karl Marx (Marx predicted many things, but he never could have guessed that his hovel would one day be Quo's private dining room, 'The Marx Room'). The food here for the last ten years has been overseen by the chef Jeremy Lee, who has run the kitchen for a decade since leaving Terence Conran's Blueprint Cafe: starters are defined by their minimalism (the famous eel sandwich is a masterclass of sandwich architectonics), while the desserts, which are what you should come for, are pure maximalist: billowy, excessive and joyous. I once had a pudding here in which I counted four different types of cream.

REGENCY CAFE

When it comes to iconic (I don't use this word lightly – these are spaces for devotion) London caffs, it comes down to E. PELLICCI in Bethnal Green or Regency in Westminster; both are art-deco institutions which feel worn-in, as if the rest of the city has grown around them. Regency edges it, partly because the food is slightly better, partly because it's less knowing about it (although Pellicci will pour bolognese over your hash browns if you ask them nicely). There's an element of ritual about Regency: the long queue, no matter how many people are sitting down; being addressed as young man or lady no matter your age; your order being bellowed by the voice of the Oracle, whether it be a fry-up with eggs like milky, glossed over eyes: crusty; a square slice of pie; or the Friday fish lunch, which is low-key one of the best fish and chips in the city. And those black cabs outside? Well, the cabbies abandoned Regency long ago. Instead, you'll find them huddled up over the road at THE ASTRAL, discussing LTNs and cashless cabs over a chaotic plate of penne-and-fusilli bolognese topped with chicken escalope, or a chicken kebab. If the Regency sells us an image of British food as we want it to be, then the Astral serves it as it is.

ARMENT'S

Think of London pie and mash and you may think of the shop itself before the food: Grade II listed buildings, bottle-green patterned walls, old names in gold curlicues, Formica tables, cold tiles. But, by and large, the days of the grand central London pie and mash shops, like the Viennese cafe before them, are over. Pie and mash's soul can be found in shops of little architectural distinction, like at Arment's off Walworth Road, where the architecture is all on the plate: mincemeat pie in a suet crust; boiled mashed potato sans butter, sans seasoning, sans anything, smeared as a buttress on the side of the plate, high and curled like a Flock of Seagulls haircut; parsley liquor, Kermit-green and thickened with eel juice and flour. Every Londoner worth the name should check into these shops once a year, like taking a prostate exam. Although jellied eels are frequently lambasted as food in Brexit form, at the time of writing Arment's isn't selling them – due to supply issues caused by... Brexit.

Hampstead Garden Suburb, a 243-acre planned neighbourhood, was founded in 1907 by Henrietta Barnett as a mixed-economy village. Its architects, Barry Parker and Raymond Unwin, had worked together on Letchworth Garden City, and brought the same blend of town and country to north-west London. The Suburb, as it became known, was soon characterised as parochial, insular and conservative (Ian Nairn, incensed by the lack of pubs, decried its 'blankness of imagination'), yet it was never intended to be a self-sufficient neighbourhood. The Suburb's lack of shops and restaurants means residents must interact with, and are fed by, the shops around it – particularly those on its west side, in Temple Fortune. Inscrutable to outsiders, you can read the Suburb's ebbs and flows like a haruspex in the entrails of these shops, which range from chopped liver at Ashkenazi delis to Jerusalem mixed grills at Mizrahi falafel joints. These foods mark the shifting tastes and immigration patterns of Jews, both in London and worldwide, played out in miniature.

The Jewish food writer Claudia Roden is among the Suburb's most famous living residents. Born in Cairo and arriving in London in 1954 to study art, she has not only witnessed the changes happening on the edges of the Suburb, but also set them in motion. It was here, in her cloistered house, that she wrote her seminal cookbooks, *A Book of Middle Eastern Food* (1968) and *The Book of Jewish Food* (1996), the latter of which is one of the supreme works of culinary anthropology, compiling a fragmented cuisine of many countries and weaving a culinary narrative that stretches from Samarkand to America. Via Roden, in the most roundabout way possible, the tastes of this seemingly banal neighbourhood have changed Jewish food for people living as far away as Jerusalem, Tel Aviv and New York, now forming the bedrock of a new London cuisine flourishing right on the Suburb's border.

How long have you been living in Hampstead Garden Suburb?

> Since I was 18. Actually I first lived in Temple Fortune, just behind
> Corney the fishmongers. My brothers and I had a flat in a house
> where the landlady treated us like her children; she used to
> leave food for us in our kitchen upstairs. It was through her that
> I discovered there was a Jewish food of the Ashkenazi world.
> She went on to live for 105 years! Really, I've lived here all my life ...
> almost, and so I've seen it change hugely.
>
> When my parents suddenly arrived in 1956 as refugees,
> leaving everything behind, the landlady said they could come
> and stay for free until they found their feet, which was very
> generous, but they did that very quickly. My mother had a British
> passport, and all the British-passport holders got £5,000 if they
> had been thrown out of Egypt. They bought a house in Golders
> Green; at the time, Golders Green was already very Jewish, while
> the Suburb was a mix of very English Christian and a bit Jewish.
> I always remember, as soon as they moved in, the Jewish neigh-
> bours came to bring flowers. So my mother said, 'Will you come
> for tea?' She prepared all our traditional foods: filos, stuffed vine
> leaves, hummus. When they came, they were absolutely astound-
> ed. One of them said, 'Are you sure you're Jewish?' We were the
> first batch of Sephardi and Mizrahi refugees; it was unbelievable
> to them that we didn't have Jewish food that they knew.

When did the Suburb start to take on a central role on London
Jewish life?

> It changed maybe 25, 30 years or more ago. Of course, now, since
> it's an eruv [since 2003 the Suburb has been part of the 'North-
> West London Eruv', an area exempt from Sabbath laws which
> forbid the carrying and pushing of items], it's more than ever.
> It has this very, very Jewish identity; you can see it from the streets
> on Saturday night, how it comes alive between Golders Green

and here. You can see from the restaurants that have gradually opened with very different Jewish styles, and of course from the kosher Chinese restaurants. Also Japanese restaurants.

I noticed there is also a sushi section in Kosher Kingdom!

Yes! The Jews aren't just trying to remember the shtetl. I remember going to New York where all the Hasidim live in Flatbush, to go and ask them for recipes. When I went, I asked, 'What kind of cuisine are you doing? Heimish food?' And they said, 'No, we're doing Thai, Japanese. Everybody else is, why shouldn't we enjoy it?' They didn't feel they had to cook the foods that their ancestors in Eastern Europe had done – except for on Shabbat and Jewish festivals.

How have those shops on Temple Fortune changed since the 1960s?

The Jewish food shops didn't want to change, because enough people went for what they had. In the beginning, it was just delis because people would go there for their Saturday-morning smoked salmon, their pickled cucumber. Now they sell cooked foods. I love going and getting a whole range of Jewish things: chopped herring, chopped liver; I love it all. When I started my book, I first went to Bloom's in the East End, and I bought everything I could. For me, it was exotic! There were things like stuffed neck. I had invited my parents, my brothers, everybody to come and eat. My mother started eating and she said, 'I'm sorry, I can't eat this. It's awful.'

But gradually, more and more of the Jews came from the Arab World and from Israel too. There are little synagogues in houses in Golders Green. Sometimes I would go in and think, 'Are these people Jewish? They don't seem like Jews.' But they were Iraqi. There were Jews from India, Jews from all over.

Tell me about the diversity of shops that feed all these different tastes in the Suburb.

A shop that I've gone to regularly for years is Iranian, but you can see they're not religious because they sell wine. Sometimes

I brought film crews there from abroad. One time, when the owner was away, they told me 'No, you can't film'. It turned out it was because they have pictures of the Shah! It's sort of a mix: as soon as there is a Jewish festival, this Iranian shop has all the Jewish things. They have horseradish at Passover, pomegranates for the new year. Whatever occasion it is, they know exactly. Before English people started eating this kind of food, it was one of the only places you could get molohiya, which is adored by Egyptians, and frozen artichokes from Egypt.

There is Platters – the owners are from Egypt as well and do better smoked salmon than Waitrose and Marks & Spencer. And, of course, the best shop for meat, that people from all over come to, is Silvermans. I just went this morning: I got chicken soup and I got chopped liver. Years ago, there was a butchers called Frohwein's where you could get chickens that were not roasters but boilers. You could get unborn eggs – tiny baby eggs that were full of a kind of milk. You know, the kind of things that you would get in a shtetl. But Silvermans is more attuned to the modern Ashkenazim. I should say that the shops here mirror the different types of Jews who are here; the older Jews, the conservative Jews, the modern young families who want to be fashionable and follow influencers. All the kosher people go to the Finchley Road Marks & Spencer and Waitrose to buy vegetables and fruit and other things, and also shop in Golders Green.

When did you notice your book having an influence on Jewish food in London?

My mother used to go and play cards with her friends and suddenly they had things like mezze that we made, just as we made them. They said they bought it at Marks & Spencer. She just couldn't be-lieve it. Soon after I was invited by Marks & Spencer to go and taste things for them and I found that my book was the only book there; they had asked the producer to do my recipes and he was there! I told him my cousin had said that the hummus in Waitrose is the best, and this man replied, 'I also do the Waitrose hummus. I do all of them, and each a little bit different!' Sainsbury's called to ask what they should stock; I said things like bulgur and couscous. Then I ran a bonding weekend for Waitrose managers of Middle Eastern food.

It was when Yotam Ottolenghi came on the scene that this kind of food took off, and it is really his influence that has made it the fashionable food all over London. But here, in the Suburb, I noticed it earlier – much earlier, with caterers who catered for weddings and bar mitzvahs needing a book, because none of those countries had cookbooks. It's only usually people who come here who are immigrants that start writing cookbooks, because they are nostalgic. All the caterers here use my books, especially the Jewish ones, for all the weddings and bar mitz-vahs. They can look at the book and they can say, 'Yes, this is Jewish', because they couldn't always do that. They could look at my Middle Eastern book, but they couldn't say for sure a recipe was Jewish. But eventually, it was the influence of my books in Israel that was felt the most on the food in Golders Green and Temple Fortune.

Even though these shops are round the corner from you, the book had to go all the way to Israel and back for it to have this effect?

When *A Book of Middle Eastern Food* first came out there in Hebrew, the publisher said 'I don't think it will sell. Because we don't like that food. We want all the people, all the Jews coming here from the Arab world, to leave their food behind, to leave their culture behind.' When children from Arab Jewish families were asked at school, 'What does your mother cook?', they all would say 'steakim and chipsim', as if they came from nowhere! But then right away the book was a bestseller with the Ashkenazim and Sephardim. When *The Book of Jewish Food* came out the local media were asking, 'Where is all this "Jewish food" we don't know?' Then chefs began contacting me about what they were doing with my recipes. Inspired by the home cooking of the wider diaspora, they were creating a kind of fusion Middle Eastern cuisine. The influence I had in Israel affects what is eaten here, because many people here go to Israel and they want to eat what they've eaten there.

What's funny though is that those recipes I wrote for *The Book of Jewish Food* were all tested on my friends and neighbours, and they would make suggestions like 'It needs a bit more of this, or a bit less of that.'

So the tastes of the Suburb have shaped the trajectory of Jewish food worldwide! You've been in the Suburb for almost 70 years now. Why haven't you left?

There is a community here and it's very strong. It's because of the Henrietta Barnett spirit, where people really do help each other. When I couldn't go down to the shops because of the pandemic, all of a sudden I had so many phone calls saying 'I can shop for you.' I should move because it's a big house but because of this community, I feel I don't really want to leave.

What's nice is that I can see the Suburb changing again; there are more and more people from other countries coming in, or serving the community. They are appreciated hugely. Of course not all of the spirit of Henrietta Barnett is here: the whole idea of the poor living next to the rich isn't there at all because even the little houses have become 'boutique'. But there was always a social mindset about doing things for people in the area.

Sometimes the synagogues invite refugees or homeless people round, very often Syrians. I went to one synagogue on the other side of the Market Place, a Masorti synagogue where my grandchildren go. There was an event run by Syrian refugees, who had been – and are still being – invited to come regularly, not only to be given things but to see lawyers or a doctor or to be helped in a general way. They wanted to return the friend-ship by doing an event, and they came, they played music, and they sang and they made kibbeh, all the exact food that we made when we first came over! You see, three of my grandparents came from Aleppo. I was just really moved. I felt: this is how it should be.

AMBA IS THE NEW CHRAIN

The story of Jewish food in London is one of simultaneous decline and ascent, one necessitating the other. One story starts in the first decade of the 20th century, when Hampstead Garden Suburb was formed and J. Rogg's delicatessen opened in the East End. Rogg and its slow death rattle is documented in Jenny Linford's book *Food Lovers' London*, where it is described as selling the exact stuff that Claudia Roden would so memorably call 'a cold world': schmaltz herring; snappy new pickles; fried gefilte fish balls; chopped liver; cold tiles that spell 'CUT HERRING, anchovy, shmultz and pickled'. Nine years later, the most famous Jewish deli ever to exist in the city, Bloom's, opened on Brick Lane. This was back when Whitechapel's *lingua franca* was Yiddish rather than Bengali, and its warehouses and ramshackle housing still had the feel of the Eastern European shtetl.

Bloom's operated within this peasant tradition, serving salt beef, smoked tongue, salami, beef and veal viennas, and pastrami, many a sandwich forming the ballast for meetings advocating socialist and communist foment. But cities change. The working-class community that fought at Cable Street moved out; working-class Bengalis came in. The north-west suburbs of Golders Green and Hampstead Garden Suburb became the new refuge for Jews who had fled Europe. Bloom's in Whitechapel closed, and Bloom's in Golders Green opened. Another opened in Edgware, which proved to be at least one stop on the Northern line too far. The death knell for Bloom's came in 2010, after it suffered a final humiliation of losing its kosher licence. Yes, the clientele had moved, had changed, but ultimately it no longer cared enough to be good. The energy had moved elsewhere.

Yet a couple of decades prior, up the street in Hendon, another story had been unfolding. In the early 1990s, a wholesale bakery owned by Yael Mejia had started making challah and rugelach for Jewish businesses in the area. The bakery would eventually take on the anglicised name of the founder – Gail – and dominate every bougie high street until the end of eternity. Mejia's second venture, Baker & Spice, was where chef Sami Tamimi fatefully met pastry chef Yotam Ottolenghi; together they would go on to change the way Jewish food is perceived in London, integrating the food of Israel, Palestine and the Middle East into a new common language. Because, for all the decline, this food has never been more popular: from the Tel Aviv-style central London restaurants that euphemistically call themselves 'Mediterranean', to the hummus bars and falafel joints of Temple Fortune, where the new salt beef sandwiches are sabichs the size of cannonballs, and amba is the new chrain. If Jewish food is dead, then long live Jewish food.

B&K SALT BEEF BAR

Like that other London Jewish institution, the chippy, the stewardship for smoked meats has fallen to Cypriots – like the brothers of the Georgiou family, who have opened three B&K Salt Beef Bars since the original in Edgware (one of them, in Crouch End, now no more) as well as several Tongue & Briskets, the quicker, easier-to-get-to-from-anywhere-that-isn't-Zone-5 version of the original. But the original is where you should go. There are certain rules here that can make the experience better: according to Marina, the youngest member of the Georgiou family, you need to tell Michael to add extra mustard, according to food writer Daniel Young, tell both of them to give you extra fat, and, if you're at the Pinner branch, try to convince them to let you put a fried egg and ketchup in. The Edgware branch is for the purists, who only want sandwiches as easy receptacles for soft tongue, and salt beef with strata of snowy fat. Get fish balls, get latkes, get soup with kneidlach, and leave full and happy.

SALT BEEF BAR

Another Greek Cypriot-run salt beef bar, this establishment (featuring Ronseal-like name) is in Temple Fortune, just as it hits the North Circular, and is basically a workman's caff where, instead of bacon-and-ketchup sandwiches, you get salt beef and mustard – but aside from this discrepancy, they are spiritually exactly the same. Connoisseurs will do two things: first, they will ignore the salt beef and get the ambrosial tongue, so soft you could eat it through a wired jaw, and secondly, they will order at least two of the zeppelin-shaped latkes. One should be eaten by itself, or kept in a front pocket as a snack for later; the other should be immediately halved and shoved into the sandwich for ballast, fulfilling precisely the same function that a hash brown does in a breakfast McMuffin.

REICH'S

Mention Reich's to anyone who grew up around Golders Green and they may shudder with traumatic memories of bar and bat mitzvahs catered with exactly the kind of food a young teenager doesn't want to eat. I once mentioned Reich's to my dentist in Temple Fortune who, upon hearing the name, paused, mid-examination of my mouth, to say 'wow, that is old-school'. For some it is slightly too old-school. Reich's is where you go to get pareve lasagne, where dairy and meat haven't touched each other. Reich's is where you go to get five types of kugel. But Reich's is also where you go, on Thursday, to get cholent, that long-cooked stew of barley, beans and brisket that is the great-grandmother of all old-school dishes, the final boss in the video game of heimishe Ashkenazi foods. Cholent at Reich's with a side of burnt potato kugel and kishke is something that gets to the very core of being a Londoner: you might well suspect that the wobbly bit of brisket fat in the stew is propping up the entire city, like ravens in the Tower.

POCKETS

The pocket at Pockets in London Fields' Netil Market doesn't quite sell itself with its unassuming name. What the pocket actually is: a pitta steamed for maximum elasticity, like a pair of good jogging bottoms, thick and fluffy, puffed up like a whoopee cushion and assembled by, and only by, the owner, Itamar Grinberg. He layers

every single item – falafel, hummus, tahina, cabbage – with the gestural precision of a master performing tea ceremony, turning a bowl angle by angle, swirling the inside with amba like a doctor taking a swab, before balancing a red chilli and a fried potato on top. Quite frankly, it makes almost every other pitta and laffa shop look amateurish. It's just a shame it's in London Fields.

BALADY

If you had to name one takeaway that sums up the new diversity and direction of London's Jewish food, it would be Balady in Temple Fortune. The shopfront, the pale blue of a morning sky, has the same word repeated three times in three different scripts – English, Hebrew and Arabic – and which roughly translates as native, or local. The first time I went, I got talking to the Sabbo brothers about the sign and found out that they were from Israel but also had Moroccan heritage, that although the cafe was vegetarian they cooked their grandmother's fish recipes on Fridays, and that the sign above the door was a mark of respect and also one of welcome. They have opened a second branch, bringing sabich and falafel to Leather Lane, which is like bringing coals to Newcastle (by my unofficial reckoning, Leather Lane has the highest concentration of falafel wraps in the UK, a legacy of the Jewish involvement in Hatton Garden's jewel trade) but also their roughly cut chips, which taste like your mum's chips, no matter where you were brought up.

stephen buranyi

the baths

The bistro at the New Docklands Steam Baths in Canning Town isn't the best in East London, but it may be the best placed. The food is uncompromisingly local (heavily oiled, fried cutlets, chips, dumplings and kippers) and the decor tends toward the basic comforts of a local social club – particle-board furniture, worn couches, and a muted television in the background. But neither the food nor the decor is the point here; in fact, the lack of frills is the draw. The bistro sits above one of the last serious baths left in the capital, and there may not be another room in the city that draws a more dedicated or diverse crowd: East London cabbies, Caribbean stall-traders, businessmen who have been attending for decades. Worked in seamlessly around them are groups who have often travelled miles to attend for the love of bathing: Baltic and Belorussian tradespeople, city workers, and nearly always a large contingent of Hasidic Jews from North London, conversing quietly in Yiddish or Russian.

The baths themselves are sparsely appointed (verging on run-down, regulars would admit), with worn white tile-work and clear vinyl strips serving as curtains between the atrium and the steam rooms. It is nonetheless busy nearly every night of the week. Long-time bathers talk about it like a religious service: private yet public, intimate, intense, and deeply relaxing. There is teasing, knowing banter in the harshly lit public areas, hushed and contemplative repose in the dense steam. The bistro, then, is the church hall that solidifies the community; a simple setting to relax and socialise, shared by a diverse group with a single common bond.

If you want to find a good sauna or bath in London, it helps to look for the ones that also serve food. Most baths that remain in the city are attached to over-designed luxury hotels or recently redeveloped and subcontracted council fitness facilities. They are often billed as health spas, and subscribe to that particular modern notion that anything you do for pleasure must simultaneously be good for you. The term 'wellness' is used frequently. These places do not, as a rule, serve food in the baths; if they did it might be smoothies, salad boxes and protein pots.

The Finnish sauna, Turkish hammam, and Russian banya, on the other hand, are places of pleasure and excess, sensual overload, and, most importantly, communal experience. Health is a by-product – sometimes a rationalisation – but it's never the main event. In London, food provides a reliable guide to the dwindling number of great baths that remain: the New Docklands Steam Baths, but also the Finnish Church in Rotherhithe, which serves up brain-numbingly sweet pastries and dense, gritty rye-flour Karelian pasties filled with buttery sugared egg, and Banya No. 1, where carafes of ice-cold 90% proof vodka and blini, pickled herring and pelmeni are served by slipper-clad Russian chefs. It is a signal, when an establishment foregrounds pleasure over utility, that it won't be sterile – in presentation or attitude – and, crucially, that it doesn't want to hustle you in and out for a pre-arranged booking. Food suggests you might stay a while.

photos by malcolm glover

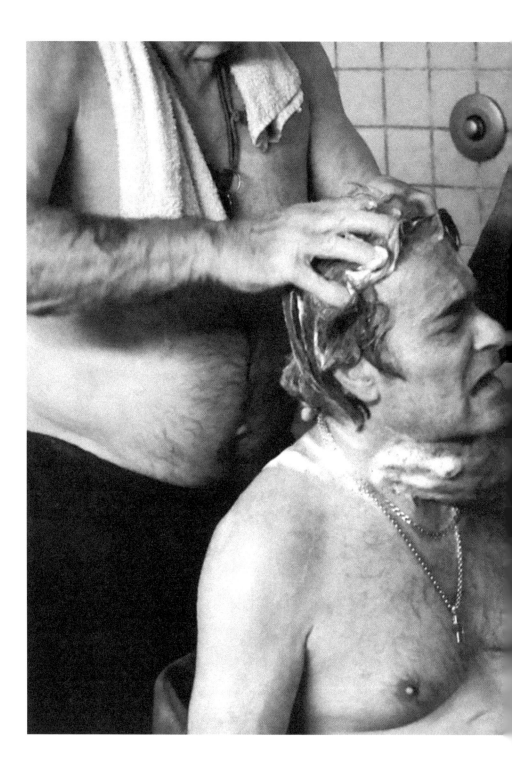

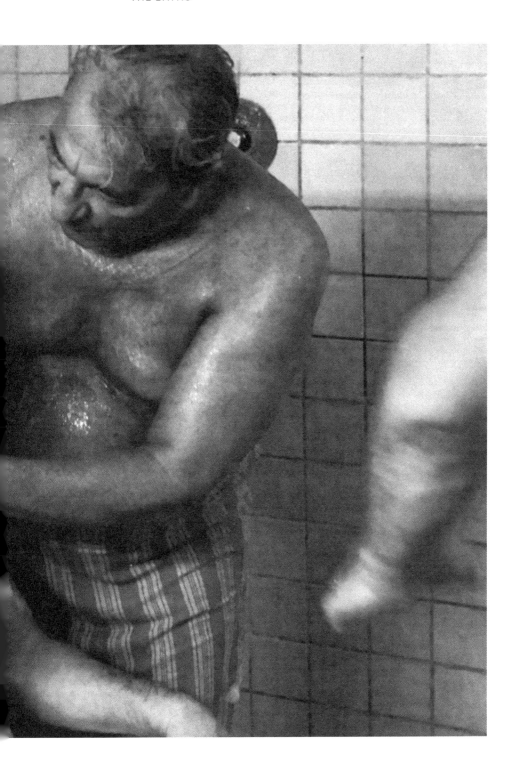

London has always seemed somewhat culturally unsuited to bathing. 'We are not a bathing people', the *Illustrated London News* proclaimed in 1858, 'too busy, too indolent' – and besides, averse to heat and nudity. But London still became a city of baths. The 1846 Public Baths and Washhouses Act encouraged councils to construct facilities so the masses could bathe and wash clothes. In the tradition of the Romans, bathing was seen as both virtuous and a matter of pleasure. The historian Malcolm Shifrin estimates over a hundred Victorian baths were opened in London alone after the act was passed.

Most of the baths that were built in the early 20th century were grand council projects, often planned decades earlier and coming in stupendously late and over budget. Between 1929 and 1939, the Poplar, Ironmonger Row, East Ham, West Ham, Porchester and York Hall Baths all opened or were refurbished. They were comically over-appointed, generally with a capacity of more than a thousand patrons, all finished in an overstuffed art-deco style of marble and stone with columns and arches all over.

When you speak to patrons who were around for the 1960s and 70s heyday of London's bath culture, it usually prompts recollections of a sepia-tinged social utopia: the rich and poor bathing together. Most remember the baths as remarkably egalitarian – entry was cheap and residents from the local area were encouraged to attend, so people from different communities met on a sort of nude neutral ground. Drinks were often allowed. Larger-than-life figures slipped by you in the steam. Well-known MPs massaged cab drivers. Terence Stamp came in, as did several members of a Jewish street gang who fought the fascists at Cable Street. Most of the legends centre on men, but there were dedicated women's bathing groups as well. Nell Dunn's Olivier-award-winning 1981 play *Steaming* – about a group of East London women who express their true selves in the baths – is derived from her experiences at Ironmonger Row in the 1970s. The bathers were diverse in other ways too; in the Porchester there used to be a massive mahogany table where groups would gather to eat the cafe food or packed lunches. Jerk was always present, alongside South Asian pastries, kosher sandwiches and fry-ups from the kitchen.

There are differing ideas of when the true high point of London bathing culture was, but most agree that there was a clear decline in the 1990s. Some of the traditions and communities that had fed it were already faded: boxing, working men's clubs, the entire profession of dockworking. But councils were also spurred to sell or redevelop their properties and set new priorities. The Poplar and East Ham baths were closed in 1988 and 1990 respectively, later replaced by more modular and family-friendly leisure centres.

As council budgets cratered in the new millennium, these facilities were increasingly contracted out to the companies offering 'spa services' that run them today. The Ironmonger Row and York Hall baths retained their architectural glory but not their original culture or clientele after prices went up and rules changed. Few similar spaces – cheap and oriented around formless, pleasurable leisure time – have been offered in their place. Of the grand old baths, only the Porchester retains nude bathing, and patrons have spent years fighting attempts by the council to outsource, commodify, and otherwise regulate them.

New Docklands Steam Baths was founded in 1977, using equipment salvaged from the East Ham Baths, but took on its current form during the 1980s and 90s in response to these shifts, as a refuge when London's other council-owned baths began to close or change. A charitable trust situated on an industrial estate beside a scrapyard, it was initially started as a squat and seen as beyond the currents of privatisation, profit-seeking, and soaring property prices that killed off the previous generation of London baths. It was also considered a bit rough; when it opened, Porchester bathers told the *Evening Standard* it was run by the Canning Town Mafia, and that its patrons spoke in a 'sub-Kray argot'. The baths' most recent head of trust, Wayne Gruba, an irrepressible storyteller, always said the roughness was part of the point, and vigorously denied any criminal element as incidental, claiming that 'everyone came together in the baths'. The bathers, he said, simply wanted to be left alone by anyone who wanted to change their traditions, and joined by 'anyone: any race, sex, colour or creed' who prized a proper bath above all else. Aesthetics would always be secondary. One illustration of this is his choice of 'homely' as a descriptor in advertisements for the business. Perhaps a better one is the presence of a DIY goat pen, complete with actual goats, in the parking lot.

When the EU expanded in 2004, an influx of banya-loving Baltic Slavs found a home at New Docklands, as did London's rapidly growing Orthodox Jewish community, who were always in need of a schvitz.

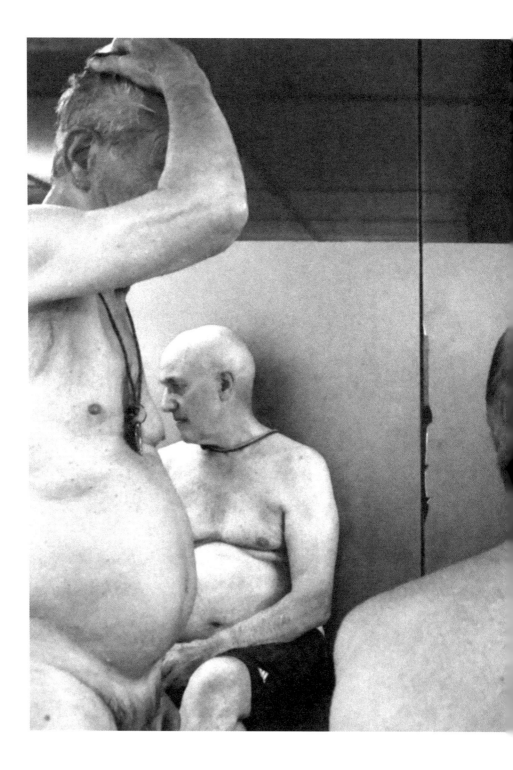

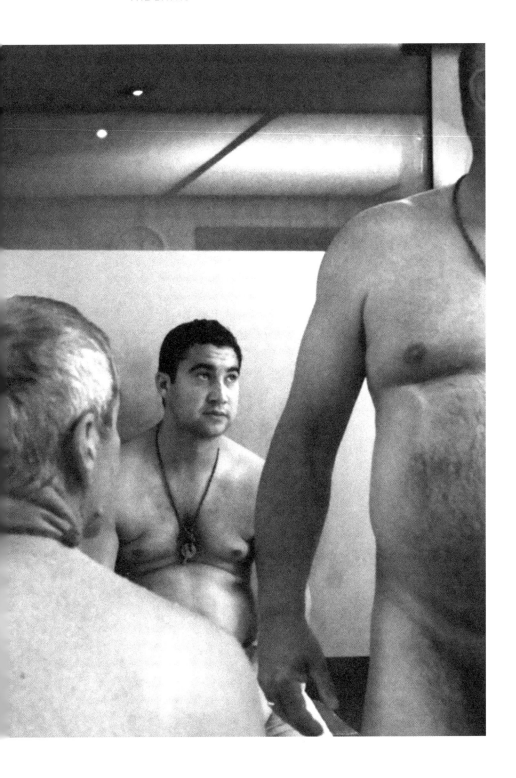

This openness to newcomers with different bathing traditions has always been part of the city's appeal. In the early 20th century, London boasted one of the most unique and diverse bathing cultures in Europe. Private institutions brought specific bathing traditions into the city, and they were melded in the grand council projects that followed. David Urquhart, an MP and diplomat with a senior posting to Istanbul, helped build the first private hammam in London in the 1850s, and gave lectures to Chartist groups and working men's clubs on the pleasure and benefits of Turkish bathing. Meanwhile, Russian Jews fleeing Tsarist oppression over the same period opened vapour baths in the Russian tradition all over the East End.

From the Jewish vapour baths, New Docklands picked up the tradition of schmeissing, a washing style that uses a palm-fibre mop to both strike and scrub another bather. The most obvious antecedents for schmeissing are the plant boughs from the Slavic Banya tradition, and the body scrub found in the Turkish hammam, but long-time bathers claim it also comes from a line of Jewish ritual cleaning. Schmeissing is talked about with semi-mystical airs; only an experienced schmeisser may wield a schmeiss to wash others, for example. It also imposes a structure and continuity in the bathing community. Entire bathing groups form around the responsibility of making and caring for their schmeisse, along with a loose hierarchy of mutual washers and masseuses who volunteer to perform the spa-like services of the baths for free. It is the core thread that anchors the London tradition, sets it apart from others, and inspires the kind of hardcore devotees required to sustain a multi-generational culture.

Today, the long table at the Porchester is gone, and the cafe sells only takeaway sandwiches. New Docklands still struggles with funding, and the travails of running a decades-long charity project. Modern London exerts a terrible outward pressure on anything that fails to produce not just a profit, but a big return. Instead of being central to neighbourhoods, baths have been pushed to the margins of the city, or transformed by its new commercial logic. But it would be a mistake to describe them only with nostalgia, as a charming holdout of a dying culture. London bathing is still a living tradition. At New Docklands you will find lockers full of schmeisses kept by regular bathing groups. The old steam rooms rival anything that can be found in the city's high-end spas, and available much hotter if you'd like. A new 20-person sauna and outdoor plunge pool were added as more Eastern Europeans and Russians came through the doors. Part of it feels like a portal into an older era of the city, but the clientele is, on the whole, surprisingly young.

These bathers come and sustain the place for the same reason the old bathers fight for Porchester to stay the same. A place where time unfolds slowly and every instance of personal pleasure won't be squeezed for profit. They are the inheritors of London's bath culture, built on foundations of Victorian morality and the utopian dreams of the 20th century welfare state, and fed by the great migrations and industries that constituted the city. The newer 'spa style' baths offer wellness as coping, as if whatever relaxation you may receive is being kept on a ledger, to be used in a later transaction against the stress of the world. But great baths tap into something different – they are slower, more elemental, accountable only for their own traditions. In an increasingly expensive, atomised and unmoored city, they feel like an escape. The outside world truly vanishes in the steam.

Wayne Gruba sadly passed away in October 2021, following a battle with Covid. Wayne was wholly dedicated to preserving the New Docklands baths and their traditions, and his stories told in the Docklands cafe, about East London baths and the larger-than-life characters who inhabited them, sparked my own interest in this history. Another long-time trustee has succeeded him as director of the baths and intends to keep them running. The baths, and the goats, are safe for the moment.

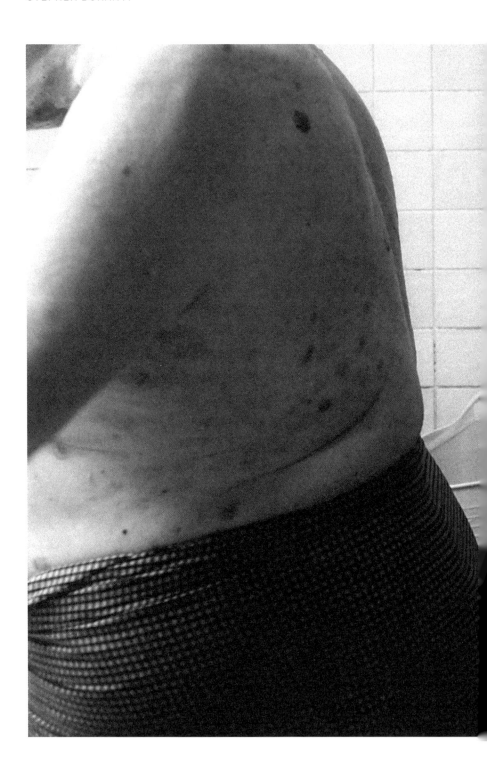

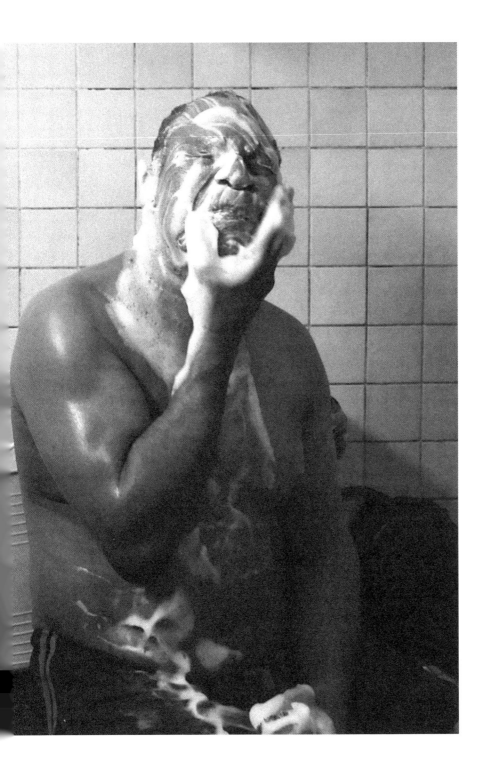

THE APRÈS-SAUNA MEAL

Baths and food usually shouldn't go together. Certainly, food should never be consumed in the bath, or else the experience becomes a zero-sum game of cleanliness (as it surely was for the person covered head-to-toe in tattoos who was observed by a friend of mine eating a whole poached fish with his fingers at New Docklands Steam Baths). And food before a bath is ruinous, weighing you down, making you too aware of your own body at the exact point that you want it to melt away. No, the only thing that should be consumed during a hot bath is either cold water, refrigerated champagne or vodka from the freezer, all things that you wouldn't mind spilling over your naked body, cooling you from the inside while you're being gently oven-roasted on the outside.

But food after a bath? It's obligatory, needed even. Sweating out all your insides and electrolytes is liable to leave you feeling famished and depleted, which is why all the best baths serve some kind of après-sauna food. Often this food is as wet as the baths themselves: dumplings steamed and slick, like the bald pates of retired boxers in the steam room; soups and stews – hearty food to sate a body now working like a machine to stop itself from drying out. At the New Docklands Steam Baths, this is the food of the old and new East End coming together: salt beef from Ashkenazi Jews, pelmeni from Russians, kippers because they're the British version of pickled herring, kebabs (not for the old Turkish hammams but for the new Londoners, from the Middle East to the Baltic countries, for whom kebabs are vernacular foods). More importantly, it's where the real world starts to fade back in, like a Polaroid: in the baths we are all one body, like the Borg, we all experience the same heat, we suffer equally, but it is in choosing our food that we once again assert the individuality of taste.

BANYA NO.1

If you want an experience, a story, you go to New Docklands. But if you just want a really good steam, some good food, and to luxuriate for three hours, then you can pay five times the price and go to Banya No. 1, a private baths in Hoxton (and now Chiswick) that caters almost solely to homesick Russians and people who have been given gift vouchers and aren't quite sure what they're in for. The big draw here is the parenie treatment, where your naked body is slowly beaten to death with birch branches on an altar-like table in the sauna, while other naked people look on. And then, once it's all over: shots of vodka; carmine borscht with garlic and pork fat; plump pelmeni, well-filled, bouncy, and genuinely better than most Russian restaurants in the city. Yes, it's expensive, but you could spend the same sort of money at Novikov and be red and nude only from embarrassment.

ALBINA

The real move at New Docklands is to skip the bistro and walk up the road to King's, the Ugandan-owned bar that serves food from Guinea-Bissau, or Albina, a Ukrainian restaurant whose copious use of raw garlic makes Richard Olney look like a coward. The menu might provoke the same exhortation as a compilation of risible Adrian Chiles columns – cold herring and onion, beef tongue and mayonnaise, liver in 'delicious sauce', and, most appealingly and appallingly of all, salo: lard with garlic, unnecessarily wrapped like a marzipan cake decoration into a pork fat flower, and served with chopped raw garlic on the side. The borscht here uses chicken stock and tomato as its base, ruby-hued and pungent with dill, with an island of sour cream that spreads into an archipelago over the course of eating. It is, of course, served with a clove of raw garlic which should be nibbled between gulps. 'If one of you has it, you all have to have it,' the waitress once advised me. 'Otherwise it's unfair.'

BERNELIU UZEIGA

Beckton was once a mythical realm for me, a place where my dad told me everything from the bathroom ended up. He was right, of course, but 30 years later Beckton, a short trip on the DLR from Canning Town, is now the place to come for Lithuanian restaurants which feed one of London's newest demographics. Berneliu Uzeiga is actually a chain, a pub with decor somewhere between a castle and a school holiday chalet: lurid pink-orange walls, plush benches, melancholy Lithuanian electro-trash, and Guy Fieri on the TV. It's a riot. Lithuanian cuisine is perfect post-sauna food, an exercise in how many combinations of pork, potato, and dairy it's possible to eat before exhaustion sets in (with enough sauerkraut and beetroot horseradish, the answer is 'all of them'). The best and most evil of all options can be found in the snacks: soldiers of brown toast rubbed with garlic and covered in a snowstorm of grated cheese. This is cuffing-season food.

BALZAMBĀRS

Down the road from The Porchester Spa, and down the stairs of a five-storey Victorian town house, is the bar of the Latvian Welfare Fund, Balzambārs, which holds the distinction of being the only Latvian bar in the entirety of the city (so secret that even many Latvians don't know about it). Go on a normal day and you might find beers refreshingly labelled from 'light' to 'medium dark' to 'dark' (rather than increasingly baroque versions of IPA), bar snacks which range from dill crisps to chip-sized stale toast sticks that vibrate with garlic, and a Russian guy propping up the bar quizzing the waitress on Latvian sayings. On Friday and Saturday, you can book yourself in for a three-course menu (remember those?) which might be something like frikadeller, a soup of meatballs that squeak on the teeth; a delicious fried pork schnitzel with melted cheese, tomato and roast potatoes; a salad made almost entirely of chopped raw leek; and a meringue roulade. Food how it used to be, and sometimes still is.

UMUT 2000

A bath and massage at the Turkish Hamam in Dalston, followed by kaburga at Umut 2000 next door, is maybe the perfect one-two hit of relaxation in London: one a dying breed of Turkish baths that have almost vanished from the city, the other the best of a very crowded field of East London grill houses. Umut 2000 is where you go for the close-up, elbows in, lamb-fat-in-your-hair feel of a good ocakbasi. Sit by the mangal and order a plate of ribs, which are cut across the bone, creating raised dimples of meat you'll have to pull off each rib with your teeth. There is bread on the table, painted with a red woad of hot pepper paste and MSG, and if you're considering using this to rip off the crispy hubcaps of creamy fat before exploring the bone, saltier than sea water, with your tongue, then finally stripping it bare: you should give in to temptation.

the canteen

The Euston Road is a great river of capital, it flows it flows it flows and never stops. When I emerge, blinking, from the British Library in search of food, I have the dizzying feeling that I am about to slide into a current that is too strong, and which will rob me of my bodily autonomy. The pace on the Euston Road is different to that of my desk; standing at the edge of the pavement, I feel its quickening movement against my ankles.

In Joris-Karl Huysmans' 1882 novella *À vau-l'eau* ('Drifting'), the protagonist Jean Folantin searches Paris for a meal that will not make him feel wretched. Folantin drifts from disappointment to dis- appointment with ever greater desperation. Brief glimmers of hope are snuffed out: 'It was a mistake to leave one bad restaurant in order to go to another no less bad, and after all that to end up eating rotten vol-au-vents from a patisserie!' In the end he gives up and goes with the flow – 'à vau-l'eau' – unable to swim against the current in search of something better. Folantin and all who serve him food are afflicted by being the bodies from which capital is extracted; then, exhausted, depressed, and grimy, they drop like sediment to the bottom of a river and become the bedrock supporting its onward flow.

If I go with the flow, it only ever seems to take me through (not *to*) Pret A Manger, where it is difficult to stop or even really pause for more than a few seconds. The space is devoted to fast-moving queu- ing, the lion's share of which is given in most branches to pathways towards the bank of tills. *Beep beep beep!* Pret A Manger keeps the queue moving and we shuffle along the aluminium floor that has just enough grip on its surface so we do not slip before we have paid.

I feel the ghost of Jean Folantin on the Euston Road each time
I paddle desperately away from Pret A Manger, seeking a meal that
makes me feel alive – until one day I follow a tip and escape up
Ossulton Street, landing at Nata28 at the Somers Town Community
Centre. The cafe-cum-canteen is a slip of a space snatched from
the lobby of a centre offering medical and social support to local
residents. Lodged in a nook that just escapes the reach of the current
coursing along the Euston Road, it is a catching place, where life can
get a foothold. I dig around and find the notes about the first visit in
my journal from November 2019.

> Despair at the erosion of institutional provisions
> → Twitter conversation about the British Library canteen
>
> A recommendation from X about a cafe for lunch. No time
> to go, too difficult to extract myself from institutional
> architecture which should have a canteen that is cheap
> because it is so very difficult to exit.

One month later:

> Still without a secure contract, returning from a meeting
> with a very nice academic who will support my application
> for a project about – eating in public – on the tube, making
> my way to the library.
>
> I go to the library and put my backpack in the locker
> (after a security check, of course). Then I leave and walk
> to where the Twitter conversation told me to go and find
> a tiny space that shares the institutional flooring with the
> community centre – grey-white tiles.

Nata28 is not particularly visible from the outside and appears unexpectedly as I walk along the residential street. The windows are small, and it is difficult to see in, unlike the hyper-visibility (or is it vigilance?) of the glassy walls at Pret A Manger. The space is like a thin stretched-out semi-circle. I enter halfway along its length.

At the entrance, a cabinet is devoted to the Portuguese nata custard tart, with signs advertising discounts on multiples: '4 NATAS = £5 MORE THAN 10 PLEASE ORDER THE PREVIOUS DAY ☺'. Another display unit carries, from top to bottom: doughnuts and cake, macaroons, and biscuits, wrapped sandwiches, and on the bottom, deep-fried breaded rissoles with different fillings.

I have a peach iced tea, a suckling pig rissole, a hot sandwich. The iced tea makes me think of Europe and the rissole is garlicky and soft and sweet in a thin chewy pastry, coated in cornmeal. Then a small coffee and a nata tart: 'Do you want cinnamon on the nata?' asks the woman at the counter. 'What do you think?', I ask. 'I, as a Portuguese woman, always have it because it opens up the egg yolk flavour.' All sorts is going on around me; the double doors to the community centre swing back and forth. A man says loudly 'I have a urine sample!' and there are people who will listen.

When I return in November 2021, the scant notes in my journal show there is still a lot happening –

Nata28
Sequestered in Somerstown Community Centre building.
Three young women with a baby and chips. Other kids are
at school. Drs and nurses. Beautiful pancakes with berries
on come out for the women. A road sweeper comes in
and uses the toilet. Wooden Christmas decorations,
decorated by children with flags of different nationalities.
A carer-type figure asks after the welfare of one of the
young women, who says, 'I feel better. Not depressed.'
Do you feel ready to work from home? Do you know what
you're doing? 'Yeah'.

Few things make me feel more romantically full of hope
than a cheap cafe or canteen.
to encounter a menu like this
it is to encounter oneself
– in a safe, holding space.

£1.60 suckling pig rissole
£1.20 prawn rissole
£1.30 side salad
£1.20 coke
£2 flat white and nata tart made in house

£7.30

The architectures of welcome in Nata 28 are multilayered. The easy connection to the community centre through the double doors, the pricing (my meal is less expensive than one dry sandwich and a drink at the British Library cafe), and indistinct purpose make the space navigable to many people, and allow diverse forms of living to take place inside. The space is carved out of the community centre and the spirit of public service has left a residue in the cafe, making it into a public canteen on a tiny scale.

My body is quick to tell me if an eating place will acquire the status of 'canteen': it has to do with how comfortable I feel stopping moving. Can I remain seated for long enough that I can eat and digest and feel rested? Since I began experiencing periodic spells of fatigue several years ago, I have become acutely aware of whether a space allows me to rest, and I experience architecture in a new way. If stopping moving for too long means that a business will not meet its KPI for profit generated per square foot, I find out via a dizzy feeling in my head and a sense of panic that I will not be able to sit down. Spaces that are designed to keep me moving moving moving with the current of capital more often make me unwell.

In Pret A Manger on the Euston Road I am whooshed through, minimising the interval of time between crossing the threshold, spending money, and leaving. It is difficult to imagine a 'lunch *hour*' there. At Nata28, once I am seated at a table on the right or left side of the entrance, there is no urgency to move. The layout does not channel me out of the door as soon as I have paid. I extend my time there with a second order of coffee and a nata tart after finishing a savoury dish. People do not hurry away – but nor do they stay all day on laptops or having a business meeting. Varied needs – to eat, to rest and have a nice time, and to receive care – are allowed to be visible in the cafe. Perhaps that is why customers are mindful that others should have use of its space, too.

Like Folantin, I dream of a place to eat that does not make me feel physically wretched. I keep a mental list of sites where I can feel fragments of a utopian, dreamed-about canteen that a few years ago I defined as 'a seat, a table, a glass of water, a plate of food with the calorie density to sustain a life for a good while; the space and the time in which to unfold.' At Italia Uno on Charlotte Street, I might have a cannolo and a coffee after a plate of parmigiana di melanzane or a ciabatta sandwich, and I can disappear peacefully into the ambient sound of Italian TV. In Wong Kei in Chinatown tea is brought in a stainless-steel pot as soon as I sit down: refreshment is given before money has been spent (or even promised). The IKEA canteen in Croydon is cheap – there are enough chairs, toilets and plug sockets, and the space is large enough that one never feels pressured to leave. I love the atemporality of cafeterias on the top floor of department stores where I might have been sitting next to white-haired shoppers eating large slices of cake for five minutes or five hours.

On a work trip into London following a week of fatigue in late March 2022, I held Nata28 in my mind as a beacon in which to seek respite. I did all I could to limit my energy use on my journey: I took the train at a less busy time, I moved slowly, I did not hurry, I sat down whenever possible. At lunchtime, I began walking in the direction of the cafe.

It is very cold after a week of warmth. Grey, a chill. I walk out of the library building and turn right away from Euston Road. A grey, blurred-edge moment in the spring. I walk along past the gargantuan new Francis Crick Institute building and note the new brightly-coloured stickers and a sign saying, 'Living Centre' on the glass walls of entrance and 'Somers Town Community Association.' I am confused and a little worried, as it reads like a displacement of where I am headed.

I keep walking and begin to feel unsure if I am on the right street as I cannot see the A-board ahead, though I recall that on other occasions the modest scale of the cafe had also left me feeling like I was on the wrong street or have not walked far enough.

These are things I tell myself to feel reassured. I begin watching a woman walking in front of me. She is walking intensely, holding a cigarette and drink in one hand and veering slightly in a zig-zag and she goes. She begins to veer towards the entrance to the cafe which suddenly comes into view, as well as an A-board. I feel relief but then I see the A-board does not say Nata28 as I expected, but other words in a different font. Then I think, maybe they're advertising a special, or maybe the A-board is being used by one of the community organisations that use the adjacent space. There are often people who appear to be receiving medical treatment or social care walking through or eating and meeting in the cafe.

Then I notice no chairs outside and wonder if it was due to the chill in the air. But then I see the door was locked shut and a sign saying

'POP-UP CAFE OPPORTUNITY AT SOMERS TOWN COMMUNITY CENTRE'

and I feel distraught, lost, unmoored, very tired. I take a photo of the poster to confirm the situation. I feel wounded by the closure.

I search online and find a note on their Facebook page: 'hard times and the increase of the cost of living took [from] us the capacity of continuing with our beloved cafe.' The canteen has been eroded away. 'The simplest thing is to go back again to the old eatery, to return tomorrow to the awful fold.' I become a despondent Folantin disappointed once more, and drift along the street, back into the library and buy a very bad, expensive sandwich.

WHEN DOES A RESTAURANT BECOME A CANTEEN?

Answering this riddle is a bit like wondering when a fish stops being a fish, or what constitutes pornography: yes, there are many different indicators that what you're seeing may be a canteen, but one of them alone doesn't necessarily make it one, nor does every canteen need to abide by each rule to qualify. Rather, the canteen-ness of the space is always in flux, dependent on a mixture of variables constantly being twiddled like a hi-fi's sound system.

Take institutional canteens, for instance. These are, indisputably, canteens. They are the ur-canteens, the canteens that are, almost always, the first canteens we will ever experience, birthed as we are into a world of turkey dinosaurs, spongy pizza and cold custard. They are a respite from the day, a one-hour leisure sandwich between two slabs of hard work. But you don't experience time there the same way you do in some of the best canteens, where it spreads out before you, shapeless, with no horizon except closing time. In her essay *I Dream of Canteens*, Rebecca May Johnson cites IKEA and McDonald's as the two consumerist models for a modern canteen. Johnson is under no illusions: these spaces are not in any way utopian – they are there to sell us more things – but she notes that they function differently to most other restaurants, one example on the city's edges and the other in its centres. 'No one is asked to leave and no one feels anxious about out-staying their welcome. Of course people *do* leave, but still, staying is not suspicious', Johnson observes.

Yet cafes catering to anxious millennials trying to work outside of their house – where the price of day-long entry is a flat white – are not canteens, nor are restaurants where long lunches blend into dinner. A canteen must not only be cheap and utilitarian (indeed, some kind of subsidisation is always welcome, which makes sure the food punches above the price), but there must also be a sense of commensality – that you might be able to start a conversation with your neighbour, as long as they don't want to be left alone – and also of equality: that no table is worth more or less than

the next. And, at the very least, if the food is served from metal trays then you can definitely say it's a canteen.

WONG KEI

If I was put in charge of the UK's National Food Service and was given the chance to set up new British Restaurants, my own personal canteen would look something like the notorious Soho Chinatown restaurant Wong Kei, where the menu choices are as infinite and recursive as Borges' library: the food cheap and hot, the tea hot and free, and the chilli oil free and plentiful. The curt service puts you on equal terms with your server; the communal seating allows you the same with your fellow diner. The chilli oil makes the worst things on the menu taste good, and the best things, like the beef brisket noodle soups and the stuffed tofu, green peppers and aubergine, taste every bit as satisfying as a Michelin-starred dish. And all for less than a Pret meal. Now I'm not saying we should nationalise Wong Kei, but also, nationalise Wong Kei!

DAPUR

To get the full choice at Dapur, a nasi campur (mixed rice) canteen in Bloomsbury, you have to come at 12 on the dot – once a tray has gone it's rarely replenished, and by 1:30pm you may as well not bother. Over the years I've enjoyed shatteringly crisp fried chicken and sticky ayam kicap berempah here, as well as beef rendang simmered down to fraying point, but I've particularly loved the lesser-seen dishes from Johor, the Malaysian peninsula's southern thumb, like the pinkish ayam ros Johor, or steamed tofu dipped in egg, deep-fried and stirred in sambal. But the unsung heroes of the Dapur menu are the vegetables – stir-fried green beans that still retain a snap, squash cooked down in coconut milk until it is almost baby food. Nasi campur is a mixed plate that you need to zoom out from, like a pointillist painting: when combined with their other components – a pool of sambal, two halves of a boiled egg, coconut rice, peanuts and some crispy anchovies – eating these dishes has the same satisfaction as watching the last piece of a particularly complex puzzle lock into place.

LA PLACITA

Whether La Placita is a canteen, or a hawker centre, or a market hall, or a mode of eating imported right out of a Bogota strip mall, is debatable. What isn't up for debate is that this Tetris block of stalls, piled up on top of and next to each other, some-where on the bend where Old Kent Road fades into New Cross, is completely unique in London: not even Latin Village in Tottenham gets close to the chaos of La Placita on a karaoke night, when the whole place is rocking to Spanish pop, beer is flowing, someone you don't know has just handed you an empanada, and you've realised that every dining room is a dance hall waiting to break free. The stalls are generally Colombian or Ecuadorean, with a smattering of Dominican and Cuban food, but if you can't choose, then don't worry: you will be rushed by a cadre of aunties each trying to sell you something that they have cooked especially for you.

MALAYSIA HALL CANTEEN

There are dynasties and then there's Malaysia Hall Canteen, an institution within the Malaysian High Commission which has incubated a whole swathe of London's Malaysian cooking. At the time of writing, the Canteen is closed due to permit issues, after having gone from a public canteen to a private one, accessible only with a Malaysian passport (however, if you were brown enough and knew how to say 'hello' in Malay, you could usually get through). Now the canteen's diaspora is spread throughout London, with their old audiences following them for their 'air tangan' – their hand water, which imbues every dish with a signature taste. Pak Awie, the chef here during the mid 2010s, is now at MELUR in Paddington, while Kak (Sister) Anie is at MAKAN CAFE under the Westway on Portobello Road, where nasi campur

is dished out canteen-style, in a space that looks like a rundown caff. Anie's nephew Shubli, by the way, now runs an outstanding outfit called MALAY FELLAS @ PUTERA PUTERI in Bayswater, while his brother owns RUMI'S CAFE, in Rumi's Cave. As I said: dynasty.

INDIAN YMCA

Supplying guests at the YMCA with food, and journalists with cheap copy on 'Why it's Fun to Eat at the YMCA' alike, the Indian YMCA is that rare thing: a genuine central London canteen that's open to everyone. Breakfast here is a split continental/Indian affair, and under strip lights it has a nightmarish hotel buffet effect, but lunch is fully Indian, with a slant towards home-style dishes – dal, green beans, curries that only need the name of their protein and nothing else. The trick here is to treat it like a school canteen and not overload on a variety of food; rather, stick to one route (one side, one main) or go for the set menu of the day. If you go *à la carte*, it's now possible to spend as much here as at Dishoom, which kind of kills the point.

the housing estate

THE EVERYDAY LIVES OF THE MEGASTRUCTURES

It is difficult not to return to the scar across south-east London left by the demolition of the Elephant and Castle shopping centre. This blue, and formerly pink, globule was one of the only truly democratic, comprehensive public spaces in the capital – one disguised as a failed 1960s shopping mall. The destruction of what had become a multifunctional, largely Latin American retail and restaurant complex had many causes, but one of them was the consequence of a town planning theory: the notion that modernist architecture couldn't possibly create a successful 'street'.

Increasingly accepted as the source of 'iconic' public buildings and housing, modernism is still blamed for destroying an imagined world of corner shops, pubs and the ability to leave your door open at night. The fact that the Elephant and Castle shopping centre included many of South London's most interesting 'streets' was something that current town planning doctrine would judge to be impossible, and few clues were given by the building's monolithic exterior: the only way you could find it out was to go there and look.

When you did so, you could see an urban space of considerable complexity. There was the market surrounding the centre (which was a later addition, not envisaged by the architects Paul Boissevain and Barbara Osmond) and inside, there were some of the things you'd find on any ordinary street – a chain supermarket, a bank – but there were also many kiosks and mini-shops serving Walworth's Latin American population. There were community functions like the bingo hall, with its extremely cheap British and Caribbean food, and at the top, a bowling alley that was maybe the only place in the whole of south-east London to be used by almost all of the various social groups in the area.

What happened in Elephant, curiously enough, was that the unpredictable, 'unplanned', grass roots changes in the area happened through the intersection of post-war planning and working-class multiculturalism: the places that feel like an imposition, like a contrivance, are those which have strived to follow the organic and unplanned 19th century models, and which are now routinely used as an example of the only sensible way to build cities.

owen hatherley

HOW TO KILL A STREET, OR NOT

Not everything in modernism can be blamed on Le Corbusier – but the suspicion of streets can. One of the Swiss architect's slogans in his celebrated and notorious mid-1930s outline of a 'Radiant City' was 'We must kill the street'; that is, we must destroy the 19th-century planning model, where a through-road is lined on either side by tenements or terraces with a row of shops underneath. These were considered by Le Corbusier to be congested, polluted, chaotic, unsafe, and best replaced with, well, what Elephant eventually became: large slab blocks of flats in green space connected to community amenities. This was executed pleasantly at the Heygate, and more harshly at the nearby Aylesbury, but in both cases with no obvious old-school thoroughfares (though the nearby 18th–19th century conduits of East Street and Walworth Road survived the Elephant's replanning).

Illustration of the Elephant
and Castle Shopping Centre,
designed by Paul Boissevain
and Barbara Osmond,
from a brochure produced
by the Willets Group, 1965
© Southwark Archives

Conversely, since the 1960s, writers such as Jane Jacobs and James C. Scott have looked at the bustling streets of areas like the pre-war Elephant and found a spontaneous order which they often associated with restaurants, hardware stores, corner shops and other small businesses – the 'vibrant' spaces that attracted middle-class people back to the areas depopulated by bombing and planning. Since then, the notion has become fixed: an architect, or the state, cannot successfully plan these sorts of spaces – in fact, to do so would kill off the anarchic energy and serendipity that multicultural retail and food spaces thrive upon.

This criticism is not completely without merit. The early London County Council estates such as the Boundary in Shoreditch and Millbank in Pimlico, for all their arts-and-crafts grandeur, replaced teeming and messy conglomerations of pubs, butchers, bakers, greengrocers and brothels with a couple of cafes and a store (and never, ever a pub). Looking at the suburban council estates of the 1930s, George Orwell praised their comforts, their heating and their spaciousness, but lamented how the old shops were usually replaced with one big Co-Op. But the fact is that London has dozens of planned, council-designed and often modernist high streets. Scores of cafes and restaurants thrive on them, and they are as complex, unequal and unpredictable as everything else in London. In fact, one thing that is perhaps specific to London is how much diversity can be found in local authority parades and precincts.

Of the 22 years I've lived here, I've spent the last ten on public housing estates in south-east London. Each of these has its own council-built and designed 'high street', and the differences between these are instructive. The first of them I lived by, on the St Mary's Estate in Woolwich, was a typical 1950s shopping parade, with a large and usually empty tree-filled green next to it and a slab-block of flats on the other side. Its fare was the same as you'd find in the council precincts of a new town or a provincial city, tweaked just a little – there was a Post Office, a newsagent run by a Vietnamese family, an old-man pub, a Turkish-run chippy, a West African bakery. Near the small estate of two post-war blocks where I now live in Camberwell, the precinct restaurants can pin magazine reviews to their windows: the Iraqi-Kurdish restaurant Nandine occupies one of the units in the shopping precinct of the low-rise, bricky Lettsom Estate, while Zeret Kitchen is on a more dramatic Brutalist precinct beneath the tower block of Castle Mead. In Jane Jacobs' thought, this gradual ageing of bureaucratically planned units into complex, multifunctional, multicultural spaces, should not have happened. But it has, and any analysis of local authority planning and council housing in London has to take one fact into account – that, eventually, it worked.

A TAXONOMY OF COUNCIL ESTATE HIGH STREETS

Council high streets range between the precincts around squares (the most common type, exemplified by the Dickens Estate in Bermondsey), corner spaces such as the greasy spoon Cat & Cucumber cafe – which elegantly uses the ground floor of the Red Vienna-style St John's Estate – and the sometimes slightly bleak suburban parades of interwar cottage estates such as St Helier in Morden, which nowadays as often contain Bulgarian restaurants as branches of the brightly lit greasy spoon chain Star Express. Aside from in Globe Town on Roman Road, where two rarely-discussed precincts by Denys Lasdun and Berthold Lubetkin face one another, major architects have seldom had much to do with them.

That is, except for the exemplar, the model which many councils tried hard to follow in the 1950s and 60s: Frederick Gibberd's pioneering Lansbury Estate in Poplar, originally built as part of the Festival of Britain in 1951. Its streets and precincts were planned – and have always functioned – as an ordinary, warm and friendly working-class centre, formed around the then-new Chrisp Street Market and its clock tower. Gibberd's innovation at Lansbury was to try and combine the Corbusian approach – blocks oriented to the sun, buildings suspended above thin pilotis, lots of greenery, clusters of identical towers – with an idealised, slightly nautical idea of 18th-century London, all bow windows and jaunty details. On weekends, it is one of the liveliest bits of the East End, with Medina Bazar and Maureen's Pie and Mash standing opposite one another and, until recently, London's only pease pudding stall. The many schemes inspired by the Lansbury include the fabulous Central Parade in Walthamstow designed by borough architect F. G. Southgate, where shops and cafes stand below a wavy concrete canopy.

Another approach to this problem – maintaining 'neighbourliness' while throwing out the old world of dysentery, rickets and landlords – was to retain the existing century's high streets as a spine between the newly built council estates, as opposed to replacing them completely with a mall. This is what happened a few miles away, on Deptford High Street, which has long had one of the lowest levels of dereliction and the fewest number of chain stores of any British high street – though in an era of landlordism ascendant, this hasn't stopped it being criticised. In a particularly egregious episode of the BBC's *The Secret History of Our Streets*, a claque of former market traders and slum landlords insisted that Deptford High Street had been 'destroyed' by 'the planners', while one of the busiest, friendliest streets in Europe bustled around them. (Remember: a photograph of a group of teenagers hanging around on a street in Deptford in the 1940s is indicative of the good old days, but witnessing an actual, existing group of teenagers hanging around on a street in Deptford in the 2020s signals 'Anti-Social Behaviour'.)

Ironically, though, the most sheerly exciting spaces are often products of 1960s–70s Public–Private Partnerships which, like the Elephant, combined successful social planning with inadvertent retail failure; this caused collapses in rents, after which they became interesting. The bizarre Catford Centre, a design of Owen Luder, is an elaborate 'casbah' (to use the architect's oft-used term) of car parking, flats and shops piled up dramatically over a pedestrian precinct and currently dominated by a giant fibreglass cat. A less dramatic version of the same can be found in the flats tucked away at the top of the megastructure that is Wood Green Shopping City. In Cumbernauld New Town in Scotland, a similar megastructure's penthouse flats have been derelict for years, but in London, where people are used to living in odd places and strange corners, these spaces work – why *not* a ziggurat of council flats, on top of a mall, on top of a market?

INVASION OF THE STREET-SNATCHERS

The evidence of what actually happens in the socially planned municipal spaces of London is not usually enough to save them. The example
of the Elephant shows how wide the gulf can be between contemporary planning ideology (in which planning's role is a self-abnegating
one, there to aid the free market and the property industry) and social
reality, where something that would be 'vibrant' if it were taking place
in a 19th-century street or a cluster of reused shipping containers is
deemed worthless because it is taking place in a modernist megastructure surrounded by Corbusian council estates. Today, the Elephant
and Castle shopping centre's introverted form, its abstraction, its formal complexity and multi-level plan has been replaced by the standard
model for urban architecture and 'real streets': rows of mid-rise flats,
facing stark pavements, above shops. This can be seen in a particularly
patrician form in the wannabe Manhattan grid of the new Elephant
Park development, where you can find Mercato Metropolitano, an old
postal depot turned by developers into a desperately sanitised and
inorganic parody of the unpredictable, complex multicultural commerce of the shopping centre.

Developers know what they want in their new shop units. Aside
from an estate agent, they want a 'vibrant' restaurant, but in the
Dishoom vein: a comfortable version of an imagined, slightly
frightening thing. They might even want a 'street food market'
in the private-public space outside, as well as a branch of Albion
greengrocers. There are many of these spaces now; in Stratford and
the Elephant and Kings Cross, and they are strikingly similar. In
the 2010s, seeing Mercato Metropolitano near to the Elephant and
Castle evoked the scenes in *Body Snatchers*, when a pod containing
a lobotomised, controlled version of a person would dangle in wait
next to a sleeping human being, a body that it would soon replace
with a heartless parody superficially resembling the original. Now
the Elephant has been taken by the street snatchers, it's urgent that
we stop them from killing again.

THE ESTATE RESTAURANT

If you had listened to the way chef Philip Harben told it, you might have concluded that the biggest influence a single housing estate had on London's food was the surprising introduction of the kebab. In 1937, there wasn't much in the way of Turkish restaurants in the city, but at the bar at the Isokon in Belsize Park – an extraordinary Wells Coates-designed constructivist housing estate whose sensual lines and whitewashed walls give the vibe of a Bond lair, or a building in a city with much better weather than London – you may have found kebab on the menu, hiding somewhere between old stagers like hare terrine and stewed rabbit (although back then they were very much new stagers, and the kebab positively avant garde). Dig a little deeper, into Harben's cookbooks though, and you will find recipes for kebabs which are literally just unseasoned kidneys and chipolatas on skewers – a combination which would today get him laughed out of any Green Lanes ocakbasi.

The Isokon was a rare housing project that centred food and its consumption – even the rooms were linked by a pulley dumbwaiter so meals could be delivered from the canteen – but since then the idea that restaurants and food provision should be part of a housing estate has pretty much vanished. When Thamesmead was built in the 1960s, 70s, and 80s, too few food amenities were built nearby or on the town's estates. 'There is a lot currently lacking I think in terms of communal places where people can get together, have a coffee or food,' says resident Bhajan Hunjan in *Tastes of Thamesmead*, a local community cookbook. Even today, in a restaurant-obsessed culture, the town centre contains a KFC, a McDonald's, two chain supermarkets, a pub, a Chinese takeaway and a Pizza Hut. To get an inkling of Thamesmead's true food diversity, you would have to go to the hidden African Cash & Carry, or all the way to Erith to eat ogbono, to discover that the area has a higher concentration of West African residents than Peckham.

The primary link between housing and food today is the way that most restaurants seem to exist solely to drive up house prices in the area: fronts for landlordism. Houses are now advertised by estate agents like The Modern House, with a list of nearby restaurants cribbed from national reviews used as bait. But there are a few – just a smattering of restaurants, unplanned and serendipitous – that act as Thamesmead's street, and use its estates as armour, like a snail in its shell, becoming central to the lives of locals already there.

The third link is perhaps the future: in a world where any home kitchen can become a ghost kitchen for delivery, it is the housing estate itself that can *become* a restaurant: in 2016 Prince Cofie Owusu started cooking from his mum's estate in Camberwell; today, Trap Kitchen is the trendiest restaurant in Balham, of course.

BAKE STREET

There's something about Feroz Gajia's Bake Street, near Rectory Road station, that seems to straddle two worlds. On one hand, it's a generically named halal brunch spot giving a splash of colour to Heatherley Court (with the absence of its name on the awnings, it was destined to become known as 'the yellow cafe'). And yet, on weekends, this housing estate has as many out-of-towner pilgrims as the Barbican or Neave Brown's Alexandra & Ainsworth, all hoping to get their money shot of the expansive brunch menu that flits between about ten cultures in five dishes, like a frenzied Eisenstein montage. What is extraordinary and unique about Bake Street is its sense of play: it is really the only restaurant in the city trying to encompass everything interesting about London in one place (where else could you find the head chef of Quality Wines making a biryani?). The smash burger, the fish cutter, the Nashville Chicken and the Makhani burger are four of the most well-composed sandwiches in the city, while baker Chloe-Rose Crabtree's crème brûlée cookies are maybe THE essential London bake of the moment. Really, this book is just theory; Bake Street is the practice.

NANDINE

Anyone who says breakfast is the most important meal of the day is a liar, your boss, or both. Breakfast in England is a Puritan affair: cereals, toasts and porridge; fuel for the day and eaten swiftly to get you working as early as possible. The only breakfasts really worth eating are the long, leisurely ones which actively resist the idea that meals are punctuations to labour. At the original Nandine on Vestry Road, which forms the backside of the Lettsom Estate, you can get all this in the Kurdish breakfast: a blank canvas of fresh yoghurt and home-made white cheese, fig jam, honey, warm bread just out of the oven, a zingy salad, olives; simultaneously frugal and completely luxurious. Upon starting it, you may feel the day stretching out before you like plates on a table, full of endless possibilities. Yet by the end, if you've done it right, all you'll want to do is go back to bed.

ZERET KITCHEN

To find the best Ethiopian restaurants in London, just check under housing estates. GENET CAFE in Tottenham is beneath a dour set of flats, and a Brutalist housing estate off the Walworth Road – on a makeshift town square that also contains the marvellously named West Indian bakery, Margaret's Cakes of Distinction – houses Zeret Kitchen. Here, Tafe Beleynah works alchemy with lentils that any number of molecular gastronomists and meat-free burger companies would sell their soul to learn the secret of: misir wat – lentils spiced with berbere – which has the uncanny meaty depth of a slow-cooked ragu, or the defin misir wat, a much milder lentil stew, which has a rich, acidic butteriness approximating cottage cheese. The veg dishes are so strong that Zeret frequently gets mislabelled as a vegan restaurant, but the meat is every bit as good: the dulet, the most obviously meaty thing on the menu, combining kidneys and tripe finely chopped into springy anonymity, could convince even the most ardent offal sceptic to convert.

FISH CENTRAL

There are three categories of fish and chip shop: the first is an old-school sit-down place, like The Golden Hind or The Fryer's Delight, which are all past their best and frequented by tourists ticking off a bucket list. The second is one of those handsome new-school fish and chip shops that ikejime their fish, charge double the amount fish and chips should cost, and should actively be avoided. The third is what a chippy should be, a neighbourhood spot that you would go to if you lived nearby. The only central London chippy in this category is Fish Central, forming the north side of an tripartite estate courtyard which contains all the amenities you could need: a corner pub, a launderette, a bookies, a Korean restaurant. Owned by Cypriot George Hussein, the fish and chips here is the highest expression of the Mediterranean-influenced London style: fried to order, cooking gently inside its batter which protects it like a crunchy exoskeleton. A sit-down restaurant is attached, but one of London's great pleasures is to take the package outside, unwrap it like a Christmas present, and greedily eat the steaming chips out on the concrete.

OSLO COURT

Originally a members' club straddling the ground floor of Robert Atkinson's art deco apartment block of the same name in St John's Wood, Oslo Court is perhaps London's most reviewed restaurant. Pretty much every critic has done it once, because it allows the writer to meditate on such grand things as 'the meaning of the restaurant' and the nature of this unchanging institution in a city that does nothing but change. 'Why do people come here?', they wonder, tasting the food which ranges from mediocre to unfuckupable (there's only so much you can do to steak Diane), before noting that restaurants are actually not about food at all, but about fantasy, to be taken somewhere else for an evening where things are precisely as you remember them, where grapefruit segments are on the menu, where Neil is recommending the best dessert on his trolley which he's saved just for you. It could be London's best restaurant, but only if you're in on the joke.

the shopping centre

'It meant a lot to the locals
on Edmonton Green...'

Let us start with a song, for I will bet a paltry sum that none of
the other locations in this book have had one written about them.
You may know Chas & Dave – dimly, at best – for novelty hits: money-
making abominations such as *Glory, Glory, Tottenham Hotspur* and
Snooker Loopy. But get past those songs and two things stand out:
Chas Hodges and Dave Peacock were among the most technically
able musicians of their day, and they sang about working-class life
in London with a precision and pleasure matched only by Madness
or Ian Dury.

Edmonton Green is a prime example. Its subject is unpromising –
who in their right mind writes about a market on the outskirts of North
London and sets it to waltz time? But listen:

They took away Tubby's takeaway
And they've torn down Flash's Tyres
In fact, there ain't an old sight to be seen

Singer Hodges is remembering a world that's disappeared, the one that raised him. Born in 1943, he lived a five-minute walk from the Green and intermittently attended school just around the corner. His first job was in one of its jewellers, repairing old clocks. It was skilled work for which he was well suited, aside from the part about getting up in the morning: one too many late starts finally landed him the sack.

Early last decade, a friend sent me a link to a YouTube video of *Edmonton Green*. Someone had taken the Chas & Dave lyrics and matched them to black-and-white photos of the places the pair sung about. There was the Edmonton Empire, where music-hall singer Marie Lloyd (famous for 'My Old Man [Said Follow the Van]') gave her last show; she collapsed on stage and the audience hooted and clapped, thinking it was part of the act. There was Raggs the chemist who, when faced with certain ailments, would bring out a jar filled with leeches. And there was the open-air market where, as one writer noted before the First World War, the road was 'given up on Saturdays to the coster class on whose barrows are displayed for sale goods of nearly every description for the poorer classes'. The council thought the market lowered the tone, but the traders fought off all attempts to move them on. Hodges sings about paying a penny for jacket potatoes so warm that 'on a winter's afternoon you could make believe that it was June'.

Where others saw an ugly jumble of stalls flogging cheap tat, he saw memories, and his song is less a tour of a place than an itinerary of a childhood. It ends in adolescence, with a nudge in the ribs about 'that night in Pymmes Park':

It was the first time
I'd had a good time
Without laughing

Just as Hodges reached his early 20s, his world was razed to the ground. In the mid-1960s, Edmonton went from being its own municipal borough to getting absorbed into the London Borough of Enfield, and the Green was demolished. An official report argued that 'nearly all the shop property is without special architectural merit,' ignoring its mix of handsome red-brick, timber-framed cottages and coaching inns dating back to the 18th century. It went on: 'The Comprehensive Redevelopment Area is characterised by obsolescence and is ripe for redevelopment'; in other words, they smashed up the historic centre of a centuries-old district simply because they could.

The new council spent £4 million (around £80 million in today's money) on a new shopping and leisure centre with large car parks and tower block housing. It pledged a civic centre – none came. It promised the new covered market would come 'attractively laid out with mature trees, shrubs, planting and a plentiful supply of seating.' The actual result, notes Matthew Eccleston in *Enfield: Portrait of a London Borough*, was 'a concrete jungle replete with all the grace and charm of Erich Hohnecker's [sic] East Berlin'.

I was born and raised on the same streets as the late Chas Hodges. Although a few decades apart, we share a geography – a working-class part of a post-war capital seeking to wash, wax and polish its working-class past until all that is unsightly and unsellable disappears. And I have my own memories of bunking off to Pymmes Park for reasons that would be hard to justify to teachers, but my Edmonton Green was built on the rubble of his.

Sometimes, the very things most dismaying to his generation filled me with excitement. As a child who spent all his school and university years under Margaret Thatcher and John Major, it amazes me even today that a council could find 80 million quid to build anything, let alone a shopping complex. Or take the massive grey flyover that took you into the main entrance of the shopping centre: an absurd structure, given that the high road it towered over could be crossed in seconds, yet it had spiral steps at either end that you could cycle down, slow and bumpy at first, then faster and faster and faster and with less and less control until by the end your bike and your little body could be hurled into the metal railings. It felt *just* scary enough to make it mandatory.

One afternoon this spring, I went for a stroll around the centre with Danny Birchall, who works for the Wellcome Collection and grew up just a few doors down on the same road as me, a fact we only discovered upon meeting last year. This walk was our chance to compare memories as well as to see what was new.

We meet close to the main entrance, where as a teenager Danny put in lots of weekends imploring locals to buy his Trotskyist newspapers. 'We'd shout, "Hate Thatcher? Then you'll love *Socialist Worker*."' With luck, they would make a few sales. With even more luck, they'd make their point. Then they'd go for a beer.

This is the first March in three years that the shopping market is operating as normal, and it is the same thing sung about by Chas & Dave, only under a roof. The scene is barely different from the one I knew as a child, trailing behind my mother as we worked the market late on a Saturday afternoon, me pulling the wheeled shopping basket, my mother bargaining down the greengrocers. The trader I remember best sported a brown moustache a little bigger than a toothbrush head and a look of lordly bemusement that allowed him to cut prices on unsold spinach and act like he was bestowing a favour.

Back then, this suburb was white as Daz and my mother was the only shopper in a sari. Some clearly wish it had stayed that way. Under that YouTube video are commenters discussing the 'slum' of modern Edmonton; one asks: 'Where have all the white faces gone?' Back in the early 2000s a senior Tory councillor likened the place to 'a UN feeding station'. Today, the traders are nearly all Black or Eastern European, and a stall specialising in Afro-Caribbean fruit and veg adjoins one offering Mauritian produce, which is next to another selling Ghanaian sugar bread in dense white loaves from a warehouse in Tottenham. One of the stallholders catches me jotting down what's for sale. Big mistake. Taking photos no longer arouses suspicions now everyone has a camera in their pocket, but who carries a notebook apart from coppers? A bit of explaining, though, and Omar Bowlyn is giving us the rundown of today's items. He has cassava from Brazil, cocoa yam from Jamaica, white sweet potatoes from Uganda; the list goes on…

When economist John Maynard Keynes sought to depict the glories destroyed by World War One, he looked to shopping: 'The inhabitant of London could order by telephone, sipping his morning tea in bed, the various products of the whole Earth.' An Edwardian gentleman could enjoy 'conveniences, comforts and amenities beyond the compass of the richest and most powerful monarchs of other ages'. This is the version of globalisation that still haunts today's Sunday supplements: well-heeled Westerners gorging on stuff grown or made far away, in Black and brown countries. But a different dynamic is at work when the people originally from those parts of the world are also the consumers. In hyper-diverse Edmonton, for instance, it is impossible to ignore the history of the items on sale in this market: those long, thick sugarcanes in the corner once harvested by slaves in the West Indies, the breadfruit intended as cheap food to keep their bellies full and their spirits pacific.

The middle-class chains that were here when Danny and I were kids have mostly gone – some, like Woolworths, to retail heaven, others such as Sainsbury's to wealthier areas. The old swimming pool is today a big Asda, outside which five vans are cooking everything from pink Bulgarian karnache coiled sausages to rotisserie chicken. At the end is an orange van with 'The Midyeci' written on the front, where a man in a cap beckons to us. This is an outpost of the shop of the same name in Dalston, which claims to be the first in the UK to specialise in Turkish stuffed mussels. On the evidence of this after-noon, the concept excites Edmonton shoppers less than the van next door rolling out halal pizzas. Luckily for The Midyeci, Emir Ogut – the man in the cap – is a consummate charmer. He hands over a plate of black shells that we prise apart to reveal orange mussels packed into little brown balls of rice. The intricacy of the arrangement and its hint of labour appeals more than their somewhat flat taste – until he starts adding spice. Emir tells us he has been in the UK for only a few months, giving up a career in Istanbul. 'I sold medical equipment!' he laughs – whether at his past or his present, I don't know.

We order what the van advertises as 'Fish bread', also known as balik ekmek – mackerel fillets freshly grilled and stuffed into a hunk of baguette, handed over with half a lemon. Even excluding all of Emir's free samples, the prices come in at about 25% cheaper than what you'd expect to pay a couple of TfL zones in. And for the first time this year the sun has got his hat on, which means Danny and

I can perch on a bench and for half an hour pretend that we're by the Bosphorus, rather than in the shadow of a 'Sam 99p' store.

Even though the Edmonton Green that I grew up in is the one that obliterated Chas Hodge's childhood, perhaps he would have recognised the spirit of improvised entertainment that persists today. But over the next few years, it will be altered beyond recognition. The shopping centre's relatively new owners, Crosstree, want to knock down the lot and put up 13 new tower blocks, some 35 storeys high. The emphasis will be on housing rather than shops, although not many of the planned 1,500 new homes are genuinely affordable.

Back in the market, Omar and his brother are excited about the prospect of a new cinema and a bowling alley. What about those residents who can no longer afford to live here, I ask them: where will they go? 'London's always expanding. There'll be some place for them to go,' says Omar's brother, 'like Luton.' He shrugs, and in the air I can hear the faint resignation of that Chas and Dave song:

Edmonton Green, Edmonton Green
You're gone but you'll always live on
in my dreams …

'GIVE ME THE CHILD...'

Why does the shopping centre loom large in the memories of so many Londoners? Part of it is certainly because of our mums, harried and time-poor, using the efficiency of the shopping centre to get errands done, screaming kids in tow. I think many of us grew up hating shopping centres for this reason, seeing them only as sites of inertia and trauma. Lay a Londoner down on a tan chaise longue and delve back far enough, and I guarantee that repressed memories of a Zone 4 mall or a giant Matalan will come flooding back.

You can find these shopping centres across the UK, yet there is something about their particular geographic placement within London that makes them more appealing once you slip into teendom. If you were born in a London suburb, you either grew up in an area where not enough was going on, or too much was going on. The area with too much going on had a shopping centre. It is the difference between Bounds Green and Wood Green, between Enfield Town and Edmonton, between Hampstead Garden Suburb and Brent Cross. If London is many different towns combined into one, then shopping centres are those towns' economic and social hubs, reorienting the city centre away from the West End and towards them. Londoners rarely grow up in Zone 1, surrounded by culture; in the absence of anything else, the local shopping centre is where we first learn to experience the city on our own terms.

Food is a huge part of this. The thing about suburban shopping centres is that they are 90% the same – the same shops, the same kiosks, even the same smells – a mixture of new clothes, old leather and, somehow, chaat, despite the fact that no one ever seems to be selling it. They might contain a Cineworld, a Costa, a Primark, a Lidl, an Argos, an Avogadro's number of shoe and accessory shops, and nothing more aspirational than a H&M. Food is the missing 10% which makes each shopping centre different. 'Give me the child for seven years', Wood Green, Brent Cross and Edmonton Green shopping centres all tell us, 'and I will show you the man who reps his postcode'.

Just ask the drillers who launch postcode wars against Tottenham with Wood Green's red brick shopping centre in the background. There is something of your local shopping centre that doesn't leave you; it is neither love or hate, nor nostalgia, but a kind of ownership and protectiveness from the outsiders who don't understand their banality or grim unloveliness. Squint, and that trauma might even look something like affection.

UNCLE LIM'S

Sometimes shopping centres create culture before it's reproduced centrally: in Croydon's Whitgift Centre, people travel specifically to go to Uncle Lim's, a Malaysian-Chinese restaurant on the upper floor which was selling notably good Hainanese chicken rice years – if not decades – before anywhere in Borough Market made it 'a thing'. Being an actual part of the open-plan shopping centre, with no doors or barriers separating it, Uncle Lim's has the feeling of a canteen or kopitiam in KL or Singapore rather than a part of South London that has the distinct feel of a chainified city-centre somewhere in the Midlands, and is perfect for a very casual bowl of laksa, har mee (prawn noodles) or just a plate of that chicken, which comes served with rice cooked in its own stock.

MAURITIUS PARADISE

Mauritius Paradise Catering is a long-standing feature of Wood Green Shopping City (now pretentiously called The Mall, as if it were located in an anonymous American suburb), the end point for thousands of family trips spent traipsing around miles of shopping centre. It is located in a scruffy section of The Mall which has stayed defiantly unchanged since my childhood, while everything else changed around it: the same grocers, fishmongers, butchers, the same discounted fake jeans. Here you can buy gateaux piment and gateaux arouilles with chutney if you're in need of a snack, or larger diaphanous rotis stuffed with soft chicken livers or the sweet Mauritian-Chinese preparation of peppers, onions and chicken simply known as chop suey. Either way, both heave appealingly with oil; a worthwhile treat after hours of shopping.

SHEN MAURITIAN FUSION

At Edmonton Green shopping centre, the serpentine sections of retail corridors all coalesce into a central courtyard of ramshackle stalls, selling fresh produce and everything from Turkish hot nuts to kenkey. It was a food court before food courts existed. If the owners weren't already thinking about building housing on top of it, then it could serve as the next location for Market Halls Edmonton. At Shen, a small Mauritian caterer, you can sit down at one of two tables and order whatever is available that day: dholl roti, or chicken biryani or, if the owner is in, some noodles which display the hybridity of Mauritian-Chinese food.

KAIETEUR KITCHEN

Greatness is usually measured in terms of high water marks, but there is another kind of yardstick that goalkeeper Peter Schmeichel used to describe the greatness of Paul Scholes, as someone whose absolute worst performance never registers as noticeable: a high 'bottom level'. By this metric, Faye Gomes of Kaieteur Kitchen has the highest bottom level in the city: it is impossible to have a meal here that is anything less than good, and the best of her Guyanese dishes have the sublime quality of a spun-on-a-dime 50 yard cross-field pass. Kaieteur Kitchen used to be located in the doomed Elephant and Castle shopping centre moat but has now moved to a temporary wooden structure opposite the station, with a small dining room to show off Gomes's hospitality. There is technically a menu here, but far better just to talk to 'Auntie Faye' and be fed; although, on Friday, the pepper pot, bittersweet with cassareep and containing cow foot with the texture of good *pâte de fruits*, is unmissable.

ROTI KING

Roti King's journey is the ultimate example of how the centre is always about a decade behind the suburbs. It started off life as a stall in the food court of Oriental City – a shopping centre in Colindale for the East and South East Asian community – run by Kalpana Sugendran Sugendran. When Oriental City was sold off, he moved to the kitchens of Malaysia Kopi Tiam in a Chinatown mini-mall, a precursor to the idea of residencies. It was only when he took over a defunct Chinese restaurant in Euston that everyone beyond his cult following took notice. Now his kingdom is huge, with several spin-offs, but the original is the best, as is the original dish: the roti canai, crispy and oily with rugged topography, served with a side of dal.

And isn't that city too full of themes, of monuments, enclosed squares, national shrines, to be able to enter *tout entière* – with every cobblestone, every shop sign, every step, and every gateway – into the passerby's dream?

— Walter Benjamin, *The Arcades Project*

It would be beautiful to be able to walk up and down Peckham still, because I love it; it's where I grew up. But it just doesn't work.

— Ashley Walters

the arcades

yvonne maxwell

I have spent most of my life in Peckham. I was raised on the bricks and mortar of the Friary Estate, wedged between Peckham High Street, the Old Kent Road and Burgess Park. The yellow brick of Bells Gardens and the high-rise towers of the flint-faced Ledbury Estate designed by the GLC Architects Department formed my daily view, while the number 36 bus route marked out the boundaries of my life – from New Cross to Oval. As I journeyed within the geometry of these South London borders for school, social rites of passage, family gatherings and, eventually, work, I would see faces just like mine at every point.

Everyone has their own memories of Peckham, even if just from TV. My own recollections order every street, block and shop spatially in my mind, like a topographic map. I remember racing down Peckham High Street on my way home from school, thinking about how I was going to conceal the Morley's burger sauce stain on my shirt from my mum. A quick detour down Rye Lane to fantasise over the new window display at Clothing Club, then down the aisles of Blockbuster in search of any new Black American movies that may have come in. A stop at Woolworths to spend my last two pounds on some pick 'n' mix and play with the sample toys and games before getting kicked out by the security guard. The new Usher album would have been released, so we would make our way to the CD Bar in Rye Lane Market to listen to the sample. Walking back down the high street towards Rye Lane Market, we'd witness Black aunties and uncles selling live giant snails, aloe vera leaves and Dudu-Osun; see shops with bundles of premium human hair hanging from makeshift lines, and salons where hairlines got stretched from intricate corn-rows and 'pick and drop' braids.

The covered arcade of Rye Lane Market, as I remember it then, was a vibrant multifunctional space packed with a variety of small businesses and cafes which somehow mirrored and condensed the energy of the high street and the character of the communities that it serviced. The entranceway sloped in such a way that allowed visitors and shoppers to see the stores on the retail horizon, each simultaneously offering everything and nothing: leather goods, bamboo earrings in every size and colour, affordable fashion items, technicolour pashminas, shoe repairs, beauty treatments, toys, holistic medicinal treatments, religious artefacts. The smell of freshly made popcorn from a local vendor attracted flocks of schoolchildren, while the sound system of the CD Bar played the soundtrack for the day, a mix of latest releases, local artists and the oldies. The walls of the CD Bar were painted a deep, palm-oil orange, with shelves stacked with CDs, vinyls and cassettes of artists from across the Black diaspora, from Lynden David Hall to Beenie Man to Ladysmith Black Mambazo. The owner's gold tooth would glisten under the harsh yellow arcade lighting when the riddim hit him right. I would spend hours there, just listening to music; hanging around long enough to hopefully catch a glimpse of Peckham's elite from the various estates.

I fail to recall the exact moment I learned that the CD Bar had closed, but neither can I precisely recall any of the moments when I realised that most of what I had known, experienced and lived alongside was no longer there. I thought that I would have more time in these spaces. I thought home would always be there. But this version of Rye Lane Market is now as fictional as the Peckham of Del Boy and Desmond Ambrose – it simply does not exist. This version of Peckham lives on only in my memories.

We don't like outsiders.
We don't like outsiders.   — Giggs

In 2009, another tour of a lost Peckham was captured in an infamous video which came to be known as 'spot the white man'. In the video, a BNP supporter filmed his walk through Rye Lane, lamenting the absence of all he once knew and bemoaning the non-white faces that walked so freely in a space he once called home, a space that was at one point saturated with faces just like his. I also remember that version of Peckham – his Peckham – which he speaks so longingly about. In that Peckham, I entered a pub for the first time and was chased out of a pub for the first time, swiftly exiting the smoke-filled room followed by a group of white men holding back a dark-haired staffy. I also remember looking on in confusion as a child while National Front skinheads goose-stepped down my road, chanting at us to 'go back home'. This was the Peckham that we endured – we grew into the space, filled it, and re-shaped it. I do not mourn the loss of *that* Peckham.

Go back further and you'll find that the arcades that we filled were a remnant of yet another Peckham, when Rye Lane was a bustling retail hotspot rivalling the likes of the West End and Oxford Street. Rye Lane Market (formerly Rye Lane Bargain Centre) was open between 1938 and 1946, in what was then known as the South of Peckham Arcade, and provided a space for local traders. As the demographic of residents changed across South London, a surplus of social housing and cheap land made Peckham an attractive prospect for Black and global majority ethnic groups and working-class families. The arcade space was reclaimed by those who could not afford the rates of a high-street storefront. Low rents, similar to Granville Arcade in Brixton, enticed small-business owners, and there was a surge in multi-ethnic businesses: Nigerian aunties selling their imported handbag-and-shoe sets, matching and made of crocodile skin to accompany the finest Asoebi styles; Colombian fashion moguls hawking bespoke denim waist-cinchers; and West Indian herbalists recommending black seed oil mixtures and digestive remedies.

There has always been an uneasy kind of hybridity to Peckham – with each community forming its own silo around estate perimeters – but the arcade was where Peckham's diversity became dynamic. Here (and maybe only here) you could be accosted by an African auntie wanting to 'make your hair' while witnessing a South Asian market seller, who still retained a Cockney accent, greet a Nigerian customer in Yoruba. Today, however, the arcade has assumed a more ambiguous identity, where remnants of the 'old' are noticed only by those who know what to look for. The auntie selling tiger nuts, kilishi, and zobo imported from Northern Nigeria. The family that stocks grocery items from across South America, with shelves and walkways so jam-packed that you are sure to miss the person sitting at the counter camouflaged among the piles of yerba maté, bocadillo de guayaba, and countless brands of natilla de coco ready-mix. The vegan Caribbean restaurant Zionly Manna, serving up Ital staples, from stewed black-eyed peas to peanut stew, dhal puri roti and a range of seamoss drinks.

But the energy that once engulfed this space is now muted – there is no music, no vibe. Street-corner preachers and mixtape sellers have been replaced by voyeuristic diners and rooftop-bar revellers. Shortcuts and beaten pathways have been replaced by ornamental benches with floral displays and perfectly trimmed AstroTurf. The old BMX park on Bird In Bush Road lies derelict, no doubt awaiting its fate as another set of new-build apartments. Just a few yards away from Rye Lane Market, new arcades have opened, such as Market Place, which aspires to serve the newcomers.

Some would simply call this gentrification – the process whereby communities which once survived invasive policing, aggressive stop-and-search campaigns, community centre closures and rising rents succumb to boutique cafes, overpriced restaurants and rooftop bars. But gentrification is to colonialism what orange squash is to an actual orange: it is diluted, pumped with enough of the sweet things to make it palatable. They are not the same things, but to someone who has been impacted by both, a familiar taste lingers. Many of the old Peckham residents, those I now consider *native* to Peckham, were once from elsewhere, having uprooted their lives from their home countries and been placed here by local authorities and housing associations. There was very little choice in terms of placement for them, and this makes all the difference; unlike our white counter-parts, who opted for white flight as a means to escape their perceived displacement, and the newcomers who possess the financial freedom to choose to live here, we were not afforded the privilege of agency. We *had* to live in this Peckham.

Perhaps this is merely history repeating itself. It always seems to come down to those who feel they belong versus those who they feel do not. Those who believe they belong possess a strong sense of terri-torial pride and view Peckham (and its communities) as a defensible space, a place that poet Caleb Femi calls 'A paradise of affordable bricks, tucked under / A blanket, shielded from the world.' In direct opposition to this territorial pride are those who do not believe these spaces and communities are worthy of protection. I guess, ultimately, people only protect what they feel is theirs. Is it a coincidence that the only Peckham building that got burnt down during the 1985 Brixton Riots was the pie-and-mash shop?

Walking through Peckham today, it is *me* who feels uncomfortable. I can draw a thread of discomfort from those white working-class

Peckham natives who first met their new immigrant neighbours with despair, to those immigrant communities who are now ingrained in the very fabric of Peckham. I can trace this same thread of ill feeling as it carries through and positions immigrants like myself and the previous white working-class residents as oppositional to our new and more affluent neighbours – the *new Peckham natives*. The reasons for ill feelings along the thread differ, but the human emotions borne out of this displacement are felt just as deeply. These spaces are now filled with new and unfamiliar lives, people who not long ago would have baulked at the thought of stepping foot here. I watch them; they seem to walk with so little purpose as they make their way to the various breweries, creative studios and restaurants on Blenheim Grove – past the new Nandos, past the Aylesham Centre, past all the halal butchers, past Peckham McDonald's, past the arcades.

I no longer live in Peckham. I once could have walked through here with my eyes closed, but walking around now, I feel like an outsider. I do not know this place. There is something very jarring about walking down a road that you have walked a thousand times and suddenly looking up and seeing the unfamiliar. It's not so much the newness, but the presence of something that simply does not seem to fit, and the sobering reality that, in order for this new thing to exist, something else – something loved – had to perish.

THE BRIXTON VILLAGE EFFECT

The single most consequential act in changing the fabric of London's restaurant scene was not the invention of no-reservations restaurants (Polpo, 2008) or the 'discovery' of Thai food (some guy, every single year since 2010) but the intervention a company called Spacemakers made in Granville Arcade in 2009.

Granville Arcade was built in 1937 by Alfred and Vincent Burr, and soon became Brixton's shopping hub away from the high street – a maze of wide-open alleys and a dramatic vaulted ceiling that housed around 100 small units. The movement
of the Windrush Generation to Brixton turned the arcade into a thriving market of garment shops, butchers and grocers, who sold the hitherto-unknown-in-London plantain. But by the late 2000s, the market had declined and the vast space lay dormant except for a few businesses which still served the local community. The owners of the arcade submitted a plan to tear most of the market down, move high street shops into the remaining units and, in place of the former market, build a ten-storey tower of flats.

This is when the 'utopian regeneration agency' Spacemakers stepped in, who proposed that instead of this, any empty unit could be leased out, rent-free, for three months to anyone who had an interesting idea. Slowly, the market filled up, mainly with food: a third-wave coffee shop, a bakery, a fromagerie, a burger restaurant, a Thai restaurant; they joined the old guard of Colombian butchers, Nigerian produce shops and caffs already there. For about a year, in 2010, the arcade seemed radical: a genuine mixed economy of eateries balanced between the old and new. The papers hailed it ('Not long ago, Brixton was known mainly for riots', said the *Evening Standard*, ludicrously) and the critics came in, praising the new restaurants and mainly ignoring the old ones. By the time the arepa stand and butchers on Pope's Road were demolished to make way for a big Sports Direct, Granville Arcade had become Brixton Village.

The Brixton Village effect is being copied all over London, including across the Atlantic (Road) to Market Row, which has now been grouped together with Granville Arcade as one big Brixton Village by its new owners, Hondo Enterprises – a company with a backstory slightly too on the nose to be believed (the CEO is a Texan billionaire ... called Taylor McWilliams ... who moonlights as one quarter of a house music group called ... no, really ... Housekeeping). Economically, it makes sense: new businesses can trial ideas at low risk, with the arcades becoming incubators (Honest Burgers in Granville Arcade, and Franco Manca in Brixton Market opposite, started in Brixton Village and are now nationwide chains), while property developers can slowly turn the screw on rents as the market becomes more successful. They will all succeed, for sure, if making money is the definition of success, but it seems likely that the thing which made Brixton really work, at least briefly, will never be replicated.

CHISHURU

Hondo, in between trying and failing to evict Nour Cash & Carry, have done one good thing, and that's to run a competition to fill a unit at Brixton Village. This was won by Nigerian chef Adejoké Bakare, who went on to set up her restaurant Chishuru in Market Row. Chishuru is that surprisingly rare thing: a chef cooking pretty much exactly what they want to cook, ignoring those who want the food to be more like their mother's, and those who find the scotch bonnet 'a bit much'. Bakare's food takes in not just Lagos but the north of Nigeria and outside of it, a pan-Africanism influenced by shared agriculture and spice routes; like if Burkinabé Marxist revolutionary Thomas Sankara had taken up cooking instead of running a country. The tasting menu constantly changes (goat ayamase with the dark-chocolate bitterness of irú, onglet with garnet-hued shito); the only consistency is Bakare's joyful presence.

EL RANCHO DE LALO

One of the few units in Brixton Village that existed before the Spacemakers regeneration, El Rancho de Lalo has been putting out better food than its well-reviewed neighbours for over ten years. The menu contains empanadas dense as bricks, stuffed to bursting with strands of spiced pork, then fried to order so the casing satisfyingly cracks and spills out its contents, and an excellent rendition of the Colombian national-dish-slash-fry-up, bandeja paisa – an enormous platter of meat and protein, including standout crispy chicharrón and kidney-bean stew. Typically, as of 2022, rent increases have forced El Rancho de Lalo out of the market, but you can now find it behind Lambeth Town Hall, while the original restaurant is now an Argentinian grill house simply called 'Rancho'.

SAM SANDWICHES

Shepherd's Bush Market was bought in 2020 by Yoo Capital, who had one eye on regenerating it, for obvious reasons. It's a lot of space, for one thing, bending in an arc following the railway line from Shepherd's Bush Market station to Goldhawk Road. And from Uxbridge Road, the entrance to the covered indoor market is hardly striking – a gap in the street and some corrugated metal – but it's a portal to some very good food, from the Filipino stall Adela's to the Palestinian Mr Falafel. Sam Sandwiches, run by Samir Ladoul, is maybe the market's most popular stall due to Ladoul's understanding of sandwich architecture; he carefully constructs a loaded sandwich filled with strong flavours like merguez and liver, offsetting these with acidity and bitterness from olives, then pocketing the sandwich tightly so none of it falls out, and topping it all with an outstanding use of chips.

ZIONLY MANNA

It is only the outside of Peckham Indoor Market that ever seems to get any attention (mainly used for music videos to signal to the viewer that this is Peckham), but inside Zionly Manna still reigns supreme. Jahson Peat's food wears all its influences lightly – sometimes pan-African, sometimes Caribbean, sometimes just Peckham – and ranges from Jamaican dumplings made with wholemeal flour, to Ethiopian-ish vegetarian stews, all made with a low-salt, low-spice ethos that shares the strictures of Indian Jain food. Make sure to get pasta and noodles if they're on – they're unlike anything in China or Italy – while the creamy butter beans have more vitality than anything found at a Chelsea cafe run by a Home Counties influencer.

CHEF JOJO MANALO

Tooting and its two 1930s indoor markets have undergone a similar pattern to Brixton, with a mix of old and newcomers and a potential 'sky market' to be built on top. It currently looks like what Brixton looked like ten years ago, but with all the tension turbocharged: chains move in, while the Mauritian and Filipino places are sidelined by new Tooting residents looking for a night out. One of the market's units, an ex-Chelsea FC caterer called Chef Jojo Manalo, is currently the standout: a whiteboard of specials lists all the -silogs, a suffix that promises breakfasts of sweet longanisa or oily fish, all atop garlic-scented rice, as well as an exceptional kare-kare.

A few years ago, a friend talked me into going to a vegan Christmas pop-up at a warehouse in Clapton because he fancied the event organiser. Having never been a wingwoman before, I dutifully agreed to go; one of us had the opportunity for companionship that winter, after all. The event was called 'Chuffed and Stuffed'; I would quickly find out that I would leave as neither. How could you when given flapjack as a main?

Yet in the midst of all the dissatisfaction, the evening transported me to another realm. Running late, I did not stop to take in my surroundings but, as I rushed into the three-storey warehouse building through the side-entrance stairwell, fragments of memories crept up behind me. I knew this stairwell. I remembered my six-year-old feet going up these stairs; holding my baba's hand. As I walked through the wooden double-doors it was as if through a tear in time and space, straight into the textile factory where, 25 years ago, my parents used to work.

the warehouse

Hidden people, hidden spaces. The warehouses were the places in which Kurds, Alevis and political exiles took root during the 1980s and 90s, escaping the economic disparity, oppression, imprisonments and forced disappearances that have littered Turkey's recent history. To be Kurdish then meant a banned language, criminalised music, and an identity so unpalatable to the myth of the new nation that to even have a Kurdish name was unfathomable. The initiation into this new republic involved relinquishing your Kurdishness or not existing at all.

In London, cultural and historical invisibility became spatial; you were seen as a Kurd but you couldn't take up space because you were not invited. The industrial pockets of Hoxton, Shoreditch, Dalston, Hackney Wick, Tottenham and Edmonton harboured our new lives: illegal factories, wedding venues, community centres, spaces of ritual and faith. The Clapton warehouse I'd been at, the Palm 2, is now used for yoga and pop-ups, but in 1986 it was where my parents, uncle and countless other Kurdish immigrants worked, often illegally. The long dining table, which is now decorated with candles and dried flowers, used to be topped with rows of grey-green Singer and Brother sewing machines. The pristine sash windows that now glimmer with the reflection of fairy lights used to be smothered in old newspaper to hide the workers. The freshly painted wall displaying posters of upcoming events used to be cinder block, and covered with pictures of martyred revolutionaries and singers. My uncle Huseyin used to work in the back of a room containing the steam machine, where an open-plan kitchen now is; he was a steamer, or 'Hoffmanci' (named after the brand of steamer). My mum and dad were sewers; Mum would sew the main body of a jacket while Dad sewed on the arms and collar. Between the three they could complete a 'bundle' of 30 jackets a day, at a cost of 30p per jacket.

Lunch breaks were an exciting scurry of moving parts. The bundles of clothes would be cleared and the pattern-cutting counter became a makeshift table. Everyone would open their tiffin boxes, sharing what they had. Mum made fasulye (green beans in tomato) and nohutlu pilav. Auntie Ayse from Gaziantep would bring her chicken-and-potato single-layer borek, 'kombe'. Ismail brought in olives and special honeycomb that he had smuggled in from his home town, and his wife's fresh kaymak. Dad would run out to buy fresh bread from the local firin, and uncle would put the tea on. In the winter, yayla corbasi was most popular with homemade yoghurt, the starter for which would be shared and kept alive among the women. It is this same starter that mama used for the mother of her yoghurt, which is alive to this day. I like to think about how the yoghurt mama makes, and the soup we have with it, still contains the hands and effort of all those people from the factory days.

The London that we occupied then has shaped the London we inhabit now. Tucked behind a Dalston petrol station on Kingsland Road was Ali Shakar's event space. It was there that we held one of the first new years' celebrations of the textile factory generation; now it is a site of luxury flats. Rona Rooms on Shacklewell Lane contained a wedding hall on one floor and a textile factory on the other – now it's a shared workspace and cafe. Sen Ola, the most popular of all, was a wedding hall on a Hackney Wick industrial estate where you entered through an iron fire-escape stairwell. This is now the site of Westfield Stratford.

The most important warehouse, the port that all those who came from Turkey passed through, was the Halk Evi – the 'people's house' – on Stoke Newington High Street. It was originally a textile factory, built in a grand Art Deco style and intended to be used by the luxury menswear firm S. Simpson. When deindustrialisation came about in the 1980s, the back of the building remained a factory – an under-ground one for immigrants – while the front became 'The Turkish Community Centre', with 'and Kurdish' quickly added after a popular vote (the building was nicknamed, with a sly sense of humour, 'the Kurdish Embassy'). This is now the flagship Beyond Retro. I joke at times that we need a blue plaque.

The embassy was the place to go for help with immigration issues; for advocacy; to congregate; to get loans in order to start businesses; to form new emerging political, cultural and ethnic identities; to hold events, celebrations and funerals; and to find housing. Nuri 'Heval' (which means 'friend' – a term not used lightly in the Kurdish com-munity, since we have 'No friends but the mountains') took the role of housing those who first arrived and had nowhere to go. 'It was where we found the bearings we never had', he tells me.

The embassy was also a place for eating. The food in the Halk Evi was legendary: rice with chickpeas and butter bean stew with lamb's neck, lentil and yayla soups, the sulu yemek of the day, lamb-and-aubergine kavurma, and 'tost' with kasar and sucuk in the mornings. The cooks of the Halk Evi canteen were not trained chefs: the people's kitchen had the people's cooks. Imagine the prison scene in *Goodfellas* when old Italian-American men slice garlic with a razor, but replace them with a bunch of old revolutionaries with committed moustaches and colourful waterproof aprons. While us children were in school, figuring out how to say 'the' (the hardest word in the English language), these men – our fathers – poured out onto the streets of Green Lanes, Kingsland Road and Stoke Newington High Street and started Istanbul, Antepliler, Mangal 1, Mangal 2 and Pide. The Halk Evi kitchen was a portal where you could go from being invisible to visible; from the hidden warehouses, Kurdish communal cooking flourished into the public spaces of takeaways, restaurants and cafes, creating the food scene Londoners know today.

New Year's Eve 1991 at a Kurdish warehouse behind Stoke Newington Police Station

Not all the children of those first generations have left the warehouses: now some of them even own them. In the fifteen-odd years that I've known Mehmet Akis, I have watched him morph from a 'button boy' into a shopkeeper, snooker-bar owner, restaurateur, caterer, and now artisan vegan cheese and tofu maker in his warehouse in Tottenham. He's a true 'East Ender', a kind of Kurdish Del Boy with his hybrid Cockney/Kurdish accent, and the way he treats rules with elasticity. He has the tenacity of the old immigrants from the 1980s, ready to pivot at the drop of a hat. When speaking about his vegan cheese and tofu-making business, he says, 'Mel – I've become a proper scientist now; its amazing how this stuff works.' His jokes are always on the fringe: 'Mate, I'm using lactic acid, potassium; let me know if there's anyone who's upset you – I'm pretty sure I can make a Molotov cocktail or two.' Mehmet now supplies tofu to the likes of Planet Organic and Whole Foods. Yes, Kurds are making tofu now!

Mehmet remembers both the factories and the community centre. He grew up in East London with his parents, who came over from Maras, Andirin in 1984. Mehmet was left behind with his hala (aunt) and nene (grandmother) when he was still being breastfed. When he was finally brought over and reunited with his parents at four years old, they shared a living space with seven or eight other families, until they saved enough to run a textile factory in Wells Street. Mehmet remembers his first job at age six: putting the spare buttons into the plastic pouch that would then be attached to the inside of a garment.

This is the story of so many parents and children of the time: promises to return home or to come back for those left behind. Auntie Zekiye, who would later open Somine canteen in Dalston (one of the first 24-hour soup and stew spots in London), knew what it meant to leave a son behind, and to yearn to return home. She recalls that her son Gurkan was just one when she left him with his grandmother in 1983, and that they were reunited when he was three with the help of Turkish pop star Sibel Can, who pretended to be Gurkan's aunt for the plane journey to London to help with his entry. She was invited to Sibel's concert the same evening she was reunited with her son. Zekiye remembers the many tears being shed in these factories, especially when sad songs came on the pirate radio stations. She figures many of the jackets made were lined with the tears of the mothers yearning to reunite with those children.

In the apex of Mehmet's warehouse, I find Cihangir usta ('usta' meaning master of a trade) – a baklava master from Maras who arrived only six months ago. He occupies the top of the warehouse by himself, where the slanted-roofed glass ceiling illuminates the whole space like a greenhouse. As the rain begins to hit the glass, I am mesmerised watching him. He has been making baklava for 30 years, and seeing him turn small discs of dough into thin silk sheets of filo feels sacred. He handles the dough, dusting clouds of cornflour between each layer like a magician doing a trick, working it at first with his hands, then a sequence of rolling pins that get larger as the dough expands and transforms into delicate transparent sheets. This kind of work requires his whole body, but he makes it look seamless.

Jackets. Baklava. The life of a Kurdish immigrant was the sum of a community's effort to be whole, a whole human being, to be counted and visible; unwanted people occupying unwanted spaces. Each person had taken great risks and a great leap of faith to get here and live here, coming to a place where they knew they couldn't ever really belong, but could at least weave an existence. This made them magicians in my eyes, capable of turning a cold breeze block room of steam and dust into a place for a feast, hibernation and taking root. For those who migrate here now, the experience is often singular and lonely, but some things stay the same: the hope of returning home, or feeling at home again; the promise of reunion.

There are trades like Cihangir usta's that help me understand what doing divine work means. Working with focus and repetition, with love and devotion. It's as sacred as any prayer or meditation. He speaks about wanting to do nothing else. How many don't understand. As he loses himself further he starts speaking about regretting coming here, about missing his family and wanting to return. He shows me pictures of them with such pride. He tells me to come back so he can show me how to make oyster baklava. I promise him I will return.

THE GREEN LANES GLO-UP

If you walk out of Harringay Green Lanes station and float along the pavement, following the smell of fat on charcoal like a cartoon dog, you may notice that, although Green Lanes has all the same restaurants it did ten years ago, the street is not quite the same as it used to be. It's not just the cafes and bakeries that have moved in, exiles from Dalston and neighbourhoods with 'coffee scenes', but the restaurants themselves. Previously the dining rooms and facades traded on notions of rusticity: a *Once Upon a Time in Anatolia*-esque combination of mosaics, wood, pastoral frescos, aunties in windows making gozleme; now they are as grand as palazzos, each taking up more and more shop fronts in an ever-expanding war of mutually assured destruction and refurbs, transitioning from browns and yellows to royal blues and gold, from bold capitals to tasteful lower-case fonts. Harringay has not been gentrified, but it *has* been yassified.

Rather than lose its identity, this stretch of Green Lanes has consolidated its Turkishness, or rather, its Kurdishness. In *The Alternative Guide to the London Boroughs*, Aydin Dikerdem walks with his Baba from Green Lanes' source in Newington Green and up the road, discussing the fragmentedness of what has been portrayed as a homogeneously Turkish street, from the religious nationalists in the south to the leftists and revolutionaries further north, and the Turkish-Cypriots who bridge the gap between Turkish Green Lanes and Greek Green Lanes. But Harringay, the epicentre, has long been Kurdish – indeed, in an interview with writer Melek Erdal, Zulfikar, the owner of Diyarbakir Kitchen, points out that, of the seven Turkish restaurants on Green Lanes (including his), only one of them is actually purely Turkish, with the rest being run by ethnic Kurds.

There is a new confidence about these restaurants, perhaps the swagger of someone who was once poor and has found themselves unaccountably wealthy (see: influencer Salt Bae), but also a confidence that comes from the knowledge that the food no longer needs to be explained to outsiders, that these restaurants do not need to say that they're Turkish for people to understand what type of food they serve. Indeed, as well as consolidation, there has also been a diversification: no longer just kebabs and lahmacun, but also stuffed manti, kunefe, katmer and soup specialists. And if you're nostalgic, well, Yasar Halim hasn't changed a bit.

DIYARBAKIR

If you absolutely, positively must eat as much meat as you can physically endure, then Diyarbakir is probably the best pure ocakbaşı on Green Lanes: the one nearer the station is better if you don't want any trappings except for good food and do want to come out smelling like lamb; the more upmarket one a bit further north is more comfortable and has slightly more variation. Named after the largest Kurdish-majority city in Turkey, Diyarbakir is probably the restaurant on the stretch which is most explicit about its Kurdish identity: its owner Zulfikar says it was given the name by his father, one of the first Kurdish restaurateurs in London, as a tribute to his friend who was born there. Daily stews are a cut above others on the road, and the icli kofte, buttery balls of bulgur-wheat-encrusted lamb mince, are exceptional.

ANTEPLILER

Once a small, shabby shop decked in black with cursive red letters, Antepliler is now a leviathan that sprawls across five buildings, all unified by a sleek white shopfront with demure font: a double-sized restaurant, a baklava shop, a doner specialist and a kunefe shop on the corner, whose unbroken vista onto the street outside makes it an ideal impromptu meeting spot. The food at the restaurant is more or less the same: a little less exciting, a little more expensive. But the offshoots are excellent: at Antepliler Doner, iskender – doner meat with yoghurt and a sharp tomato sauce – is baptised with hot brown butter at the table and soaked up thirstily by chopped bread croutons, while sitting down on tiny chairs at low tables sharing sweet kunefe and bitter tea at Antepliler Kunefe is the end point of all Green Lanes nights out.

HALA

Hala means 'aunt' in Turkish; this once signified the homeliness of the restaurant's food and decor – of women rolling dough in the window and individually wrapped manti stuffed with mince and pudgy icli kofte – but two refurbs in a few years have made it look like pretty much every other restaurant on Green Lanes. This was once the best restaurant on the stretch; today it doesn't hit the heights it used to but the food is still worth a pilgrimage: it is hard to imagine a more pleasurably ascetic solo meal than a late-night bowl of Hala's paça çorbasi – lamb soup, served with pickles and lemon – alongside some fried liver and bread. Groups of diners should get the manti and icli kofte to share, alongside adana, ribs and chops, or a mixed grill at least one size too big to be fully eaten.

HARINGEY CORBACISI

A new addition to Green Lanes, and refreshingly not a part of the refurb arms race, Haringey Corbacisi is a literal name, meaning soup shop, and sells pretty much only variations of soup and sulu yemek – stew made from beans, aubergine or lamb neck. Soups range from the gentle (lentils) right up to the gory: behind the counter you'll find a pyramid of lamb skulls stacked on top of one another like a warlord's threat, stripped of all their meat, which is separated out into head, tongue, brains and eyes and added to the long-simmered meat or rich yoghurt broth, as per the customer's request. The kind of place Green Lanes should do more of.

DURAK TANTUNI

Not on Green Lanes, but further up on West Green Road, Durak Tantuni is probably the closest thing London has to replicating the superior late-night snacking culture of American and European cities, except this is not tacos or tapas, it's tantuni. Long cigarillos of single or double-layered lavaş bread are filled with finely chopped meat, fried in cotton oil in a pan resembling an upside-down sombrero, and then judiciously adorned with some onions, sumac, and parsley, with a slick of meat fat sealing the package as saliva does to a rolly. Pickles and lemon are provided gratis. There is nothing else on the menu, nor does there need to be.

Park Royal, a vast industrial park that seeps across the borders of three boroughs in West London, has been feeding Londoners since the early 20th century. It was once home to Alexander Gibb and Giles Gilbert Scott's imposing Guinness brewery, and still houses some large-scale production – as evidenced by the wafts of malt that emanate from the McVitie's factory at Harlesden – but today it is mostly a warren of piecemeal, dark kitchens for delivered food, and centralised kitchens housing cute cupcake, gourmet pet food and healthy juice brands.

Over the last few decades, Park Royal has also seen a blossoming of wholesale bakeries, sweet shops and supermarkets, opened by immigrants from Syria, Iraq and Lebanon, many of whom have since opened public-facing businesses where patrons can sit down, eat and perhaps smoke shisha. Park Royal's low rent and huge warehouse spaces have meant that it has become a viable alternative to the Edgware Road for new Arab-owned businesses – a culinary hub where it's not only possible to buy manakish, baklava and masgouf, but also the industrial equipment needed to make them.

In the middle of all the concrete, between a processed-meat wholesalers and a restaurant selling broasted chicken, is an oasis: a beautifully adorned Syrian dessert parlour and library called Levant Book Cafe. When you enter the cafe you'll find antique items from Syria dotted around the space, alongside quotes of compelling one-liners in Arabic painted on its walls. On any given evening you'll find families, uncles, aunties and youngsters chatting over an ice cream and playing with one of the many handmade backgammon or chess boards available to patrons. We spoke to the owner, master chef and craftsman Sameh Asami and his family.

the library

What's the story of Levant Book Café?

> Levant Book Cafe is currently three years old, but the concept
> was initially created approximately 12 years ago. Our good friend
> Muhammad Ramadan had experience in creating a number
> of Middle Eastern spaces in the past, such as Ramadan's Tent
> ('خيمة رمضان') and a desserts shop on Edgware Road.
>   We set out to create a Little Damascus in a corner of London.
> Somewhere to get away from the busy London streets, and that
> makes us feel like home. We'd collectively thought of creating
> Levant Book Cafe and were looking for an ideal location to deliver
> on the idea.

London is a big place – why was Park Royal chosen as Levant Book
Cafe's home?

> We hadn't initially set out to start the book cafe in Park Royal;
> it was pure luck and coincidence that we ended up here. We had
> been searching for a place that had both indoor and outdoor
> space but due to the costs it proved very difficult to find [this]
> in central London. Our theory was, rather than compromise on
> what we intended to create, we would locate a place that would
> fit our specifications, and our customers would come to us –
> which successfully happened, alhamdulillah.

What experience does Levant Book Cafe give its visitors?

> Levant Book Cafe specifically represents the Middle Eastern
> area of Greater Damascus ('دمشق الكبرى'), but includes the
> Levantine cultures of Jordan, Iraq, Lebanon and Palestine too.
> Everything in our shop is carefully selected and placed. Nothing
> is displayed by accident, from the trinkets hanging from the
> shelves to the quotes painted on the cafe walls – it's all by design
> and carries meaning. We've found that a lot of our customers will

bring their children (who have never been to Damascus) to the book cafe, to show them their cultural origins.

The design and decoration of the book cafe is intentional and representative of Levantine culture and history. For instance, our stained-glass windows – if you ever walk through the roads and buildings of ash-Shām ('الشّام', referring to the Old City of Damascus), the first thing you'd notice would be the brightly coloured glass windows framed with wood, painted in a luminous baby-blue. We have these exact same windows installed in the book cafe, so that you feel like you're in ash-Shām.

Levant Book Cafe also has a wall full of books: it's pretty unique for a cafe to have a library. What was the idea behind that?

In London, it's very difficult to find Arabic books and libraries, and we're a community of people who love reading. If we truly wanted to create a Little Damascus experience in London, we would be amiss if it didn't include books. When you visit Al-Hamidiyeh Souk ('الحميديي قوس', a shopping dis- trict in Damascus), which is adjacent to the Umayyad Mosque ('الجامعالأمويي', also known as the Great Mosque of Damascus), you'll find rows and rows of books and literature in the market- place's floors and walls. It has characterised Greater Damascus, and it's a character we're conveying in Levant Book Cafe. To fill the gap we identified, we've taken [it] upon ourselves to create a space in London where we can provide Arabic books for anyone who has an interest in them. Anyone can come browse our book collection and take home any book on our shelves, and return it once read. This isn't something we charge people for.

We've received a lot of visits from Arabic authors, both domestic and international, or they'end up sending us copies of their work to put up on our shelves. For example, a Syrian poet from Scotland named Rubaa Wakhaaf ('فاقووىبر') sent us signed copies of her work. Our shelves were the first shelves that had her published poetry. Another author whose first published work we welcomed is Syrian actor Ayman Zeidan ('أيمن زيدان'). He resides in Damascus, and ended up sending his books to a cafe in London – it made us realise the power and impact of what we were doing, and how far news of the book cafe travelled.

The cafe also serves a variety of Damascus ice cream, sweets and baked confectionery, such as Baklava and Kunafeh...

> We strictly follow the recipes and traditional techniques of the foods we have in the book cafe. We always strive to deliver the highest quality bakes and sweets for our customers, which is why we're very particular about what ingredients we use, and where they're sourced from. Again, all the bakes and sweets we produce here are handmade; they can't be mass-produced in a factory!
>
> Also, you mentioned that we serve Kunafeh – we don't call it that here...

Really? What do you call it?

> We call it Nabulseyeh ('نابلسية'), because the dessert originally comes from the city of Nablus in Palestine. We think it's important to highlight the cultural origins of Nabulseyeh to our customers, because praise must be awarded to the people who produced the dish. After learning the recipe and understanding the cultural significance of the dish, we believe it's important to emphasise this fact.
>
> The traditional Nabulseyeh recipe is thousands of years old, and has also passed down from generation to generation. The recipe specifies the location [from] which ingredients are meant to be sourced – for instance, when Nabulseyeh was produced, the cheese would have come from the Palestinian city of Akka ('عكّا'). And because we follow the traditional recipe, when we make our Nabulseyeh in the book cafe, we also source our cheese from Akka.

It's apparent that you possess a strong understanding of the history behind what you provide to your visitors. Where does that stem from?

> The ethos of our cafe is: before you sell anything in the cafe, you must have a full understanding of its history. Historically, every profession had a Sheikh, whether you were a textile weaver, an architect, a farmer or a stonemason. The Sheikh was called Sheikh Al-Kar ('شيخ الكار', meaning elder tradesman). And if a young professional or tradesman wanted to set up a new

business in Damascus, they would have to seek the blessing and permission of Sheikh Al-Kar. The Sheikh's responsibility [was] to ensure that there [was] a comprehensive understanding of the trade, and that a tradesman fully [understood] Suluk Al-Tijarah ('سلوك التجارة', meaning business practises) before their new venture began. They would quiz and test you to check that you [were] performing to an acceptable standard. They'd teach you how to interact with customers, and how to treat them with respect and Adalah ('عدالة', meaning fairness).

Unfortunately, this system has died out over time due to a multitude of factors ... but the generational habit of possessing a comprehensive understanding of your product or trade hasn't. And that's reflected in our book cafe.

How culturally significant is Levant Book Cafe for the Arab diaspora in the UK?

The Levant Book Cafe is a physical act of preservation. Our family didn't choose to leave Damascus during the 2011 Syrian Crisis – we never thought we'd have to leave Syria; we were forced to leave because of the conflict. The experience of leaving a place that we loved left us with a profound sense of longing for our home. But we still had our memories. The book cafe is the physical manifestation of memories from Damascus that we love and hold dear. It's an archive of Syrian history as well as a space that preserves and values Levantine societal norms and customs.

We set out to create a small Syrian corner that could hold these memories, a place that looks like 'us' and is coloured with the colours that we grew up around – like the stained-glass windows we grew up running past on our way to school. From the books we used to see at Al-Hamidiyeh Souk to the mosaic decorations we would admire at the Umayyad Mosque, we've amalgamated them at Levant Book Cafe.

What sort of impact has the book cafe had on Park Royal?

By operating in Park Royal, we've brought an eclectic mix of customers with us. The neighbouring businesses in the area tell us that, since our existence, they've had a myriad of new faces visiting them too, as they'd either be coming to or leaving the cafe. Remember, we aren't on a high street. We're situated in the middle of an industrial business complex, so people aren't ever 'passing through'. When our customers do visit us, we're usually the sole reason for their journey into the area.

And although we occupy space in an industrial business complex, we wouldn't characterise Levant Book Cafe as a 'business' – we don't operate like one. It's a social space that houses Levantine arts, sweets, books and decorations. When you see our customers, they feel like they're at home and they care for it as they would care for their own homes. It's a beautiful relationship.

This interview was conducted by Nabil Al-Kinani and Sana Badri. A longer version was originally published in Pipe Dreams, *a zine about shisha culture in Park Royal edited by Zain Dada. Follow Levant Book Cafe on Instagram at @levant.london*

COME TO PARK ROYAL, THE REVOLUTION IS HAPPENING!

You may feel a sense of irreality as you walk through the Park Royal industrial estate. Blindfold a Londoner and put them in the middle of it, and they might swear that you had taken them to another city, Los Angeles perhaps; here there are strip malls, MOT garages, shisha bars, warehouses, bakeries and restaurants, all traversed and mediated by the car, a profoundly un-London mode of transport. Indeed, Park Royal looks like a vision of what London's food scene might be if it had limitless space and low overheads, bending the rules of what restaurants are allowed to do in the centre. A kind of Freetown Christiania of industrial production away from the cookie-cutter curation of property developers who prefer to turn neighbourhoods into restaurant theme parks; an *It's a Small World* of food.

There is too much space in Park Royal, too much to go unnoticed in 2022. The Old Oak and Park Royal Development Corporation was set up by the Mayor of London in 2015 to initiate the compulsory purchase of land and regenerate the area in the usual way: big train station; new mixed housing; thousands of new jobs. Hoardings are plastered with the smiling faces of restaurant and bakery owners, to show that they are valued by High Speed Rail 2. Already the towers owned by Imperial College (who surely promised students a 15-minute train ride into Oxford Circus) are starting to circle the park; it seems inevitable that the new food businesses will start to move in, too. Until then, Park Royal remains one part asphalt, one part double apple shisha, and one part knafah.

AL ENAM

The heart of Park Royal is the Acton Business Centre – inside, a labyrinth of dark kitchen businesses that send their food whirring across West London on motorbikes; on the outside, small growths of bakeries and restaurants that have made the leap from wholesale to retail. The busiest of all of them is Al Enam, a Kurdish-Iraqi restaurant that often appears to have more people inside than people in the rest of the industrial park put together – indeed, people come here by car from all corners of London, as well as from outside it. Lamb shawarma is at its best here when chopped fine and stuffed into soft sub rolls with chips, taking on the pleasing gummy texture of a good Philly cheesesteak. Even better is the fish cooking – butterflied sea basses becoming burnt-out carapaces of crispy skin to scoop soft flesh from – or the lamb quzi, a sweet-and-sour lamb neck stew. Still, the best thing here may just be the lentil soup, given free to every table, and served simply with bread, lemon and pickles.

LEVANT BOOK CAFE

When the gods fought to earn the right to name the city of Athens, Poseidon struck his trident into a rock to produce water, while Pallas Athene, who won, produced an olive tree from the ground. The scene must have looked something like the front of Levant Book Cafe, just off the appropriately named Minerva Road, where concrete, a water fountain and an olive tree form an unlikely oasis in the middle of the industrial park. Levant Book Cafe is Sameh Asami's love letter to Damascus; he has recreated a shard of another city within the space of the industrial park. Everything here is immaculately designed, like something out of a Syrian Wes Anderson film: ornate chess sets and backgammon tables being used by old men and families alike, jewel-hued jars of preserves imported from one woman in Damascus, with no-label labelling. Take a book from the shelf, then sit down to eat bright orange Nabulseyeh knafeh, swirls of pistachio or rose booza (Syrian ice cream, bitter with aniseed and stretchy as taffy) and 'and halawet el jibn, curls of fresh milk curds scented with rosewater.

PATCHI

If you've had suspiciously good baklava in Peckham, or maamoul in a Knightsbridge hotel, or a better-than-average sweet on Edgware Road, then they will have certainly emanated from one of two warehouses in Park Royal: SWEETLAND or Patchi. The wholesale businesses of both are integral to the ecosystem of Arabic patisserie in London, to the extent that both have gone from mid-sized bakeries to palatial presentation rooms, decked out in cool marble. Patchi is, marginally, the better and more consistent of the two, and has recently attached a small restaurant to its road-facing side where you can get Lebanese breakfast and good, hearty stews. But this is all a distraction – you shouldn't go home without becoming laden with as many sweets as you can fit in your pockets. Just make sure to eat the Nabulseyeh knafeh there, while it's hot and oozing, and ask for it to be sandwiched inside two halves of bread – The Move.

BEIT EL ZAYTOUN

With its whitewashed walls, glass conservatory, and patterned tiles, Beit El Zaytoun is the closest Park Royal comes to being self-consciously picturesque. Indeed, outside on a summer's day, shisha smoke in the air, Fairuz on the sound system, sat right on the shoulder of the Paddington arm of the Grand Union Canal, you might believe that you weren't on the biggest industrial estate in London. Beit El Zaytoun is an attempt by the Lebanese entrepreneur Ayman Assi to create a kind of haven in Park Royal, away from the wholesale bakeries, fast food manufacturers and MOT servicers, and it kind of works – on weekends and evenings the restaurant is a destination, packed mainly with families and younger couples eating manakish and enjoying double apple. On Sundays the draw is mloukhiah, a stew of chicken and the eponymous mucilaginous vegetable that, under various names and guises, conjures up childhood nostalgia for Lebanese, Greek, Turkish, and Nigerian diners alike.

HAMADIA

There are lots of hidden surprises in Park Royal: a Lebanese supermarket opposite Levant Book Cafe was once the only place in London you could find traditionally cooked masgouf, the much-loved Iraqi preparation of Euphrates carp, while FLAMES, an industrial meat factory, has now opened up a sandwich shop here, selling an absurd and delicious long, cylindrical chicken tube stuffed with mushrooms and cheese that can either be ordered as part of a sandwich or (better) on its own with chips. Maybe the best surprise is Hamadia, a shisha lounge that also happens to serve some of the finest broasted chicken (fried chicken cooked under pressure, so the outside is crispy and dry but does not compromise the moistness of the inside) in the city. The chicken, though, is really a distraction from the potatoes cooked in the same fat, that look like souffléd, ridged Pringles and are a vehicle for snow-white garlicky toum.

the club

My dad never felt particularly Polish growing up. I'm not sure if Poland ever really existed for him, beyond the language and the community of exiles he grew up in. My grandfather was a well-known Polish psychiatrist who ran the Mabledon Hospital for traumatised ex-servicemen and refugees, a stone's throw from London in the Darenth Valley. All the staff were Polish, as were the patients, so the hospital became its own little corner of Poland in Kent. My dad spent all his childhood there, before being summarily sent to a British boarding school where he had the Polish beaten out of him. I think Poland was like a birthmark for him, like the red splotch on Gorbachev's bald pate. The kind of thing that marks you out as different, but whose presence in your life you cannot adequately describe. My dad also said he never felt particularly English, but that it was hard to say exactly what he was, because his connection to Poland felt so tenuous.

Growing up in the 1950s and 60s, my dad wasn't able to visit the country, nestled as it was behind the Iron Curtain, but the next best thing was going to Ognisko, the Polish Hearth Club, where my grandfather took meetings. It has been in the same spot on Exhibition Row since 1939 – a bequest from the British government, who offered up the building as a home to the Polish government in exile during the Second World War. Soon it was filled with military officers coordinating their resistance efforts, both with the British and also with the parallel institutions of a government that existed to manage a country which, in many ways, no longer existed. Ognisko had a restaurant as well as a theatre and offices. The restaurant was decent (although speak to anyone there at the time and they will tell you that the food was better down the road at Daquise) but I was never taken there as a child.

The community that built Ognisko was defined by the war: people left as refugees or as soldiers and found themselves unable to return. Ognisko was the seat of government, of intellectuals and the officer class; it was precisely the kind of community that would have suffered the most at the hands of a proletarian revolution. The Poland that had been created in London was a simulacrum, harking back to a pre-War nation that had briefly flourished for two decades from 1918.

By the time I was born, the wall had fallen. The curtain had been drawn back. The hospital was disbanded in the 1980s, my grandparents died, and the few Polish friends that my dad had from that time dispersed throughout London and the rest of the country. I'm not really sure if any of them found their way back to Poland.

In 2016, my dad was jerked into Polish-consciousness. Whatever he was, it was not Brexit-British. Suddenly his identity – which had previously been a curlicued question mark – clarified itself into a period. He was Polish. He applied for a Polish passport. I started to notice more Polish goods in the fridge when I returned home. Cheesecakes and poppy-seed rolls, pickles and Kabanos, his favourite dried sausage. He'd dust off decades-rusted Polish with the plumber. He started introducing himself as Polish.

For his 70th birthday, we finally went to Ognisko. Aside from a few tables of dates – furtive hands held across tables, the awkwardness of couples not yet comfortable with their own silence – all of the tables in the garden were filled with multi-generational parties. That night we counted no less than seven other birthdays, which meant that every twenty minutes or so the entire terrace stopped what they were doing to shower affection in that table's direction. The birthdays seemed to get older as the evening went on. One family sang an old Polish army song and the person they were celebrating wore an army cap. My dad leant over to congratulate them and we were told the guy was in his 90s.

Truthfully, the main reason we didn't go to Ognisko growing up was that it was already well past its prime. In 2012, the members nearly sold the club; by then the dining room was musty, with peeling pink walls and a cuisine firmly rooted in the past. The club decided to lease the F&B operation to Jan Woroniecki, who was running the very successful restaurant Baltic at the time. He transformed the space, and the menu is now a sleek contemporary take on Polish classics. The dining room hums.

While the kitchen does brisk trade, the club itself is sclerotic. The events it puts on are still mostly dedicated to the Second World War or to Chopin, as if the last 70+ years of Polish history were a gloss. Over the years, as my grandfather's generation has died off, it has struggled to maintain relevance. The second generation of British-born Poles, like my dad and Jan, could lean to either side of their hyphenated existence. (Those who know Jan from childhood still call him John; it was only when he opened Wodka, a Polish restaurant, in the mid-1980s, that he started his life as a professional Pole.) Similarly, those who came to the UK when Poland joined the EU in 2004 saw no interest in hanging out in a place like Ognisko. Poland was now open; the culture was alive there. Why visit an aspic version of your culture from the 1920s?

Over at POSK, the Polish Social and Cultural Association Centre in Hammersmith, I could also feel this tension. POSK was started in the 1960s by Professor Roman Ludwik Wajda, who aimed to build a centre that could house all of the disparate associations and cultural organisations that made up the Polish diaspora – those that had outgrown the government in exile and the elitism of the officers at Ognisko. While it had a membership, it was not an exclusive club in the way Ognisko was. It was intended as a community centre for everyone. It would also house the Polish library, which comprised some 50,000 books, most of which had been banned in the USSR.

I spoke to my friend Karol, a vegan chef from Warsaw, about going to POSK. He'd never heard of it, but was intrigued to visit. We cycled along King Street until the squat Brutalist building came into view, the letters P O S K backlit against the concrete frontage. We took seats at Cafe Maja, the small cafe adjoining the building. I ordered sour-cream-and-potato pierogies and a kielbasa sausage, while Karol ordered the single vegan thing on the menu – some sauerkraut-and-mushroom pierogies. As Karol pointed out, Warsaw in recent years has gone through a vegan revolution; the fact that there was only one vegan dish on the menu reflected that POSK was a step behind both the city it served and the culture it represented.

I was interested in why Karol had never heard of POSK; it turned out he'd simply never looked for it. He wasn't interested in how Polish people lived in London. At university he'd tried not to hang out with the Polish kids. He wanted to absorb as much of the world as he could. Soon he'll be eligible for British citizenship, but since Brexit he hasn't felt particularly excited about London. I think Karol found it moderately absurd to be sat in Hammersmith in a Polish community centre, being gently grilled about how he understood his Polish identity by someone trying to figure out their own. When my dad applied for his Polish citizenship I found out that I was also eligible. I'm now in the process of getting a Polish passport. This is despite never having visited Poland, or speaking a word of Polish.

Maybe identity is best understood not as a function of what a person is, but rather what a person is not. My grandparents' generation were 'free Poles', meaning they were not under Soviet occupation, but this caused them to be so defined by the war that the generation that came after sought to be defined by their relationship to their new home. For Karol, London represented a break with Poland, but Brexit has created a new dividing line intersecting our sense of self. My dad and I are now Polish – we'll get our passports and stay in London as Europeans. Karol will be British, but he will take his passport and leave.

A few nights after going to Cafe Maja, I cycled over again to meet Marek Laskiewicz, the chair of POSK, who offered me a tour. The building is labyrinthine; we passed rooms for the Polish psychologists' society, the Joseph Conrad society, the Polish University, and an atrium recently converted for classical music. There was something dizzying about seeing all the fractals that comprise a culture vie for space in one building.

Similar to Ognisko, Laskiewicz acknowledges that the centre has struggled to keep itself relevant. His first change after assuming the chair last year was to insist everyone who works in a public-facing role at POSK was bilingual. He wanted the space to be able to speak to people like me, who might not speak Polish. He also noted that other London diasporas sometimes end up there: there's a group of Iranians who use the rooms sometimes, while the cafe is popular with Japanese tourists.

As we toured the building we ended up connecting with another group, formed of the heads of a few Ukrainian charities that were trying to coordinate relief efforts. Poland has taken a disproportionate amount of Ukrainian refugees during the war, and the solidarity shown has been a bright spot amongst the relentless darkness of the conflict. In London, the White Eagle in Balham – a Polish community centre – has been a focal point for donation drives.

At one point we stood in front of a poster dedicated to Polish resistance efforts against the Soviet regime. 'Of course,' Laskiewicz said, waving his hand towards a photograph of women fighters who had all been killed, 'Russia absolutely crushed Poland. I mean, it was destroyed. That's what a centre like this was for, to try to desperately hold on to whatever was left.' – he paused for a moment – 'And obviously the same could well happen to you. Flattened—' His voice dropped as he realised he might have slightly misjudged his comments, 'absolutely destroyed...' One of the women stifled a tear. 'Hopefully that won't happen!' He said, with eccentric cheer, 'but you never know. All I'm trying to say is, Poland has been there. And POSK is here as a result, and it can be here for you.'

We continued on and I thought about how spaces like POSK and Ognisko had once held a community in its contingency. I thought about the Polish people in exile, arriving in a blitzed-out nation, trying to affect their own healing and participate in the recovery of their new home while watching their mother country wrenched behind the

Iron Curtain. There is something quixotic about the attempt to preserve a foreign culture in a dynamic global capital, but I admire that
places like POSK and Ognisko still exist. That, despite the entrenched
old guard that constitute their marrow, they are still, by dint of their
very existence, in dialogue with the city around them.

We eventually found ourselves in an empty storefront that is part of
POSK. A 'To Let' sign was taped on the floor-to-ceiling glass windows
and light streamed in from the setting sun. The Ukrainian group talked
about the various ways they could use the space. I watched quietly as a
new group of floating exiles sought something to hold on to.

THE EU RESTAURANT

On 1 May 2004, the London food scene changed almost overnight. This was the day that seven former Eastern Bloc countries – Lithuania, Latvia, Estonia, the Czech Republic, Slovakia, Hungary and, most consequentially, Poland – joined the European Union, the endgame of a 15-year project that started with the fall of the Berlin wall, and reached its denouement with the arrival of the polski sklep as a London institution. The labour market immediately exploded (or imploded, depending on who you talk to). Net migration to the UK from the EU suddenly jumped from almost zero to nearly 100,000 people a year, primarily as a result of the new accessions. The UK was one of the very few EU countries that imposed no work restrictions, meaning that London became the primary destination for Europe's economic migrants. In 2007, the same thing happened with Romania. A decade later, Polish and Romanian citizens would make up the biggest proportion of foreign-born nationals in the UK, overtaking Indians from the old empire.

What is curious is that many members of this new wave, unlike those who came before them, did not open restaurants. They changed the London food industry through their labour: many worked across hospitality, from small cafes to high-end restaurants (the restaurateur Jeremy King estimated that up to 75% of his workforce was from mainland Europe by 2016), in shops, in bars, on farms, in abattoirs. Perhaps it has something to do with the untrendiness of the cuisine, of Eastern European food being unable to shake off an (undeserved) reputation as Soviet-style poverty food and herrings under fur coats (Barclay Bram has also remarked that there has been no Polish equivalent of Ottolenghi). But what is more likely is that the transient (and ultimately, as it turned out during the Brexit vote, conditional) nature of EU immigration was not conducive to opening restaurants that require a large amount of investment and a certain degree of being settled. Instead, it was the polski sklep – the Polish shop – that left the biggest mark on London, becoming as ubiquitous as the newsagents.

The fact that Eastern and Central European restaurants haven't become a London demotic doesn't mean that they don't exist. Polish restaurants, for instance, have a long history here, from the post-war opulence of Daquise and Ognisko to cheap dumpling and vodka cafes like Mamuśka in South London. Romanian restaurants, while rarely getting any press or frequented by anyone outside the community, are becoming increasingly common: from Edmonton to Croydon, from Barking to Ealing. And although there are a smattering of Lithuanian, Hungarian and Latvian restaurants (where you will have an extremely good time), perhaps the biggest influence of Eastern Europe on London dining is the masquerade: if you ask, rather than taking its signage as a given, you may find that your local Italian deli is run by Romanians, your Greek taverna by Bulgarians or Albanians, and that we're still waiting for the Balkan Ottolenghi to show us the way.

OGNISKO

Even though the elderly and well-dressed clientele can give the early dinner sitting the appearance of an extremely well-catered funeral, Ognisko is really one of the great London dining rooms: it is both opulent and intimate, a place you could conceivably take your date or your grandparents, or both. Yet the best place to sit is at the bar, where you have the entire tableau of the candlelit room set out before you. From this serene position – eating pierogi and fat pelmeni at the counter – you can witness well-managed chaos. The food here is better than it needs to be and, in some cases, exceptional: potato pancakes like McDonald's hash browns, served with blushing chicken livers, and a multi-layered honey cake, like a millefeuille of Graham crackers. Make sure, whatever you do, to get two carafes of homemade vodka – one for the food, and one for the road.

MIKRUS

If Ognisko is Poland as it was, Mikrus on Streatham's resurgent river-wide high street is Poland as it is now, without romance: low blue lighting, disco balls and turbo-folk. Order sledzik (mortuary-cold pickled herring – that icy, pelagic North Sea fish), with white onions, white vinegar and dill, or placuszki: hench rosti amped up on protein shakes, dipped in sour cream or gravy or, ideally, both. Mains could feed an army – a huge knuckle of pork comes with a mass of sticky, sour cabbage that has been dredged through all the fat from the pork, as if the chef scraped up the caramelised remnants of ten pans just for one portion. Or an escalope the size of Dominic Cummings' head, crowned with salty cheese. Whatever you order, if you praise the owner's homemade kompot, you should expect to receive some very necessary shots of cherry liquor to settle the stomach on the bus ride back.

MAHALA

When entering Mahala in Croydon, you may feel it has the vibe of a pub – a bar in the middle of the room, banquettes, and music slightly too loud to hear anyone – it's probably because it once was one. Now the building serves a new institution: a Romanian restaurant, and one of the few making an attempt to appeal to anyone outside of the Romanian community (the room has the feel of any mid-end pan-Mediterranean restaurant in any small English city centre). The food is excellent: the amount of garlic in the tripe soup could revive you at a Romanian wedding at 2am, while the cabbage rolls, stuffed with rice and mince and served with a square of polenta, are worthy of every central London restaurant serving their iteration of homely comfort food. With grills, burgers, sandwiches and chips on the menu, you can imagine it being rolled out nationwide as a vast improvement on Wetherspoons.

HUNGRY TUMMY

Complaining about lack of food options has become a Hungarian *émigré* sport, replacing the era of Soho's Gay Hussar, when the sport was to complain about the *quality* of the food options. There are some Hungarian restaurants in London,

if you travel far enough – The Rosemary in New Cross, or Lakehouse in Leytonstone – serving a standard homily of stuffed cabbage leaves, goulash and chicken paprikash. But the real homesick stuff, the filthy stuff that makes every *émigré* dream about a return trip (despite Viktor Orban), can be found at a hole-in-the-wall in Aldgate, Hungry Tummy, which serves langos. These are, to be blunt, fried dough, and you can buy them served traditionally (topped with inhospitable amounts of garlic, cheese and sour cream) or inauthentically, in a version which is labelled as pizza (not a leap – they are essentially Neapolitan pizze fritte). Make sure to get the paprika-red meatballs, with a thick crust and molten core, and aranygaluska, which are golden walnut dumplings – small wodges of cake – in a slow-flowing vanilla cream sauce: school dinner puddings nonpareil.

CHICKEN & ĆEVAPI

The food of the former Yugoslavian republics is not so well represented in London today – the days of the Anglo-Yugoslav cafe, serving Portobello Road traders and Yugoslavians of all stripes, is long gone, with the few restaurants left mainly divided down national and ethnic lines, serving small pockets of communities (some from countries which have EU membership; some, like Bosnia, which are still waiting). The South Ealing Bosnian chicken and cevapi cafe named, with a dose of literalism, Chicken & Ćevapi, is an anomaly: an attempt to introduce London to a new level of its citywide cuisine, the kebab. There are few options at Chicken & Ćevapi which aren't chicken (grilled breast) or cevapi (bullet-like beef sausages) – you can get them in burgers, wraps, sandwiches or, best of all, just by themselves with airy lepina bread on the side, accompanied by a healthy serving of garlic sauce, dill béarnaise and ajvar (red pepper sauce). Not to tell you what to order or anything, but no one has come here wishing they ordered more chicken and less cevapi.

the partition

A curious cartography exists in London. Somehow, as if it were planned, its west has become a hub of Punjabi life, while its east has become a hub of Bangladeshi life, mirroring the partition of India 75 years ago, when the Radcliffe Line split the states of Punjab and Bengal in two.

South Asian food in Britain tends to be critiqued in terms of its authenticity – there is little room for hybrid experimentation. Yet pubs and fast-food shops – those staples of English dining culture – have absorbed immigrant influences to better serve their diversifying local communities. A new partition is in town.

imran thupar

The west and south-west suburbs of London are my original home. My mum is white British and grew up in Hampshire; my dad is an Indian Punjabi who grew up in West London. I was brought up somewhere in the middle, between native and immigrant, white and brown, small town and urban.

My grandparents settled in Southall in the early 1960s, like many Punjabis. Southall's Broadway is a landing strip for north Indian life, full of portals to my fatherland, even if it's just the men serving masala corn or round jalebi from stalls. In Saadat Hasan Manto's short story, 'Toba Tek Singh', a small bag of sweet snacks is gifted to the main character, a patient at Lahore's lunatic asylum, by his visiting Muslim friend, Fazal Din. The exchange takes place before the decant of the Hindu and Sikh population following partition. Since reading Manto, I've come to view Southall corn-sellers' polystyrene cups as an emblem of Punjab's multi-religious fraternity.

My dada ji (paternal grandfather), Vishva Nath, was a proud Hindu, yet he spoke Urdu and enjoyed singing ghazals and qawwali, reflecting the interfaith fabric of his Ludhiana upbringing. Punjab's rivers and tolerant diversity were two features that were spliced in two by the Radcliffe Line, creating tensions with Pakistan and between religious groups across India that have hardened ever since. But back then, he would saunter down the Broadway to hang out with Muslim friends at the row of Pakistani karahi houses that encircle the mosque – a stone's throw from the small gurdwara a few doors up, and the men selling corn and jalebi outside the busy outfit shops, then as now, come rain or shine.

Migrate from Punjab's border to Bengal's, from West London to East London, one mesh of hidden subcultures to another.

In 1971, following a bloody war of liberation, East Pakistan became Bangladesh. Extending a migratory lineage that has stemmed from Bengal's Muslim-majority Sylhet region since the 19th century, when seamen recruited on steam ships by the East India Company landed on the Thames, many Bangladeshis settled in the docklands of East London following their new country's independence.

The borough of Tower Hamlets has one of the highest concentrations of both fast-food shops and Bangladeshi-owned restaurants in the UK. Most restaurants here cater for City workers, tourists and European palates, while the few that deal in authentic Bangladeshi dishes are male-dominated spaces, a bit like desi pubs – attracting an older, post-mosque clientele.

PFC (Perfect Fried Chicken) is subtly inverting this. At first glance, these three letters may appear a generic, unremarkable acronym, but in fact, they signal a rare and impressive convergence of hyperlocal microeconomics, home-style flavour and intergenerational pride – preserving culinary tradition while looking ahead to adaptive British multiculturalism.

'The chicken shop was where you gathered after school,' says Dina Begum, a Bangladeshi food writer based in East London. 'Now I see my teenage nephew and his friends stopping there. It's cheap; it's owned by other Bangladeshis. It is a space where the younger generation feel safe.'

photos by harkikaran

Pubs in Southall are another portal. If you turn right out of the train station you will see what was formerly the Glassy Junction, a pub which used to accept rupees. Its name informed the title of a chapter in anthropologist Brian Keith Axel's book, *The Nation's Tortured Body*, in which Southall's pubs are presented as a political organising space for Punjabis, where they could also adapt to English drinking culture. All that remains of the Hambrough Tavern is a boarded-up ruin at the far end of the Broadway, but it has been remembered as a defiant symbol of anti-racism since it was burned down by young Asian men and women in July 1981, two years after the 1979 riots, for hosting National Front-affiliated 'Oi!' bands.

Amongst this raucous solar system, the Prince of Wales in the old town is the brightest star. 'Princey' attracts a loyal customer base – many of them Punjabis living nearby, young and old – but it is a safe space for many breeds of men: white British lads filling up before the races; Eastern Europeans in dusty reflective gear and Caterpillar boots, feeding after a day of hard labour; Black Caribbean elders wearing flat caps, reading the newspaper and watching the cricket. These demographics mix, debate and exchange banter.

'If I raise the price of a drink by 10p, someone will protest,' chuckles manager Chandan Singh, whose family has owned the pub since 2003. He points towards a row of Jameson whiskey bottles standing in formation like saluting soldiers and notes that 'all of them will be gone by tomorrow'. The faded carpet remains unchanged from when he used to charge around as a child.

All the way up the A11, where Whitechapel Road leads into Mile End Road, tracking the District Line, PFCs serve typical fast-food menus but also naga chicken wings, naga doner kebab, shatkora doner kebab and biryanis of all sorts (including doner meat), which come with a side of daal. Naga Morich and shatkora are totemic ingredients: Naga Morich is a chilli which is beloved in north-east India and Bangladesh, while shatkora is a citrus fruit whose rind is used to flavour many Bangladeshi dishes. Before London's East End stocked nagas, Bangladeshis would grow them in allotments – a practice upheld by household elders today.

The story of PFC crosses both partition lines. For decades, as chef and writer Feroz Gajia points out, Pakistani owners of Turkish-style kebab shops in London have been chopping doner kebab meat up with masala and onions on a sizzling griddle and serving it with naans. Adding the naga to this process was the next logical step for Bangladeshi owners: it was also soon applied to chicken wings.

'Me and my brothers keep our standards high,' one worker behind the till at Stroudley Grill & PFC in Bow told me, after I'd enjoyed a mammoth plate of eight naga wings and chips for £5. Kept busy taking orders from a long queue – giggling schoolchildren, stern young men in tracksuits, women wearing hijabs – as well as by a continually ringing takeaway phone, before excusing himself to pray, he still made time to ask: 'Did you try the chilli sauce?' I had done, which is why I was speaking to him with blissfully throbbing lips.

Nestled amongst social housing estate tower blocks, next door to a competitor whose name, 'PFC Espresso', makes me

Gesturing at tables of men nursing beers, he tells me that when he tries to redecorate, regulars ask him not to.

The Prince of Wales is a 'desi pub' – a phenomenon which can be traced back to the Midlands, where thousands of men from post-partition Punjab settled – on invitation from Westminster – to fill workforce gaps. They would drink in English pubs after long shifts in the metal foundries. By the 1980s, after assimilating, mobilising in workers' unions and saving financial capital, Sikh and Hindu owners invested in their own establishments, which had bhangra and kabaddi teams and, eventually, kitchens offering Punjabi food.

London's west is dotted with these pubs too; they orbit the nucleus of Heathrow airport, whose sprawling terminals and factories also attracted arriving Punjabis who were seeking work. They range from the snazzy to the spit-and-sawdust: the sports lounge of Hounslow's African Queen; the fine dining of Queensbury's Regency; the disco-barbecue of Masala & Coal in Ruislip Gardens. Hundreds of pubs have closed in recent years due to soaring property crises and the digitisation and fragmentation of community life, but many desi pubs have stayed immovable, serving food that competes with home cooking to hold on to repeat punters. These are essentially gastropubs, without the pomp or the £7 scotch egg.

The food at the Prince of Wales is remarkably good, which is baffling on football or cricket game days, when you'll find the organised supply-chain chaos of a bustling Amritsar dhaba crammed within

smile every time I think about it, Stroudley is one of the most celebrated PFCs in a crowded market. One way to gain such a community-wide stamp of approval is by making the best naga chilli sauce: a fluorescent liquid of blended onions, garlic, tomato, vinegar and, of course, naga. Every PFC has its own home-made version, an attempt to bend homogenised regulation towards individual flair, like a teenager refashioning their school uniform as personal expression.

At Stroudley, the plastic squeezy bottle is refilled from a vat at the back. Customers of all ages wait their turn to squirt it on their chips alongside mayonnaise and ketchup. At Whitechapel Fried Chicken, you have to ask the minder at the till to ladle it onto your plate. 'Are you worried someone will steal the recipe?' I asked on my visit there, naively expecting a smile in return. But he looked at me deadpan while pouring continuously, unapologetically, until bright red filled my white china plate like a thin soup. In such a competitive ecosystem, naga chilli sauce is no joke.

Given the lack of accessible Indian Bengali or Bangladeshi restaurants in London, this vast, overlooked cuisine, which shares many similarities across the border created at partition, remains rarely eaten outside of home kitchens. PFC shops provide a unique communication stream for different generations of Bangladeshis, and a rare opportunity for their East End community's culinary heritage to slot into everyday trends. With fewer youth-friendly spaces across the UK following a decade of austerity, PFC has taken on a heightened significance. Like Morley's south of the river, and Sam's in the city's west and north-west, PFCs are reliably

its intimate, peeling walls. I've never experienced a busier dining room than when my dad and I watched India play against Pakistan in the final of the ICC Champions Trophy on Father's Day in 2017. Every inch of floor space was in use, yet our sizzling tandoori mixed-grill, karahis of paneer and daal, and naans buttered with slices of garlic and finely chopped green chillies arrived within minutes. Waiters juggled trays through the crowd with the speedy balance of street entertainers. The kitchen's metronomically swinging door revealed glimpses of yelling, sweating turbaned men in spice-stained white aprons. The head chef has worked there for nearly two decades. His deputy lives upstairs.

Desi pubs represent a postcolonial society trying to make sense of itself, authentically interweaving the cultures of my mixed heritage. They render racist door policies ancient history. Many of them are welcoming, warm and modern, with diverse, family-friendly customer bases. Others are not without their problems – as in many men's drinking pubs, female presence is a rarity. A museum can honour the past without getting stuck in it – though I would be lying if I said I think about this when I'm biting into a steaming lamb chop.

branded spots where young Londoners can access affordable food. Like desi pubs, they tell a story of ethnocultural preservation as well as raw socio-economic need.

The partition of India in 1947 may feel like a distant slice of history, rarely given focus in rear-view memories of Britain's global past. But its descendants have forged survival spaces on the margins of London life. Unlike its original iteration, the new partition is far from tragic. From two directions, it has proven that inclusivity in this unforgiving capital is possible. Just choose your poison: a pint of draft beer with your paratha, or a squeezy bottle of chilli sauce with your chips.

LAHORE – KARACHI – PESHAWAR – LONDON

Due to a combination of lazy pub quizmasters and childhood trivia books, everyone knows that the most common name for a pub in the UK is The Red Lion. But what about the most common name for a restaurant? As far as my knowledge stretches, no one has run the data on this yet, but if you counted takeaway shops and stalls as restaurants then I have a strong suspicion that the answer would be Falafel King, with each area of Britain resembling a feudal, pre-Alfred conglomeration of kingdoms, each presided over by a benevolent ruler serving halloumi wraps. But if it isn't Falafel King, then the answer would almost certainly have Lahore or Bengal in the name, the two most commonly used words to give a restaurant a suggestion of 'Indianness' without quite explicitly saying it.

There is a good reason for this euphemism. In the aftermath of the Bangladeshi War of Independence in 1971, the UK received a significant wave of immigration from the newly created Bangladesh, mainly from Sylhet in the north-east. Although the restaurant trade was already a well-travelled path for Sylhetis in Britain (the first Indian restaurant in the UK was started by one), most moved into heavy industry; it was only deindustrialisation in the late 1970s that pushed them back into the restaurant trade, and which led to the creation of the curry house. These restaurants served a food that was not in any way Bengali, but approximated a rich, saucy north Indian palate. Rather than claim Bangladeshi-ness (Bangladesh being a young country which had no resonance for the British population), these curry houses had names like Bengal Village, Taste of Bengal, Bengal Spice and Bengal Lancer, trading off memories of when the capital of the British Raj was in Calcutta. Today it might seem like a subtle equivocation, but these names probably secured the economic survival of a whole generation of Bangladeshi restaurateurs.

Pakistani chefs took a similar route, although the British desire for the theatre of the grill, of freshly made naan in the tandoor, allowed them to toe a closer line to their own cooking, particularly thriving in the Balti houses of Birmingham. Pakistan, carved out of Radcliffe's scribbles, was still a slur hurled on the streets of Southall and Handsworth alike, though; the cuisine, therefore, was 'Punjabi' and the restaurants all had Lahore, the largest city in West Punjab, in the name. Today, these pioneers of Pakistani cooking in London have been joined by new ones from Pakistan's largest city Karachi, and Pashtuns on the border with Afghanistan – those who straddle Durand's line rather than Radcliffe's – all cooking some of the most exciting, direct food in the city. The restaurants' names are still consummate poker faces (Taste of Peshawar, Khyber Pass), saying everything to those who need to know and nothing to everyone else.

LAHORE ONE

The very simple reason that Pakistani food hasn't permeated the mainstream is prosaically, almost disappointingly, simple: Brits love to get tanked while eating spicy food. Historically, the restaurants which allowed BYOB tended to get the plaudits over ones further out, which mainly cater to those on their deen who don't want their meal disturbed by what was formerly lads chugging Cobra, and would now be very polite foodies turning up with bottles of saison. This is not to say there are no great Pakistani restaurants centrally, or that BYOB is a bad sign. Indeed, Lahore One fulfils both criteria and has been around for donkey's years, its huge neon signage lighting up Commercial Road like the Bellagio. It was to Lahore One that many generations of South Asians came specifically for methi chicken, a tangy, herbal, bitter curry cooked with so many fenugreek leaves it's practically verdant.

LAHORI NIHAARI

Some of the best South Asian food in London has yet to be discovered because some people cannot be bothered to spend an extra ten minutes travelling east on the District Line. Good. People for whom Upton Park may as well be Southend or Colchester don't deserve Lahori Nihaari, a Punjabi restaurant which has the feeling of sitting in your friend's mum's living room, alongside a dozen or so uncles having a very animated meeting over some paya. The menu here is concise: a few grills, slow-cooked meat and dals, and a top-drawer haleem, but really everyone is here for the karahi, which can be ordered in cauldrons which grow exponentially in size; choose between chicken or lamb, with layered aromatics of ginger, cardamom and chilli, all under a delicious strata of scarlet oil that sits on top like a warning to your heart.

ALADIN KEBABISH

Do you know Aladin's? Of course you do. Everyone knows Aladin's – that central jewel set into the crown of a particularly blessed stretch of Hendon Broadway which also contains a Pashtun restaurant, a sheeryakh specialist and a bakery selling Afghan bolani – everyone from the Pakistan cricket team, whose signed bat adorn the walls, to the Uber driver who, when I gave it as the answer to 'What's your favourite Pakistani restaurant?', did a double-take so hard that I may as well have named his mum's house. Everyone knows Aladin's because it's really the only place in London to go if you're feeling homesick for Karachi; it specialises in the 'Karachi holy trinity' – haleem, qorma and nihari. Of the triumvirate, it is the nihari you will find on most tables: a huge lamb shank blushing ruby that can be dismantled with the back of a spoon.

CHARSI KARAHI

The only sharing plates I officially recognise are dishes that are too physically large for one person to consume; 'Go big or go home' dishes. The whole lamb sajji you can get at any good Pashtun restaurant is one of these sharing plates, big enough to cater for a whole Downing Street lawn and terrace work meeting. Charsi Karahi in Norbury must get through about a herd's worth of lambs a day for takeaway, judging by the number of cars waiting to fill their boots. An unfeasible number of south-west London parties, weddings and funerals have been catered for with this lamb. As is so often the case with these dishes, the lamb itself is just a very expensive container for the rice, steamed to perfection inside the animal's belly, plump and glossy with oils and fat. One type of person would make a beeline for the most prized cuts of meat; a wiser one would crack open the rib-cage, find the rice and squeeze the whole cooked garlic cloves over it like they were chip shop packs of mayonnaise.

NAMAK MANDI

Turn up at Tooting's Namak Mandi late on a Friday or Saturday and you will find well-managed chaos – the restaurant is essentially a three-floor flat, with multiple small, private rooms full of people reclining over a communal mat eating charsi karahi, waiters running a staircase gauntlet, and families on the ground floor arguing over who got there first, while groups of young men sit in the carpeted window, drinking sweet tea and staying out of it. But waiting is as much a part of the experience here as the karahis that start their life as a mass of lamb and whole tomatoes, steamed until they lose their skin and dissolve into the sauce, and the chapli kebabs that are sent out like funeral boats into an ocean of animal fat. The best thing to do here is book one of those private rooms and order a whole lamb, so only the Almighty can witness your *Grande Bouffe* levels of gluttony.

the park —————— santiago peluffo soneyra

After a decade living in London, I'm still not sure I would call this city Home. But I can say that, during the summer of 2015, when I was first invited to a barbecue at Burgess Park, London started to feel like a more familiar territory. That first barbecue feast on an (almost) sunny Saturday afternoon helped me slowly digest my homesickness and feel more hungry to discover a place which, though very distant, was becoming more recognisable, and somehow closer to my Latin American roots.

I remember it vividly: I was salting a Uruguay-imported tender rump loin bought from a Brazilian butcher on the Old Kent Road, tossing it over one of the permanent barbecues and carefully overseeing its slow cooking on the grill (which was kept at a steady temperature thanks to the meticulous scattering of small pieces of charcoal).

Coming from Argentina, a country known for its omnipresent barbecue culture (asado), it had taken me a while to enjoy barbecues in the UK. At acquaintances' gardens or hipster parks in North and East London, I often struggled to relate to the sluggish attitude towards grilling pre-spiced meat from Sainsbury's on a disposable grill – a device I had never seen before in my life. Yet here in Burgess Park, enjoying the conversation with my friends over a glass of

Malbec by the pond (which seemed, in that moment, like a lagoon), it felt different. Once that rump loin was ready, I cut smooth slices and passed it round for my friends to enjoy, in what I still think must be the closest possible experience to an Argentinian asado in London.

Over the years I've seen similar people find something like Home in Burgess Park: crowds of Bolivian Londoners eating juicy salteñas and dancing traditional folklore on their Independence Day; South London Jamaicans grilling and selling jerk chicken to raise funds for Windrush scandal victims; a trio of Mariachis performing for a mixed group of white British; Latin Americans grilling some chorizo during a loud birthday celebration; an all-day volleyball tournament ending with a picnic by the lake, participants contemplating one of the best sunsets in the city (who needs Primrose Hill?). These scenes have helped me understand how various communities have come to enjoy a Sunday barbecue, not for the mere act of feeding themselves but for the key ingredients a proper barbecue must also have: community spirit, a sense of party, spontaneity.

It's hard to believe that during the 19th – and most of the 20th – century, the site that became Burgess Park was a heavily industrial concrete desert, before it was all suddenly brought down into a pile of rubble, with entire council houses and factories turned into ashes

after Second World War bombardments. This horrendous wound created the possibility for planners to consider a rural replacement, giving thousands of people access to a green space where there was once only cement. After 1945 it took several decades of heterogeneous planning, with no architect really claiming its design, for Burgess Park to exist in the way we know it today. It was criticised by many for its lack of structure and vision, yet to me it seems like the park has reinvented itself while being able to honour its past as a part of the city – you'll find, scattered around: a lime kiln, the Edwards Library, Bath and Wash houses, and a bridge over a canal which is no longer there.

In recent decades, Burgess' relationship to the city and those who inhabit the park has become unique within London: the fusion of both public and private habits taking place in an open green space. In a sense, to many working-class communities, Burgess is an extension of their own doorstep. Put another way, the lack of green (or *any*, really) space in many of the flats surrounding Burgess Park, and in the wider context of an ever-more gentrifying borough like Southwark, makes it one of the few sources of open-air enjoyment for thousands. Massive, diverse and ever-surprising, Burgess Park seems to provide something for everyone: you'll find BMX-riding teens, foraging pensioners, focused early-rising fishers and all-day carnival parties.

'The atmosphere here is unique, with the cumbias and reggaeton full-on, but also our traditional Caporales Andean folklore dances,' says Alex, La Paz-born and a South Londoner since 2014, who I've played football with at Burgess Park over the years. He recalls one of the many Bolivian Independence Days hosted every August, at the north side of Burgess just by the lagoon. 'It's amazing to be able to celebrate our roots, culture and languages in such a big space, and a very significant one for us Latin Americans as it is very close to Elephant and Castle.'

'There's almost a migrant reflex attached to the way we make use of Burgess,' Juliana, a close friend I met in Elephant and Castle who is originally from Medellín, Colombia, tells me. 'Back home, a barbecue is a party you host on the sidewalk (or patio, if you have one) with your neighbours, your friends and the whole family. Sadly, we can't do it this way in London, so Burgess is the closest to that experience in that we can freely use the space and it's close to where we live.'

As the first rays of continuous sun mark the beginning of 'good weather' – whatever that means in London – I come across tweets from people saying they are craving a barbecue at Burgess Park, only to find a cold reply from Southwark Council: 'Good morning. The fixed BBQ area in Burgess Park remains closed at present until further notice. Disposable BBQs are prohibited in all our parks.'

'The space around the barbecues is going to be severely compromised by the new sports centre plus possibly a basketball court,' explains Susan Crisp, coordinator at Friends of Burgess Park. 'We have consistently made the point about the impact on the barbecues not considered with the sports centre extension. Parks [and Gardens] have now agreed to do a review of the barbecues, but in reality they are already closed...'

The much-loved and distinctive barbecue area, which came about following Mile End Park's popular introduction of fixed barbecues, is now a decade old. Originally built in 2012 as part of the overall makeover and master-plan development for Burgess Park, the area consisted of two separate sets of fixed barbecue structures – about a dozen in total. It quickly became very popular among Walworth and Old Kent Road's Latin American, West African and Caribbean communities, but the structures only lasted six years; in 2018 a ban came into place (because of the 'long dry summer and risk of fire', according to Southwark Council), and two years ago the north area was completely removed due to complaints of noise and smoke.

Since then I've wandered countless times around the lake, sadly contemplating the grey, crooked fences barring the barbecue area – now sitting on a yellowish dying grass – and cannot seem to solve this contradiction in my mind. It is perhaps only in a city like London (and with the diverse set of communities who inhabit it) that a *Burgess experience* can happen. Yet I refuse to be fooled: the barbecue ban is the latest in a long line of Southwark Council trying to police the spontaneous use of public space. In September 2020, Southwark were granted an injunction by the County Courts threatening neighbours with a ban of up to £10,000 for the use of amplified music, lighting equipment, marquees and even for gatherings of more than 20 people after 9pm.

As someone who constantly struggles to adapt to an increasingly standardised and hyper-vigilant city after being raised in at-times anarchic Buenos Aires, I find comfort in what Walter Benjamin calls a 'passion for improvisation': how we can naturally appropriate and penetrate an urban space. While a North London passer-by might feel somewhat estranged by Burgess' atmosphere, for the regulars enjoying a Sunday barbecue (or local church groups holding prayer meetings, or people celebrating Eid-al-Fitr, or even just large families having parties with lively music), the fiesta almost becomes an act of resistance to the UK's cold and organised soul. Burgess Park parties – in a city like London – can, in fact, cross the boundaries of predetermined behaviour. They constitute 'a rich network of practices … transforming every available space into a potential theatre of expressive acts of encounter,' as Benjamin would put it.

This 'act of resistance' for diaspora communities might not be a conscious one, given that a barbecue at Burgess Park has long become a ritual, a habit, even a remedy for nostalgia. But the park can also be a metaphor for these porous boundaries between a strict and regulated London and a much more fluid, open city, where the appropriation of public spaces is – at least sometimes – welcome. What would Burgess Park be without the smell of the jerk chicken and sancocho; without the spontaneous salsa lessons and five-a-sides; without the ancestral and colourful Yoruba rhythms; without the distinctive South American accents and the popular Carnivals?

Still, the regular BBQers seem to know how to *resist* the ban in their own fashion. 'It is sad not to have the fixed barbecues, but for us it doesn't make much of a difference: Burgess is still our meeting point,' explains Alex. 'We prepare empanadas and other traditional food at home, we take it to the park and we make it like a picnic party. The important thing is to be able to gather with your people.'

I recall my last party at Burgess Park: the Akolá Tambó band were drumming, singing and dancing Bullerengue, an Afro-Colombian rhythm that gathers dozens in a circle of joy and brotherhood. It marked the culmination of a day-long event of reflection and debate around the 2022 presidential elections in Colombia, which kicked off with a massive sancocho (a soup or stew), a traditional collective cooking celebration that, in the Burgess way of doing things, replaced the barbecue due to the ongoing ban. Next to this large crowd of South Americans, a group of Nigerian Londoners spontaneously joined the Bullerengue dance which they had little trouble following thanks to the common Yoruba roots. They also brought with them and shared some gbegiri soup; they were, too, having their own version of a barbecue.

'For me, it relates to the concept of sancocho en la calle (street stew),' Juliana tells me, 'where you take your biggest cooking pot and you cook for all your neighbours out on the street, and everyone comes around with their plates and drinks, making it a beautiful community lunch. This doesn't happen in London's neighbourhoods but it can happen in London ... at Burgess. And this is beautiful.'

A DRIFT DOWN THE OLD KENT ROAD

The only thing constant about the Old Kent Road is that people have always tried to escape it. Pilgrims trod the route centuries ago – somewhere in between it being the Roman Watling Road and becoming the A2 – on the way to Canterbury. They left their traces in names: Pilgrims' Way Primary School, opposite the big Aldi, and the doomed Thomas a Becket pub, thought to be the location of St Thomas' watering place, as mentioned by Chaucer. The pilgrims would have come down from Borough and made a turn to the south-east at what is now the Bricklayers Arms roundabout. Although the Old Kent Road technically starts here, spiritually it starts at the sign a hundred metres or so down, which says 'Peckham 2, The Channel Tunnel 62, Dover 72': the assumption is still that, if you're on Old Kent Road, your main aim is probably to get as far away from it as possible.

In the introduction to his 1956 essay *Theory of the Dérive* ('Drift'), Guy Debord refers to a certain urban phenomenon that any Londoner is intimately familiar with: 'The sudden change of ambiance in a street within the space of a few meters; the evident division of a city into zones of distinct psychic atmospheres' – in short, 'a vibe shift'. The Old Kent Road has at least four psychic zones that contain within them their own eddies and currents. At the top, from the Bricklayers Arms down to Burgess Park (spiritually an extension of Old Kent Road itself), the road is dominated by one thing: the handheld pie. Salteñas, empanadas, samosas, meat pies and bourek are all here, edible signs of the Latin American and West and North African influence on the road. Further south is a blank section which is overshadowed by the vast Avondale Square Estate; embossed with the City of London's logo, this denotes the sinister reach of The Corporation and its vast wealth that stretches beyond the Square Mile. Right at the bottom is the New Cross Road section, an isolated arc of Nigerian bars and Latin American mini-malls that isn't quite part of the main Old Kent Road ecosystem but has not rejoined the rest of the city. Between these poles is pure industrial estate and retail park. It's here you'll find Lidl, B&Q, Asda, Aldi, Homebase, a builders' depot and at least ten competing white garment churches, hidden on the second floors of former warehouses with names like 'Holy Ghost Zone'. If there was a nuclear apocalypse tomorrow then you could find redemption, plus all the tools and food needed to rebuild society, right here.

JENECHERU

Most places on the Old Kent Road are content to serve specific demographics without explaining or adapting the food for anyone else. Their isolation is precisely what Jonathan Gold discusses in his celebrated essay on Pico Boulevard in Los Angeles: how the area's lack of centripetal force allowed whole communities of restaurants to thrive, well away from the prying eyes of outsiders. These restaurants do not abide by the rules of the rest of the city: just look at the unnamed, makeshift Honduran restaurant at 204 Old Kent Road serving baleadas and pastelitos and decorated with balloons like a children's birthday party. Jenecheru, next door, run by brothers Gabriel and Diego, is one of the few places on Old Kent Road actively looking for an audience outside their diaspora, but their hand pies are still legendary for every Bolivian in South London, with a menu that includes their fabled salteñas, a cross between a pasty and a soup dumpling, fried empanadas with shredded beef, cheese pies and plain tamales wrapped in banana leaves. Carne, carbs, corn and queso.

EL MARSEM

Something happens as soon as you cross to the east side of Old Kent Road, one of those sudden changes in ambience that Debord loved to go on about. From El Marsem onwards, the street is spiritually North African, full of patisseries with names like 'L'Auberge' and 'Le Panier a Brioche', plus a Moroccan paella shop. Even the chippy is an Algerian cafe now. It is perhaps the only part of London with a genuine outdoor cafe culture; in the summer heat, this strip has the vibe of one of Haussmann's vast Parisian boulevards, with men out on the street in small chairs, gossiping, drinking small cups of coffee well into the night, and eating bourek – mince, tuna, and prawn pastries, mixed with salty cheese, tangy olives, mashed potato and sharp harissa, all brought together with oil, which glistens through their takeaway paper.

SERYBI'S GRILL

For a good mile south of Burgess Park, there's almost no cooked food on the Old Kent Road (except for a Subway) but between a shuttered Latin nightclub and a big Asda is a peripatetic street food van called Serybi's, owned by Fabrice Sery Bi. This is one of the few Ivorian food businesses in a city generally starved of francophone West African cuisine. Just choose your protein – grilled rotisserie chicken, grilled fish, or lamb or pork suya, all topped with a sand drift of yaji powder and cooling, raw white onion – and then add plantains, cooked until they're almost toffee, sour attieke made from fermented cassava, and some truly searing hot sauce which has all the fruity power of the Scotch bonnet. It's probably the best meal you can eat in a supermarket car park in the city.

HONG KONG CITY

At night-time, Hong Kong City appears out of nowhere like an apparition, lit up like a Las Vegas casino in hot red and purple neon on a stretch of road that contains nothing more glamorous than a Millwall pub. If you don't expect it, it might seem out of place, but it's entirely congruous with a road that was once home to a restaurant run by a Chinese Elvis impersonator which doubled up as a shrine to The King. On Sunday morning, which is when you should actually come, it feels a bit more prosaic: a drab white square flats with a banner announcing 'EAT AS MUCH AS YOU LIKE' sitting atop a faux pagoda. But inside it is exactly the right intersection of cavernous and kitsch

that you want from a dim sum restaurant, all red carpets, bridges and fish ponds; everything needed to turn good but unremarkable dumplings into the most auspicious start to the day imaginable.

SMOKEY JERKEY

The washed-out aquamarine signage at Smokey Jerkey may not have changed in the last decade, but that's because owner Louie McPherson only spends time on things that matter, such as tinkering with his custom-made furnace that both barbecues and smokes his meat, leaving pink smoke perimeters on every bit of jerk lamb that passes through it. This small spot on the New Cross end of the road is in the very top tier of barbecue in London: the pork and chicken are good, but the lamb is untouchable, long marinated in cayenne chillis and cooked in big cuts, which break down under hickory smoke until the bark becomes sweet and chewy, before it is all chopped up and served with rice and peas, and a side of scorpion sauce.

the viaduct

I   When I first set out to find the place called Spa Terminus, I didn't arrive until a fortnight later. I don't remember if Spa yet had a name and I also had the impression that what I was looking for might not yet fully exist. I believed that Spa was a kind of market and I was curious about it as someone who was, at the time, curious about produce. I was told – a gesture between making a mark and crossing it out – to follow the Victorian viaduct south from London Bridge and the way I interpreted those directions was: that I should follow the viaduct as if it was a road. This, one summer morning circa 2010, is one way of beginning:

But would this be a mistake? Viaduct, I soon discovered, is a peculiar kind of path, one which exists at an angle to another, which in this case was the road that I was on. Viaduct crosses over, but withholds the possibility of a crossing. It protects its distance and as such, it frequently escapes me.

I seemed to have two options: I could follow the logic of the viaduct or of the city, but I could not do both. Should I follow the one, follow the viaduct back into its memory of open space, marshland and market garden, I would come up against the limits of the city. (A brick wall.) I started to see how, for all its seeming to exist within, the viaduct is instead above, before, between and against the city. It frustrates the urban fabric which it has forced into inelegant reversals and abrupt turns (which revenges itself by covering the viaduct up; as such I also found it imposing certain limits on me and my attempts to grasp it. Standing perplexed on one of those squashed, terminated streets, I felt thwarted but I also felt excited. The viaduct flares up again: irresistible. Like any flirtatious, Barthesian 'text of bliss' it provokes *a state of loss, unsettles, brings about a crisis in relation* (Barthes) to the city; with what I think I know about it and how I presume to use it. I get annoyed, give up, but two weeks later all this is what brings me back. Now, I really, really wanted to find Spa Terminus. The viaduct had tempted me with it, but kept it hidden; my relationship with it was now personal. It was about desire.

virginia hartley

II Spa Terminus became a place I imagined before I found it in the world, so that when I finally arrived it should have felt familiar. Instead I had the uncomfortable sensation of trespassing on other peoples' idea of it, their personal space. I felt jealous of these people who might be closer to it than me. I was not, at the beginning, a favourite there, and even met with suspicion. In an intimate community where everyone knows anyone else, I felt I had to prove myself, and although it is of course very odd to think that I might want nothing more than to prove I was worthy of some vegetables, this is also how I felt. I had never seen such beautiful, soulful, intelligent, vegetables. I wanted to make this place mine, for it to fall in love with me in the way I so suddenly and inexplicably had with it. I wanted it to need me, and I went about this by not only buying produce there, but in time starting to work there, casually at first. Over time, it became my full-time job. I sold the vegetables. Those beautiful vegetables came to depend on me to be sold. I made the pastries. They needed me to exist. I even looked after the cheese and helped it mature. These days, I blame the viaduct for this experience of falling.

167

Yet Spa is not – it is firm about this – a market. It is not a market despite the fact that, every Saturday, it seems more like a market than anything else. On Saturdays, along a line of viaduct, arch tenants who produce, mature, and distribute wholesale during the week, briefly open their doors to sell to the public. Recently, in the Saturday farmer's market of a provincial town in the Auvergne, I encountered much that reminded me of Spa Terminus: the quality and type of produce (viennoiseries, salami, raw milk cheeses, low intervention wines, seasonal produce) the intimacy with the produce being sold (by the people who make it) and its sense of time and place (its temporal rhythm, dependence on the memory of *having been* and the trust of *will be*.) It is nevertheless important to reiterate that Spa is not a market, because this is what its founders say firmly and this is one key reason why it feels continuous with the viaduct: as unclassifiable within a system of knowledge (the city, its language.) The viaduct and the Spa community housed within it, are both within, outside and above what we think we know. Not only in its name, not a market, also not not a market, as a 'terminus' which is both a destination and a point of origin, a sign which is both itself and its opposite, over a period of ten years Spa would keep me coming back for what it does not reveal about itself, what it keeps hidden, for what it doesn't entirely say.

III At the beginning of my relationship with Spa, there were almost no signs. The large signs there were, like 'Booking Office' (remnants of a failed destination, the terminus of London's first railway, Spa Road) pointed to what was no longer there. Identical blue shutters concealed highly individual internal architectures. The signs of industrial production – freight lorries, forklifts, pallets – could be seen at work even at the weekend, so that although this might well be a weekend market, could we really be sure? To truly come to know Spa Terminus, you would have to get inside the viaduct. To have the courage to make your way inside an inscrutable, dark railway arch, at some personal risk to your ego. You might – as I once was – be met with laundry (cheesecloths, uniforms) being hung out, emptied out of the kind of washing machine you might have in your kitchen. You might find people eating lunch around a table, ladling into bowls from a casserole dish, startled to see you standing there (you would also be startled). You might also, after a brief exchange, be able to buy fresh yoghurt and ricotta there. When you left, you might not be sure what had just happened, whether you had got something wrong. Outside, you would see people using the industrial park as if was really a park: sunning themselves and eating ice cream.

Another project might have sought to clarify itself, but from the beginning I liked how Spa was not interested in doing so. If anything, it felt like Spa might be interested in keeping people away. Like me, you had to really want to be there not to be put off. And although Spa has today become venerable – a matriarch within the food industry, internationally respected – it has protected much of its initial obscurity.

As I learnt more about Spa's history (as with any relationship, I was particularly interested in what preceded me, what Spa was doing when I was not there), I developed some thoughts on why. I learnt about its industrial origins in Neal's Yard in Covent Garden, back when Neal's Yard was not a destination, but a site for experimental food production. Spa Terminus founders Monmouth Coffee and Neal's Yard Dairy had their first premises there. I learnt about the loss of this space – also, later, at Borough Market – to rising rents and development, and I came to see how the viaduct and its offering of concealment, of margin, of inhabiting the city in a way which is also outside it, might be about self-preservation. As long as Spa remains hard to categorise or define, evasive to those who want to see all of its secrets, it keeps itself safe. It strikes me that the speculators, investors and developers who could be dangerous to Spa often lack imagination. They are not interested in what they can't have. Desire is ultimately useless to them. What they need to know is what exactly they are looking at, so that there is no uncertainty about the ways in which something might be appropriated, modelled, made viable and sold.

Spa's previous iterations did not last because they could be grasped in this way. By making its space legible, others were ultimately able to understand it and turn it against them. Each of Spa's previous spaces have become highly attractive commercial districts, inhospitable to such core industrial activity. Spa Terminus understands that, if it is to survive within London, it must by no means give itself away. It does not call itself a market because this word does exactly that.

IV   Once I had found Spa, I found it hard to leave. I went on to work for over four different businesses there: with bread, cheese, wine, fresh produce. I remember someone once described me as 'the slut of Spa Terminus'. It's true I didn't care about who I worked for, as long as I didn't have to forgo the intimacy I had found there.

There is something inevitably womb-like about these vast, curved arches in which all manner of things are gestated, matured, and shaped. In seeking to lodge myself there, not to have to leave, I may have sought refuge from a city in which I had as yet no shape or distinguishing feature. There was certainly something about that strange experience of getting lost – trying to walk the viaduct – which thrust me out of one experience of space into another, in which I caught a flash of myself, of something I had not seen before, for the first time. Maybe it was that, as well as what I glimpsed in the gaps of the city (the viaduct) which was so exciting: I was seduced not just by my Barthesian text but what interrupted that reading: myself. Working at Spa, also doing my shopping there, spending weekdays and weekends there, I took shape, gathered, cohered. What the via-duct had revealed to me about myself became something more. Yet for a long time I was not sure what I was making there would survive in the world.

Something is lost in the transition from viaduct to city, within the gap. Today, finally just a customer again, I find that the produce which I bring back from Spa inevitably starts to fade. The pastries and bread are not only ever fresh from the oven; they age and become stale. I have even struggled to use the produce I buy; I try to preserve it, keep it in my fridge, but do not eat it out of anxiety at its loss. When I throw it away without having used it, I think about how I have failed to bridge the gap. When I use it, make a good dinner from it, I have better mourned whatever it is I have lost.

V   Today I could restart my journey, return to the beginning, and
I would not get lost trying to follow the viaduct. This is because
it is truly becoming a road. The Southwark Low Line – inspired
by New York's High Line – will attempt to transform the viaduct into
what it was not for me: the kind of place you absolutely can't get
lost along, which is designed to be used. Apparently, this is called
a 'walking destination', and it will take many more people to Spa
Terminus. As with most relationships which didn't quite end, I find
that this matters more to me than it should.

If the city is in constant fear of being discovered, then the railway arch is the ideal place to hide in plain sight and pray to God you won't be found by the wrong people. These nooks, beloved by people who tend to use the word 'liminal', have historically been the city's refuge for light industry: mechanics, garages, workshops. The scramble for affordable London space in the last few decades has given the railway arches new identities as homes for food producers, who have in turn opened up the wide, hemispherical frontages to face the public. Breweries have become taprooms; wholesalers have become grocers; roasteries have become cafes. Marginal spaces, like those under Brixton's railway, have essentially become a second high street of newsagents, grocers, butchers and fishmongers.

The arch, in its ingenious reappropriation of London's archaic railway system, has been so successful that its days are surely numbered. Prior to 2018, the arches functioned as what writer Francesca Froy, in an article in the *Independent* that same year, called a 'lucky anomaly' – publicly owned space, slap-bang in the middle of the city, that wasn't subject to the caprices of the private property market. But to assuage its debts, Network Rail sold its portfolio of 5,200 businesses across the UK for the bargain price of £1.46bn to the innocuously named The Arch Company (which was, in truth, a venture between the largest private property company in the UK, Telereal Trillium, and everyone's favourite American alternative asset manager, Blackstone). The arch is now the front line in the redevelopment of neighbourhoods – restaurants and bars line the arches to feed the residents of the 'affordable' new builds opposite. You can see the pattern in Hoxton, Shoreditch, Peckham, Deptford and most recently in Battersea, where the arches cater to the newcomers of the Nine Elms development.

Still, there are some stretches of viaduct in London that remain hidden, at least for those who aren't looking for them. You see (or unsee) them particularly in Elephant and Castle, where the Latin American community use them as closed economies within an economy, partitions and mezzanines making spaces for not just bakeries, grocers and workers' cafes, but also hairdressers, nail salons and dance venues – often all in the same arch. It's in this hybridity that the arch can create a new way of interacting with communal space, away from the eyes of those who would see them as the next big opportunity.

40 MALTBY STREET

An early beneficiary of the creation of Spa Terminus, 40 Maltby Street followed the usual private-to-public pivot of the arches, starting out as a wine importer before opening up the front of the arch as a wine bar serving small plates of food. Under the stewardship of Steve Williams, the kitchen has consistently produced some of the most straightforwardly enjoyable London cooking of the last decade, marrying a forensic attention to precision with an infallible duty to give people pleasure. The food itself defies a consistent definition – it is, perhaps, British food pretending to be continental, or the other way round – and tends to revolve in constellations of micro seasons anchored to Pole stars of pies, fritters, croquettes, tarts, toasts and ices. A marvel.

CHATICA

If Chatica isn't the heart of the Latin American community in Elephant and Castle, then it's something like its liver: a multifunctional organ that would be impossible to replace. Located in a central arch right underneath the rail station, it is both cafe and bakery, a grocery store that provides homesick shoppers with hard-to-get crisp and chocolate wafer brands, a meeting spot, a classified section, as well as being the wholesale supplier for pretty much every restaurant in the area, stocking everything from aji amarillo to concentrates of Colombian fruits used for making garish Technicolor milkshakes.

LOS CHAMOS

There is now a Venezuelan stall outside Chatica, but better to walk across Walworth Road to the other side of the arches, where Los Chamos forms a small slice of a mini-mall partitioned into various sections (a hairdresser, a Latin newspaper stand, an Ecuadorean restaurant serving huge bowls of encebollado). You can get bright corn cachapas here, but best to get the arepas, which – if you're lucky – will be rolled and cooked fresh to order, taking the best part of twenty minutes. Unlike Colombian arepas, which are ideal with just butter and cheese, or something to snack on the side, these are stuffed Venezuelan style with so much filling that they resemble an unhinged python's jaw. The wait should be punctuated with meat or fish empanadas, as well as shots that the brassy women who runs it may pour you from an unlabelled bottle of hooch.

LA BARRA DE PITO

La Barra occupies the arch right below the winner of the 2010 Carbuncle Cup, the Strata Building (which marks the South London skyline with the outline of a beard trimmer, or a lightsaber handle), and in that space you have two versions of Elephant and Castle – one which likes to make noise, and one that doesn't (the 'sustainable' wind turbines on top of the Strata have stopped work-ing). On a good night, you will find the Dominican bar on the upstairs mezzanine blasting out music to delight dancers and annoy new residents, while below, La Barra serves some of the city's best fried chicken in the form of pica pollo, a Colombian take on a Dominican dish that consists of a hillock of carefully arranged tostones, chicken, chicharron and bofes (lung jerky). Come on a weekend and you will find all of Elephant and Castle here, from families to groups of young men ordering the biggest pica pollo platter available.

MAX'S SNACK BAR

Brixton's Station Road is perhaps the best demon-stration in London of how the undesirability of the arch can become defensible. Bisect the street down its vertical axis and you will have a 'before and after' picture: on the left, facing the railway line to Denmark Hill, you have a craft beer shop and Japanese rice bowl cafe; on the right, in the arches, a row of caffs that spill out onto the street, becoming a kind of urban theatre. Max's isn't necessarily the best of these (there are Moroccan and Ethiopian arches too), nor is it the best Portuguese cafe in South London, but there is something transportative about sitting outside, in a rare spell of London sun, with a Sagres and a bifana, feeling like a steady ship in a chaotic sea. The Senegalese stall on the street opposite, selling sunshine-bright yassa, should be your second stop on a long lunch crawl.

photos by zoë cave

the market

In 2018, a chunk of toxic detritus was chipped away from a mass which had been clogging the Victorian sewer tunnels, blocking the flow of waste towards processing facilities on London's edges. The accumulation, named The Monster of Whitechapel, with sensationalist allusions to the Victorian organ-ripping murderer, was borne of flushed wet wipes, soap, fat and shit that had sedimented underground. The Monster was displayed above-ground at the Museum of London, the remnants of a feeding, expulsive, cleaning city preserved as material heritage so that we could confront it. The curator tells us, 'You can tell a lot about a society from what it throws away.'

A few roads from the museum, Smithfield Meat Market's iron gates are locked, scant remains from its overnight trade inside. A 'DEAD SLOW' sign hangs above East Poultry Avenue, cutting through the Victorian East and West Market buildings and the modernist Poultry Market. The market comes alive from midnight until 6am; traders have shifted themselves into the night to bypass the congestion charge. Artic lorries arrive from Dover, or slaughterhouses outcast to cities' hinterlands, and squeeze down the tight streets. Danish pigs, Brazilian boxed beef and New Zealand lambs are fed into the building through a corridor running its circumference, and into the traders' back rooms. By 5am, a white-coated trader stands on a palette shouting scribbled orders to a butcher stacking his van – 'You slippy git, keep count!' – and the meat makes its way back out into the city.

By 6am, shoppers browse the retail counters lining the buyers' walk, a central vein through the fluorescent market halls. On display are boxes of halal chicken, Kielbasa, Brazilian picaña and pork collars. Traders push past with pink carcasses lolling on their shoulders – 'Get out of the way, my sweetness!' – or trolleys filled with parts which have been broken down by the cutters in the back rooms. The real business takes place in the back, where deals are cut with wholesalers on phones, or with handshakes and whispers. Shoppers dawdle on the public buyers' walk, comparing prices. One mistakes a trader for someone who has the inclination to French-cut a vacuum-packed rack of lamb, shouting 'I've got some French for you, darling!' loud enough for the trader next door's ears. 'OOH la la!', the retort comes bouncing back. By day, the restaurants flanking the market serve office workers and tourists, profiting from symbolic proximity to the market. By night it's a meat rave of trade, retail and distribution as drivers, shoppers, traders and cutters tussle over the space and its clashing rules.

Under the arched Grand Avenue, posters commemorate the market's history and the area's murky past, yet its future is currently being fought over as well. The City of London, the archaic institution that owns the market, wants to redevelop it into a destination for more profitable retail, culture, offices or homes. The Museum of London has purchased the disused General Market and has eyes on the just-about-in-use Poultry Market for relocation. It is currently the last remaining wholesale market in the City: Leadenhall's once-itinerant poultry and vegetable stalls have been replaced with boutiques and restaurant chains, Billingsgate Fish Market long ago moved to the Isle of Dogs, and New Spitalfields Market, which sells fruit and vegetables, to Leyton. In 2018, the City acquired the site of the disused Barking Reach power station, complete with planning permission enabling them to move Smithfield, Spitalfields and Billingsgate to the edges of East London. Studio Egret West architects have been instructed to redesign Smithfield as part of a 'culture mile' with already familiar pop-ups, retail, food archives and flexible workspaces to transform the market buildings into an 'inclusive destination' where 'the known meets the unknown.'

Smithfield has succumbed to numerous attempts at dissection into displaceable parts. Until the 1850s, it was a live market, teeming with animals from across the nation and with a network of small slaughterhouses at its edges. Reformist Victorians rallied against its noxious business; blood, guts, faeces, noise and violence, a 'double-trade' in both life and death. Neighbouring St Bartholomew's, a hospital for the poor, had already been redesigned to include grand lecture halls where surgeons shared developments in the scientific endeavours of slicing humans. It was immoral for a modernising city to see that human bodies were close to nature. Animals were moved to the utilitarian Metropolitan Market and concealed slaughterhouses to the suburb of Islington. Smithfield was reborn as a 'dead market', designed by Horace Jones, with a celebratory facade of ornate carvings and white towers, and a functional interior of cooling airflows and underground rail specific to the production of meat. Jones also redesigned Leadenhall as a 'respectable arcade' for permanent traders and civilised retail. Between them, they encompassed the vision of how London's growing population should be fed. By 1964, Islington's slaughterhouses and live market were again rendered a pollutant to living, pushed further into rural areas, and the site redeveloped into a much-needed social housing estate.

It is odd, then, that the only remaining wholesale food market within the City is a meat one, when by logic it should have been expelled first. Smithfield, slaughterhouses and the sewers were structural solutions to suppress nature, dislocating animals from meat and our bodies from our own waste. Smithfield wasn't a dirty end point; it was a celebration of modernity's concealment of production from consumption. As Britain's tributaries of power extended into its empire and markets opened through new travel routes and technologies, producing meat was no longer reliant on enclosed domestic fields. Lambs arrived on ships from New Zealand, whole pigs in barrels from China, and poultry from France. Just as the sewers and slaughterhouses enabled reimaginings of civic spaces, the outsourcing of production dislocated a consuming city from a productive, labouring elsewhere.

Meanwhile, the market was being cut out of national supply chains. Supermarkets, which had first pick of the best meat at the market, replaced their networks of procurement with vertical supply systems, where consumers' contact with meat was limited to packaged flesh. When animal bodies became the focus of microbial and pathogenic spread, the open market halls, described as 'alive' with hanging carcasses, were divided into 32 enclosed stalls to be monitored and tracked. Smithfield became a building within a building, adapting to the changing perceptions of meat. Some traders set up wholesale businesses – retaining their stalls for their sociability, central location, and the symbolic value of being part of the market that they offered – while others opened high-street butchers, but lost trade to supermarkets and rent hikes and returned, because they 'just wanted something to do, somewhere to be,' as one market trader told me. They resist the bureaucratisation of their space with carnivalesque language, so that banter permeates the physical boundaries between stalls.

In the Poultry Market, one stall remains, 'doing a roaring trade in halal chicken.' Until their tenancy expires, the Museum of London's redevelopment is on hold. Although the market is predominantly a white, male space of manual labour, when you ask traders how they survive, they say things like 'We sell to the ethnics … the white housewife doesn't come here anymore.' The market is sustained by Chinese, Indian, Pakistani, Jamaican, Nigerian, Colombian, Lebanese and Polish shoppers. Some are restaurateurs, others are families. Admittedly there can be verbal resistance to their customers. 'That's lamb tripe', a trader tells me. 'Us, the whites, we feed that to our dogs, but the Blacks, the Africans – they love it.' Traders posture their British whiteness as a hierarchy but know who has kept them in business: immigrants. The Pakistani shoppers who reignited trade in oxtails after the BSE crisis, the Nigerian restaurateurs sourcing fresh tripe and offal, the 'ethnic' restaurant owners and the high-street butchers who now feed London, from Barking to Peckham to the West End. The market has always been a symbiotic economy that feeds the diversity of London; it is trade, consumption and distribution in one place. The known has *always* met the unknown here and been folded into its existence.

Barking Reach is described as the most isolated, disconnected place in London, nestled below Barking and Dagenham in the old dock. It sits on the river, obscured by towering industrial cylinders where, if you ignore the DO NOT TRESPASS signs, you can steal a view of the Thames and the Victorian Crossness sewage works. The area is slowly being gentrified to bring lifelong housing, transport, schools and jobs to a borough suffering post-industrial decline. The speculative markets' new home is a fenced wasteland housing piles of rubble, with CCTV watching over DHL vans, wind turbines, the white noise of generators and the smell of tar. The City purchased it without certainty of the move, and at best it will lie idle for seven years until traders' tenancies have expired. The new market designs are homogeneous rectangular metal structures, like the neighbouring warehouses that hug the unused land beside the motorway: filtration units that receive and distribute commodities efficiently. In a duplicitous, aesthetic turn, the new residential blocks nod to a return to nature and waterside living, with Bulrush, Mallard and River prefixed street names, while the warehouse opposite's facade is coloured in blues and greys, attempting to blend into the sky.

The irony of The Monster is that people wanted to see it, but the chunk needed to become a fragmented object, categorised as heritage, to be seen at all. If Smithfield is preserved under the current plans, it will be the buildings, not the market, that are protected. Smithfield's history maps visions of what is considered worthy of city space; a battle between living and production when we need both, entangled and not separated into categories of predetermined culture and anonymous production. The social life and the informality of the market's interior continues to create its value for people. Its presence is a mark of the messy resistance of difference, of finding loopholes and constructing spaces that are responsive and not dictated. There is every chance the new location of the markets will benefit East Ham's South Indian restaurateurs or Romford's traditional English butcher shop through proximity. But these markets are not being moved here for the locals; London's eastern edges are imagined by the developers as an empty place to be infilled with what the city needs but no longer accommodates in the contours of its growth. And if Barking Reach is successful as a place for living, history tells us that the markets, and its people, may again be moved on.

This piece is based on ethnographic research at Smithfield Market, and the Source to Salespoint sound archives at the British Library.

There is still technically a dock at Dagenham Dock station, a supporting act for the headliner further downstream at Tilbury, but the area known as Barking Reach, Dagenham Breach or Barking Riverside (depending on which developer you're talking to) desperately feels like it's in need of an identity. Since the demolition of the strongest silhouette on the riverside skyline – the chimneys of Barking Reach Power Station – it has been inching towards something more liveable, though not quite there yet (the credulous buyers of flats around Beam Park were promised a new train station; instead they have the best views of Crossness Pumping Station in the city). The possibility of London's three largest wholesale food markets – Billingsgate, Smithfield and New Spitalfields – taking the power station's place may make Dagenham Dock a destination, but it begs the question: for whom?

We can look to precedents: this has happened before and will happen many times more again. Writer Ruby Tandoh, in a 2021 *Vittles* article, talks about the movement of people eastward, who follow the river's flow: 'commuters, migrants, seasonal workers, students, those displaced from the eastern fringes of London, hauliers and holidaymakers'. They also follow the flow of work – factories, power stations and docks – and with them flows food (if you can measure London by the location of its pie and mash shops, then you'll find its easternmost point in Southend). Will the movement of the markets bring people with them, too? Or will they stagnate, isolated from their customer base? Or, perhaps, will the markets supply a new audience, made up of new East Enders?

The food of Barking and Dagenham is not the meat pies, liquor and eels of old, dredged from the fetid Thames; instead, it's drawn from a new population: Ghanaian, Lithuanian, Pakistani, East African. If anyone might benefit from the movement of the markets, it will be these home cooks and restaurant chefs, who will have new sources for tripe, tilapia, mutton, carp, guinea fowl – things the British forgot or never learned – to make kenkey and fish, nihari, egusi and mixed-meat soup, mishkaki, and cepelinai. (And yes, meat pies too, even if they're now more likely to be served with Nigerian pepper sauce.)

LT KEBABAI KIMO STREET FOOD

If you get off at Dagenham Dock station and walk down the inhospitable A13 into central London, you will pass warehouses, builders' merchants and London's largest go-karting track, until you find a small cabin located in a car park. Given that it's almost inaccessible unless you have a car, and there's no way you would spot it and stop if you were driving to Essex or the Dartford Crossing, it has an unusually large stream of people waiting outside – mostly builders working nearby. They have come for Lithuanian doner kebabs (yes, they're a thing): thinly shaved pork and beef, all served in lavash bread or on a plate with chips and pickles, smothered in garlic and chilli sauces – similar to what you get in a Turkish kebab shop except for the copious use of dill. Make sure you get the dumplings, deep-fried till golden, oily and crispy, covered in more of those sauces. It's supreme late-night-drinking food, even if you're most likely eating it stone-cold sober in the afternoon.

AAFIO KENKEY MARKET

Walk a bit further, along the stretch of motorway delightfully named Ripple Road, and you'll come across houses with vertiginous sloping roofs, like modern versions of Tudor thatched cottages. Move off the road and you're in Becontree, the UK's largest housing estate – a century-old carpet of two-storey homes arranged in terraced clusters along wilfully geometric street patterns. This too is a legacy of a move eastward – the first residents came from the slum clearances in Limehouse after the First World War, although many residents today are from further afield. Aafio, which has both a grocers and a food business on the same parade, is a part of modern Becontree's Ghanaian contingent, specialising in kenkey, a staple of fermented maize wrapped in corn husks which should be thumbed, dipped into pepper sauce and eaten with fish. Make sure to get akonfem – guinea fowl cooked to order – and tsofi: turkey tails so high in cholesterol that they've technically been banned in Ghana (not that this stops anyone from eating them).

INDIANA CURRY & GRILL

The location of Indiana, tucked beside a huge car wash and motor dealers, feels like something out of a Bob Rafelson film: a British version of Americana, where the roadside diner has been reimagined as a Bengali takeaway off a stretch of London A Road. You'll find a lot of the dishes you would expect to get at a curry and grill here, but look for the anomalies: wraps containing naga and shatkora-flavoured doner, a legacy of Bangladeshi and Bengali kebab owners in the East End. In the starters you'll find something almost completely unique: a samosa made, not from mince or vegetables, but from lamb or chicken doner. The samosa is made to order, the doner chopped and fried on the grill before being tucked in with pastry and deep-fried. It's a small joy, and worth the road trip.

WAKA WAKA AND KARIBUNI

Despite the movement of the City markets, there is actually already a thriving food market in Barking, mostly made up of West African, Romanian and Caribbean stalls. It's also home to the only two Zanzibari barbecue joints in the city: Waka Waka and Karibuni (subtitled Zanzibar Hot Style), which are located at opposite ends of The Broadway. Go to Waka Waka for smoke-infused barbecued chicken anointed with tamarind and hot sauce, with mandazi (fried, sweet dough) to soak up the juices. Then go on to Karibuni for East African-style biryani, sticky with caramelised onions and beef mishkaki. Finish with halwa and a cup of ubuyu – candied baobab – from either.

KURAMOH LOUNGE

While you normally find British celebs eating in what can only be described as the most straightforwardly malignant places in the city – restaurants in Mayfair called Sexy Fish if they want to be visible, cloistered Soho and St James' members' clubs if they don't – Nigerian celebrities and influencers actually have good taste, and if you wanted to find some of the best Nigerian food in London, counterintuitively and against all the rules of London dining, you might do well to follow them. You might be led by Anthony Joshua, for instance, to Kuramoh Lounge, a restaurant on a stretch of Barking Road with a simple USP: Live Point and Kill Catfish. This may sound dramatic, but the customer only does the pointing – in this case, at a tank of writhing catfish who know their time is up – while the killing, along with the careful cleaning and cooking – in pepper soup or as a stew – is all done in-house.

the vineyard

leah cowan

I'm standing in the middle of a muddy field in Enfield, tucked about ten miles inside the M25 orbital motorway which encloses London in a smoggy hug, listening to a man called Pat talk about marine water pebbles. The small blue-grey stones he clicks in his palm appear unremarkable – except for seeming out of place. However, Pat explains the pebbles are 'glacial till', natural detritus which was pushed to the front of glaciers as the field we're standing in formed and reconfigured itself 600 million years ago. Conveniently for Forty Hall vineyard, where Pat Kane is a volunteer viticulturist, these pebbles are good for drainage; likewise, the layers of chalk deep under our feet, formed by aeons-old sea creatures bubbling their last breaths and dropping to the ocean floor in prehistoric south-east England, provide great conditions for growing grapes.

Forty Hall vineyard comprises ten acres of land on a sprawling 170-acre farm owned by Capel Manor College, existing as a bizarre anode between the frantic whizzing channel of the motorway which demarcates the edge of the capital, and the gentle, generative practices of the college. Nestled in the grounds of a centuries-old Jacobean suburban villa which still holds court on green belt land, the fertile soil of the farm in proximity to the vibrant hubbub of the city embodies a paradox of urbanity and rurality. Rather than repelling one another, the farm and the urban space which surrounds it are twinned like antagonistic muscles; the land tended by city-dwellers, and visited by residents of the New Towns and beyond who slip off at Junction 25 to spend a few hours amidst North London mud and rare breeds.

Forty Hall is unique in the capital – the only commercial-scale vineyard within the city's borders. Other London 'wineries' exist, but they tend to purchase grapes grown elsewhere. (One exception is The Urban Wine Company, which invites members to bring grapes grown in allotments, supermarket yards and alongside railways to a drop point on an industrial estate in Merton.) In medieval London, grapevines were common, grown in Westminster, Holborn, the Tower of London and beyond, until a combination of the Little Ice Age (which plunged Europe into long winters and short, wet summers) and Henry VIII reigning terror upon nunneries, monasteries and their accompanying vineyards, meant wine-growing in England all but vanished.

The vineyard thrives today in part because of climate change. The warming English weather is now similar to that of the balmy French wine-growing regions in the 1950s and, as with other vineyards in Kent and Sussex, this new advantage, along with the fact that the land the hall sits on is comparable to the chalky Champagne region, is often centre stage in the vineyard's marketing materials. Associating itself with France's long (although not longer than the Armenian and Georgian) tradition of wine producing plays a part in Forty Hall's market domination, although the vineyard has also embraced the 'natural wine movement', meaning grapes are grown organically (to differing degrees) and picked in smaller amounts, often by hand. These wines are sometimes described as 'low-intervention' (meaning, where possible, no or low amounts of pesticides and sulphites are used). Forty Hall's wine is organic, does not use insecticides, and is vegan. This last descriptor isn't just flaccid marketing spin like when potato wedges or steel-cut oats are described as vegan: the wine is filtered through super-dried clay, rather than fish bladders or blood, as is typical in mainstream wine production.

The vineyard also has an eco-therapy project; this works with women's groups, including people seeking refuge from the ongoing conflict in Syria, and those navigating the UK's dehumanising asylum system (itself a colonial hangover directly linked to the extractive wealth creation which enabled the proliferation of the English country house). Forty Hall was built between 1629 and 1632 by a loaded Tudor haberdasher (Pat's comparison: 'think Roman Abramovich!'), before changing hands and undergoing various decorative facelifts. In 1698 the Hall was owned by a descendent of John Wolstenholme, an incorporator of the East India Company – Britain's infamous colonial arm in the East – and an investor in the Virginia Company of London, which did the same in the West, inflicting genocide and territorial dispossession against America's indigenous populations.

The Hall stands firm on its foundations today due to the blood, toil and exploitation of Black, brown and working-class people, both in England and in the Global South. Its education programme covers the transatlantic slave trade – presumably for this reason. Enfield's colonial connections are documented by local historian Sylvia Collicott, who notes that there were at least 15 wealthy merchants who bought big houses in the borough and together enslaved 11,156 people. (According to Nicholas Draper's book *The Price of Emancipation*, after abolition these merchants were paid compensation of just over £31 million in today's money.) As historians Madge Dresser and Andrew Hann write, the concept of the genteel English country house at this time provided a conspicuous foil to the violence and oppression being enacted overseas by – or in the name of – British merchants and slave-traders.

Skirting the farm's boundary is another source of wealth for the English gentry: the New River. This was dug during the reign of Elizabeth I in order to bring fresh water into the city from Hertfordshire, spouting gold for those who had the funds to cash in on the project. The neighbouring Myddelton House was named after Hugh Myddelton, who led work on the New River, and was lived in by the son of Henry Carrington Bowles, who owned Forty Hall in 1895. The connections between house and river run deep: Henry Carrington Bowles of Myddelton House married Anne Garnault, a member of a wealthy family who had themselves invested in the New River Company. As Ian Sinclair writes in *London Orbital*, which chronicles his 120-mile perambulation of the M25: 'Myddelton was a speculator, water was a resource'.

The aspirations for the New River and Forty Hall Vineyard – to enable London to sustain itself – were part of the same historical thread. Today, the New River still provides around 8% of the city's water, with the remaining majority drawn from reservoirs outside of the M25 via the London Ring Main tunnel system. The London Ring Main opened the same year that the Channel Tunnel began shuttling booze-cruisers between England and France, making 1994 a pivotal moment for both wine and water, which were now able to free-flow into the capital.

Forty Hall vineyard exists not in spite of, but crucially *because of* the hubbub of urban sprawl that surrounds the site. Apart from the two paid eco-therapists, Forty Hall is mainly reliant on local volunteers, particularly around the harvest. This is made possible because the vineyard is embedded within Enfield's community; Pat speaks with pride of the immense amount of help and goodwill that they receive from local residents. Because of this, Forty Hall vineyard is well positioned to reach out to people who might not see themselves represented in the very elite, white-wine-making industry. As with all voluntary work, there is a risk that knowledge and practical expertise becomes concentrated among a demographic who can afford to give up their time for free, but Forty Hall's unique approach has so far proved its viability, which bodes well for continuing a trajectory set to challenge the otherwise homogeneous landscape of the industry. Without those who tend the land for free, including people seeking support and connection, the vineyard would not be financially feasible.

Emma Lundie, Head of Operations at the vineyard, speaks to a sense of being led by the land, accepting its quirks and limitations rather than battling against it (although some setbacks are truly unpredictable: in 2017 a flock of tropical parakeets decided to tuck into the harvest). Lundie and her team are cultivating the hand they have been dealt. The purpose of the vineyard is amorphous; grapes are grown, but the harvest stretches beyond soft fruit and into the intangible terrain of 'community'. The vineyard is a place to learn, experiment, and offer coins into a well of hope, where you never know how each year's vintage will turn out, but plough on nonetheless.

It would be a disingenuous reach to suggest that Forty Hall's winemaking is a perfect community project, or represents an attempt to address the painful history of the wealth created and protected in its grounds. However, the vineyard does try to decouple itself from the elitism of winemaking, and divest from the extractive dimensions of production while forging a meaningful sense of community. This is no small feat in the shadow of an English stately home whose land is haunted by the ghostly fingers of its wealthy colonial-era ancestors. Those stewarding it in the present day are attempting to break at last from tradition by placing care and community, not profit, at the centre of these ten innocuous acres in Enfield.

HUGE ENFIELD BEHAVIOUR

In April 2021, the Twitter account @ashindestad posted one of the only ever sentences about a municipal borough that has stayed with me. 'Enfield is London's very own Florida idc', he says, before explaining what might otherwise be a gnomic remark: 'everybody here is mad, no matter the ethnicity.'

As someone who grew up one street away from Enfield's border with Haringey in the south, went to school close to the roar of the M25 in the north, and therefore travelled the entirety of the borough every morning and afternoon for seven years, I intimately recognise this madness. It's a madness that often manifests in senseless acts of suburban rage: a train crashing into its terminus, a car chase along a set of railway lines, a Tesla pretending to be a DeLorean smashing its open door into a bus; these things may well happen in other places, but they always seem to happen in Enfield (or in places like Cheshunt, which are spiritually Enfield). It's a madness borne out of a deep malaise, of living right on the edge of one of the world's fulcrums, only to be surrounded by places called Freezywater and Cockfosters. Enfield's contradictions are the contradictions of London suburbia amplified: on the one hand, the nothingness of poverty, industrial estates, concrete, grim flyovers, the ennui of being one big retail park; on the other, the nothingness of affluence, Jacobean estates, country pubs, golf clubs, bland high streets that wouldn't look out of place in a small commuter town. How can you resolve a borough that contains both the Meridian Estate and Capel Manor?

These contradictions create a disordered food culture. Enfield is so often a wasteland of TGI Fridays, cookie-cutter pub menus and Krispy Kremes, and yet there is also something here that couldn't exist unless it was in the absolute last place anyone would bother looking for it. Over in Edmonton, on the eastern side of Enfield, you will find some of the best Turkish food in London (according to the 2011 census, Edmonton has the highest proportion of Turkish and Kurdish people in the capital). Start at Edmonton Green shopping centre and walk up the A1010 and you'll go past tripe soup specialists, sandwich shops, late-night künefe cafes and ocakbaşıs more palatial than anything on Kingsland Road or Green Lanes. That you can see the countryside through the houses is half the fun.

NECO TANTUNI

Neco is Enfield's crown jewel, a late-night snack shop focusing on tantuni, the Mersin speciality of thin lavaş, rolled tightly like a Rizla around finely chopped meat cooked in cottonseed oil. Pickles and lemon are essential items; they enliven what is, at its heart, an extremely simple dish that lives and dies on the thinness of the lavaş, the quality of the meat, and the moisture lubricating everything. Or, you can go all out and get it drenched in yoghurt, tomato and brown butter, and baked like cannelloni (I've ordered this so many times that I now make my own maximalist iterations, adding chicken nuggets into the mix). It's worth the trip here for the iterations on tantuni alone, but the künefe seals it. Here it is done not to golden, but to a dark nut-brown, developing a proper bronzed crust and a rich butteriness that mitigates any syrup sweetness, with a dollop of thick cream acting as punctuation. I'm not sure there's a more satisfying dessert in London.

SEHR-I ANTEP

There's a reason why people come all the way to Edmonton for Sehr-i Antep, even though there are plenty of other Turkish patisserie shops where you can have a sugar crash. The baklava here are just that little bit better: the pastry richer and more buttery; the syrup a little less sweet; the pistachios a shade darker on the Pantone chart, gleaming like emeralds. Green and brown are the prevailing colours here: every single variation on baklava you could possibly imagine, from pistachio to walnut, from rectangular to triangular to shell-like, to verdant curd-stuffed rolls.

There are two things here that shouldn't be missed: the cold baklava made from milk and chocolate that looks like a sand dune, and the tres leches cake, something that tastes like childhood no matter where you grew up.

ENFES OCAKBAŞI

There are bigger ocakbaşıs in Edmonton than Enfes, and there are more popular ones, too – ones that have the air of a warehouse club night, and live and die on the size of their mixed grills. But there isn't a better one than Enfes, a modestly sized restaurant on a stretch of high road that is something like the last spluttering of London before it incontestably becomes Hertfordshire. Go in and take a seat at the mangal, then order a whole lamb from nose to tail – ribs, liver, heart, sweetbread, and testicles – and you'll experience something close to what it was like in Dalston's grill houses many decades ago, where you would come out wearing a cologne of meat smoke.

ÇORBA DÜNYASI

If you were to get up at 5am and walk into Çorba Dünyası, a 24/7 soup cafe decked out in wood like an Alpine ski lodge, you would find both early risers getting sustenance for the day and all-nighters putting in preventative measures to avoid a hangover. There is something incredibly un-English about this scene – very few people born in this country would go somewhere specifically to have soup, especially with company – yet on a cold night (and even better, on a boiling hot day) there is nothing more wholesome or more satisfying. Here it's possible to get işkembe çorbası, a milky tripe soup with a garlic and pul biber sting, or paça çorbası, made with tender head meat and either consumed as a puritan red broth or suffused with richness by adding yoghurt. They are served with pickles and chillies, with lemon and vinegar, with black pepper and even more pul biber – so you can season it at the table *à la mode*.

THE PILAVCI

Just outside Edmonton Green shopping centre, next to the B&Q, you'll find The Pilavci, a small van selling some uninteresting things on a cake-shaped pile of rice – and then, incongruously, as if for a laugh, an Islak burger, appetisingly advertised here as a 'Wet Burger'. If you've never had an Islak burger, it's the type of late-night snack you find all around Taksim Square – the Istanbul equivalent of a questionable hot dog stand, or those places on Oxford Street that sell roulette samosas (the 'roulette' element is whether you'll be alive by the end of the day). In Istanbul, Islaks are in high enough demand that they are kept in huge steamed-glass containers, resembling a sauna of tanned, wrinkled old men. At The Pilavci, they're whipped out from a tray at waist height and then consumed almost as quickly as the transaction. They taste like school dinner burgers soaked in garlicky marinara sauce; they taste slightly evil, like what I imagine Wario eats; they taste like regret after quick sex. I am all for it. The city would be instantly improved if every Caffè Concerto in central London was replaced with Wet Burger stands tomorrow.

the river

We talk a lot about food traditions that traverse people and places, uprooted from one place or culture and reinvented in strange new soils. But there are other food traditions, too: ones which transform not across space but over time, slowly adapting to meet the changing needs of the public they feed. In north-west London, along the banks of the Kilburn river, one such food microcosm has shape-shifted over the course of several hundred years.

There is nothing exceptional about the river Kilburn (also known as Westbourne, or Bayswater Rivulet, depending on where in time and space you are). It's a small river, emerging from the Hampstead slopes before tumbling south and west through Kilburn, into Knightsbridge and, eventually, the swollen Thames. Still, this little tributary – especially the stretch which traces what is now Kilburn High Road, and swings right towards Westbourne Park – has been a food hub for as long as people have lived alongside it.

A map dated 1824 shows the now-buried Bayswater Rivulet running through a collection of fields – one of rye, a couple with barns in them – labelled Kilburn Farm. Where there is water and food, there can be people; along this flow line into the city, the population began to grow. By the end of the century, the roads around South Kilburn were dense with housing and, in the midst of it all, there was a 'mission hall'. Against a backdrop of rapid urban growth and skyrocketing poverty, mission halls – akin to church outreach hubs, through which they could find a foothold in disadvantaged communities – were incredibly popular. South Kilburn's Presbyterian mission hall, built in 1877, was an exemplar case. Central to the mission was food; it featured things such as a bread-and-milk fund, a mothers' tea and a soup kitchen for the area's poor.

The paternalism of the mission is hard to miss: memorandums in the 1921 *St John's Wood Presbyterian Church Annual Report* detail complaints about 'anti-Christian' public sentiment, and it's clear that loyalty was felt for the mission, rather than the people it aimed to serve. But when times were hard, even the most scripture-laced hunk of bread remained a hunk of bread – the stuff of life itself. 'The year that has closed has been one of the most trying that our friends in Kilburn have ever experienced,' noted one particularly sombre annual report in 1904. For three, sometimes four days a week that winter, a Mrs Hodgson gave out portion after portion of bread and soup, filling up bellies that would soon grow hungry again.

In the years after the mission, generations grew and left. High-rises bloomed and fell. Waves of Irish, then Caribbean, then African migrants arrived and scattered along the length of Kilburn High Road which, like the river it once shared ground with, has been reinvented in the image of each new generation that calls it home. In the mid-1950s, a community hub – one that would eventually become known as The Granville – was built on the site of the old mission hall, and a new chapter of good cooking would begin.

photos by elaine a emmott

Merle Barriteau

It was 1985, maybe, when Merle Barriteau first started cooking at The Granville. *Maybe*, because it's only when it comes to dates that Merle's memory falters: she traces backwards from the age of her eldest child, adding and subtracting numbers until she settles somewhere around the mid-1980s. Nestled in the shade of a tree-lined street, and flanked by a primary school and modest residential blocks, the building seems an unlikely place to set up a food business. Nearby, Kilburn High Road is a hub for eating, drinking and spending. The Granville, by contrast, is a community centre in a residential area, a place through which people, not money, seem to flow. But wherever there are people, there is feeding to be done. It was in this building – where dance troupes, art classes and home-education groups met and worked, and in a part of the city that was, at the time, a hot spot for Caribbean culture – that Merle met local appetites with apple punch, hard food and jerk chicken.

Within a few years, Merle's Diner was in full swing, the smell of simmering stews rising from the basement kitchen while eaters streamed in. Merle spun her signature magic over platters of escovitch, bowls of coleslaw and endless ackee and saltfish. She cooked while Somali weddings dazzled in the hall above, or when the centre filled with tailors and costume makers ahead of Carnival. She cooked as the Caribbean population of the area began to age and a new generation of migrants from North and West Africa settled. By 2009, when Merle's Diner closed and Merle retired, she claimed to have fed everyone in South Kilburn. 'I didn't do it to make a profit.' Merle notes. 'By the end, a big plate of food was £4, £5. This was food for the community. That's what mattered.'

As much as cooks like Merle have nourished this tiny corner of the capital, the question of hunger remains. It has been a little over a hundred years since the Presbyterian mission, and it's hard not to feel hopeless about the remarkable flatness of that expanse of time. In 1890, roughly 20% of Kilburn's population was impoverished. Today, the percentage of people living in poverty in Brent, the borough Kilburn sits in, is 33%. In 2014, Dee Woods, a lifelong food 'actionist', and Leslie Barson – who has been involved with the running of The Granville for nearly 28 years – had grown tired of seeing the gutting impacts of austerity play out while The Granville's kitchen lay bare. It had been five years since Merle left, and people were coming to the centre hungry and stressed, without enough money to feed themselves. 'We set up this weekly lunch that a lot of people would benefit from,' Dee says. They'd already planted a community garden in the yard at the front of the centre, sending roots down deep into the soil of Kilburn's farming past. 'So this was like: right, we're growing all this food, why don't we use it?' Granville Community Kitchen was born, with weekly free meals for people in the community and food education.

This isn't local food, Dee emphasises, but *localised* food – food traded fairly, across people, cultures and places. 'Local food tends to be hyper-local and not inclusive; you can't just drop everyone else in it after 500 years of a global food system. People need access to culturally appropriate food, for their health and happiness.' It's this question of food sovereignty – ensuring that people have some control over the food systems that nourish them – that sets Granville Community Kitchen's aims apart from the work of the old mission hall, as well as its modern analogues: food banks, food waste redistribution schemes and soup kitchens. Where the mission hall was a charitable project, with well-intentioned ideas, resources and volunteers parachuted into the slums from outside the community, Granville Community Kitchen is created by and for the people of South Kilburn, its aims inseparable from the myriad cultures, desires and needs of the people it serves.

Yet The Granville is in danger. There are the big threats: the pandemic, lack of funding, 'regeneration' at the hands of developers and the council. But there are ordinary dangers too: Leslie explains how it's in Brent council's small print – in curfew times and noise limits likely to be brought in after the construction of proposed new social housing on the site – that the centre risks losing its heart. 'The needs of housing will be prioritised over the needs of the centre,' she warns. 'It will be a painful death of community.'

In the gardens at the front of The Granville – which will be lost if the site is redeveloped – beds contain echinacea, lovage (fondly referred to as the Maggi plant for the flavour it shares with the stock and seasoning brand) and a sprawling sage bush. There are strawberries and Masai bush bean, sweetcorn with jewel-coloured kernels and callaloo. There are bountiful tomatoes, too, and runner beans clambering up makeshift frames. On mild, late-summer evenings, people drift through this small Eden in ones and twos, picking up food aid parcels.

Out of the gate and one minute's walk west into the sun, there is a residential housing block, Merle Court. Named in honour of Merle's services to the community, it was built in 2012, with flats available for rent and shared ownership. Five years after the block was built, it was revealed that its cladding was the same type used on Grenfell Tower, just under two miles away.

Around the corner, Merle bustles around her home kitchen, enjoying the time that retirement has brought her, but never losing that urge to feed. The smell of chicken, stewing callaloo and frying dough float at intervals from her kitchen window and into the quiet streets outside. Sometimes she likes to walk, tracing the pavements of the neighbourhood she has made home. Her walks are seldom her own, though. At every corner, she is met with a shout – 'Auntie Merle!' – from the other side of the street, a balcony, a garden. 'Everywhere I go,' she laughs, 'I see the children, and the grandchildren, of the people who ate my food.' In the golden-hour haze, they reminisce about the meals they've shared and the meals they might have, someday, if circumstance ever allows. Far beneath their feet, old farmland lies buried, the Bayswater Rivulet still trickles, and layer upon layer of Kilburn rubble sleeps.

An alternate version of this essay was first published in Vittles.

THE THAMES RIVIERA

Cities take on the characteristics of their rivers: Paris and the Seine's stately sinuousness; New York and the vast, unknowable Hudson. Naturally the Thames is chaos, a swirling vortex with hidden eddies that might suck you under if you're not careful. Although most Londoners don't interact with it daily, the Thames is never too far from a Londoner's mind; its west-east flow divides the city into north and south, and with it two mentalities; one which orients itself north, with the Thames at its back, and the other that looks towards it. More pertinently, it is the reason the city exists in the first place, a natural trade route bringing in the rest of the world: wealth, commerce and food. Ecosystems sprung up by the river – of docks, of theatres, of pubs, and of gallows.

Running from north to south and south to north, you'll find other waterways that spring from the Thames and mark the city in a calmer fashion. Some only run underground and leave traces in names: Kilburn, Tyburn, Fleet Street; others – the Lea, the Wandle, the Brent, and the canals that connect them – form the city's visible liquid skeleton. The Thames itself generally doesn't lend itself to evocative riverside dining, but these tributaries do, breeding their own ecosystems of cafes, coffee shops and casual restaurants. It is here most of all, while nursing a coffee, a pastry, or even a Cypriot sandwich, that we are reminded that London is still a city of water.

TOWPATH CAFE

The restaurant and the river are both spaces that have the ability to transport us to another place, or another time; restaurants by water perhaps doubly so. And yet London never really utilised its man-made waterways for dining purposes until the early 2010s success of Lori De Mori and Laura Jackson's Towpath Cafe, spread across three warehouse units on the Haggerston stretch of Regent's Canal. Since then, the Towpath template has been copied everywhere – in Hackney Wick, in Camden Wharf and in the rest of Haggerston – but nowhere understands the appeal of waterside dining as much as Towpath, whose menu follows only a logic of 'things you actually want to eat', whether that be a ham-and-cheese toastie, Ashkenazi Jewish comfort food of brisket and tzimmes, or simply peas in their pods. Spotting that Towpath is finally open is like Eid for white people; in an inverse of the oyster season rule, Towpath eschews the harsh London winter weather and only opens in months *without* R in their name, realising that there are limits to how transportative a restaurant can actually be.

VRISAKI

Part of the joy of the New River Path is finding a way of moving through North London that completely bypasses its roads and pavements; if you can fly on wingèd shoes across the North Circular you can pretty much walk from Enfield to Hornsey only touching grass. Just before the river goes underground at Bowes Park, the New River path auspiciously collides with Myddleton Road, a shopping thoroughfare filled with Cypriot football bars and men's clubs, named after the New River's architect, Hugh Myddelton. It's precisely here you'll find Vrisaki, a stalwart of 1990s soap stars and Greek boy band members, serving comically large portions of meze that arrive in endless waves of meat, fish and taramasalata. PANERI, down the road, is the better restaurant, but the best things here have always been the sheftalia – loose mince kebabs wrapped in caul fat – and the hand-shaved doner, but since the pandemic half of the restaurant space has been turned into a cafe selling excellent zestosandoutiz (hot sandwiches) and soups; small and gradual changes, just like on the road itself.

CAFÉ CECILIA

Writer Fernando Pessoa once wisely said in *The Book of Disquiet* that 'wasting time has its own aesthetic'. What that aesthetic actually looks like is unclear, but it might be similar to the languorous breakfast service at Max Rocha's otherwise spartan restaurant by the canal in London Fields:

Guinness bread, yoghurt, granola and a puréed compote of sweet plums, a cream cheese bagel topped with fresh figs, a morning roll with a glossy egg and fat sausages, a ramekin of tart brown sauce, a milky coffee, a cold glass of pale pink Discovery apple juice. There are lunches and dinners here too, a bit less influenced by Rocha's Irish heritage and more by his time at that other great London riverside restaurant in Hammersmith: silky pastas, whole fish, little fried things in lemon and oil. But do make room for a deep fried bread-and-butter-pudding with cold custard, the kind of things your dinner ladies would have made for you, had they been deranged.

LIQUI LIQUI

Picture dining by the river and you might conjure an image of a Venetian bacaro or a garden on the Nile, but how about Venezuelan arepas by the River Wandle in Colliers Wood, overlooking a drive-thru Burger King? Liqui Liqui marks the spot where the Wandle splits in two, forming an *Île-de-France*-shaped island that houses a Sainsbury's and a Premier Inn instead of the Notre Dame. This is not everyone's version of paradise, but there's still beauty to be found here: tequeños, spiral wands of pastry and salted cheese, are made in-house by the owner's Cornish husband, while cachapas the colour of a Caracqueñian sun provide a bright sweetness to what are essentially meat or cheese sandwiches. The arepas are a cut above what's available in Elephant and Castle, but if you don't mind feeling like a dumbbell for the rest of the day order the patacon amarillo, a rarely seen Maracaibo speciality – a sandwich where the bread has been replaced with fried ripe plantain. And if the sun comes out, the vista onto the A24 is majestic.

THE RIVER CAFE

It is only further west on the Thames, where the river becomes narrower and less manic, that you'll find London's only truly great riverside restaurant: architect Richard Rogers' monument to electric blue, hot pink and £30 antipasti, The River Cafe. Started in 1987 as a canteen for Rogers' architecture firm, it soon became known for the canniness of Ruth Rogers and Rose Gray's sourcing and unadorned cookery, matching its location on an otherwise deserted stretch of the Thames that would allow you to pretend, just for the night, that you were somewhere on the Amalfi coast. There are two schools of thought with The River Cafe – the first that its high prices are a kind of performance art to see how much you can charge the rich for tomatoes in exchange for privacy; the second that this is the correct cost of good ingredients, cooked and served by people paid fairly. The correct view is that the space itself, not the food, is the thing you are paying for – on a balmy evening, sat outside on the terrace, it is perhaps the most magical restaurant in the city (as long as someone else is footing the bill).

The tension between use of land for produce versus for building has been part of London life for centuries. In the late-18th and 19th centuries, London was a thriving market garden city and fed itself mainly from farms on the outskirts of the city and the rural countryside. This changed as London became more urbanised and the UK began importing more food. Today 59% of London's green belt is agricultural land. In the words of Sarah Williams, the programmes director at Sustain, that's '94,000 hectares that could be farmed for local markets, but sadly is more often used for grazing horses or sitting in a developer's portfolio'.

The answers to our food sovereignty lie in our rich social history of growing food, both within the city and around it. The allotment movement emerged in the 17th century, with the protests against parliamentary enclosures, and played a powerful role in two world wars, keeping the city fed. In London, food growing – as well as bee- and chicken-keeping – has bloomed into the 21st century, with allotments, back and front gardens, community gardens and orchards, as well as edible bus stops, pavements and pocket parks.

This interview with Jeremy Corbyn, arguably the country's most famous allotment-user, highlights the need for stronger local government powers, better planning legislation and access to land for food production, but also celebrates the joys of growing food in the city, where the allotment is a place of community, diversity and sanctuary. With multiple crises impacting our global food systems, from climate change and biodiversity loss to the Covid pandemic, conflicts, and increasing poverty and food insecurity, now more than ever we must seriously consider London's agrarian and food future.

Jeremy Corbyn

interview by dee woods

More than any political leader I can think of, you're associated with growing. Your North London allotment and growing food feel central to your public identity. When Alexandria Ocasio-Cortez asked Twitter about taking on a community garden plot in New York, you replied with advice.

> She got in touch because she wasn't sure what to grow. She had very good instincts because she wanted something that would promote biodiversity and insects, so I suggested lavender and comfrey – both pretty hardy plants. Even in New York, which has rather horrible winters, both would survive. Comfrey goes to nothing in the autumn and then comes back, big time. As I explained to her: take the leaves as it dies down in the autumn, put the leaves in a bucket of water and leave them there. It stinks to high heaven, but it's fantastic liquid fertiliser. She took my advice, I believe.

Can you describe your relationship with food and growing?

> I grew up in the countryside in Wiltshire, then Shropshire, and my parents were scientists, teachers and engineers, but also very environmentally conscious. They would always try to grow a lot of stuff. As a child, I found it extremely irritating being asked to weed cabbages – you know, everybody else is playing football, and I'm weeding cabbages! As life went on, I worked on farms for a while – potato-picking, pig-keeping, ploughing, that kind of stuff.
>
> In the 1950s and 60s, there was an obsession with big fields, lots of inorganic fertilisers and high levels of production and yields. The Department of Agriculture, Fisheries and Food was subsidising the grubbing up of hedges to make larger fields – some of which had probably been there 500 years. It was appalling, and obviously the biodiversity effect was huge. As a child I noticed the soil run-off and erosion – places that had been lots of small fields suddenly became one huge 20-hectare field. Machinery would go up and down it twice a year, and that would be about it – nothing there beyond that. So it's that relationship – between the natural world, growing, productivity and our lives – that I think we have to explore. I spend a lot of time in our local schools promoting gardening, because growing food is not just

about clearing a piece of land, or planting something in it to prevent anything else growing there. It's recognising the relationship between the crop you grow and the natural world around it. On a wider level, it's a huge lesson about how you deal with soil erosion, soil loss, desertification, forests, and so on, which is very important. I've always been very interested in that. I've travelled quite a lot, and I always look at farming methods in the places I go. And in my own life, I have a small garden at home, and our allotment in Finchley.

Can you tell us about your plot? What are you currently growing and how do you feel when you're there?

I really value my allotment. I first took it over in March 2003, at the time of the outbreak of the Iraq War. I spent time during the spring and summer preparing and growing my first crops on it. What a relief to have such a contrasting venue to return to, whilst the horror of what was happening on the international scene at that point, and our activities against it, unfolded. We are a co-operatively run allotment, self-managed and self-repairing with a wonderful sense of community and mutual support, including a small trading shed supplying seed, potatoes, onions and more. I grow a big variety of produce, vegetables (potatoes, spinach, parsnips, turnips, maize, beans) as well as fruit trees (fig, apple), all enabling me to make excellent jam, especially with the abundant local blackberries. I strongly recommend allotments to anyone who wants to seriously grow things and be prepared to work in the cold and wet days of winter, as well as the balmy days of summer.

Did your relationship with – and understanding of – growing change when you moved to London from the countryside?

I thought it was a bit weird that I grew up in a rural area with a large garden, lots of space, and I ended up representing the smallest, most urbanised place on the planet. That's how it goes! But there's a point here: after the Rio environment summit in 1992, Islington council set up what they called Agenda 21. The idea was to make the borough more sustainable by 2020.

I figured: you can make Islington more environmentally sustainable, but you can't make it zero carbon. It's too urbanised for
that, but you can go somewhere down the road towards it.
We had an agenda surrounding council buildings, council
development, planning, applications – all stuff which is now
totally mainstream within the envelope of COP25 and 26 – but
also promoting community growing and small growing spaces,
which we now have quite a lot of.

   I'm very happy with my allotment, but I recognise that it's
very hard to provide allotments for everybody that wants them
in London. So what we've developed are community gardening
projects where people have a small area for their own growing, but a more communal approach to the garden as a whole.
We've got King Henry's Walk, just near Mildmay, which is a piece
of land that was saved from developers, I think because they
wanted to put the Channel Tunnel railway tunnel under it and
they couldn't sell it. Because of that, we got all of it and it's now
a community garden. All open spaces are a community victory
in London. Every single one is a victory over developers and,
sometimes, local authorities.

Imperial College has published research indicating the net number
of allotments is going down. They say that London has lost about
40 allotment sites over the last decade.

   That would probably be where they are informal allotments
   and not registered as such. Barnet Council wanted to sell our
   allotment in Finchley and develop it, and we pointed out they
   couldn't because under the existing allotment legislation,
   if you can prove need – which isn't difficult to do – then it can't
   be sold. They then tried to increase our rent by 300%, so we
   went to court over that, and we won. They got totally fed up with
   us and gave us a 50-year lease – just said 'Go away and never
   talk to us ever again'. That's absolutely fine – we're all agreed
   on this divorce! So goodbye Barnet! They'll come back for more,
   but that'll be quite a long way down the line.

Britain has a long history of campaigns around land and growing.
I'm thinking of the Diggers and the Levellers' attempts to reclaim

land following the Enclosure Acts. Do you see a relationship between the work you're doing and that radical history?

> It goes back a very long way – the skill of what would his-
> torically be termed the 'peasant farmer' as opposed to the
> industrial landowner. The skill of the peasant is greater
> than the skill of the landowner but unfortunately they don't
> have the capital the landowner does. So the mechanisation
> of farming, which has gone on for a long time, and the
> Enclosure Acts, and then the vicious mechanisation of the
> 19th century, the Swing Riots and all that, was essentially
> about the wish of the rural people – to be able to have their
> own space and grow their own food – which was taken away
> from them. In a sense, the allotment movement, which is
> largely urban but not entirely (most villages used to have
> quite substantial allotment patches), was a thirst from
> former farmworkers and rural residents, who had moved
> into industrial areas in the 18th and 19th century to still
> have some connection with the land so that those skills
> were not totally lost and they could provide for themselves.
> So it *is* the argument for land, all the time.

In her chapter on Forty Hall (p186), Leah Cowan examines the links between land ownership in London and the transatlantic slave trade. Land In Our Names is a Black-led organisation who argue that land justice could play an impor-tant role within reparations. They see land for growing within a 'reparative framework of compensation, repair and restitu-tion for the enslavement, indentureship, extraction of wealth and the loss of life perpetrated by the British Empire.' What role do you think land could play in reparations around British imperialism?

> Good question. The whole point of imperial occupation
> domination was and is control of productive land, and if
> you look at patterns of land ownership in many parts of
> Africa and Latin America, you can see a complete discon-
> nect between sustainable small-scale farming by local
> communities, which is often protective of the environment

and non-invasive, from the ranch and plantation-style farming alongside it now – often owned by global corporations and a product of the European occupation in the 18th century onwards.

If we're serious about reparations for colonialism and the slave trade it is about the restoration of important cultural items and works of art, as well as about genuine fair trade and reparations that begin to compensate for the poverty left behind at the end of colonialism. It's worth noting that at the time of slavery Jamaica was the place in the world producing the most individual wealth of any country, all of which ended up in the City of London and with wealthy families in Britain. That is just one example of the long-term effects of colonialism. I'd strongly urge our National curricula to include within it Walter Rodney's 1972 book, *How Europe Underdeveloped Africa*.

What do you think of the idea of food sovereignty – of people in London having control over the food system, whether it's through growing or other methods?

I like it, and support it. I don't think we have enough open space to grow the kind of quantities that are needed, but we do need a planning policy that helps to do it. From roughly the turn of the 19th and 20th century onwards, the Lee Valley was both a place of industry but also [contained] a huge number of market gardens and small farms. Farming changed in the late-19th century, away from big crop production in areas surrounding cities into market gardening around Birmingham, Newcastle, Manchester, and so on. I think what we need is a planning strategy that brings back a lot of that. An awful lot of the tomatoes and things that we import now, from the Netherlands and Spain, could very easily be grown here. And of course, that helps with [reducing] the pollution from transport.

Do you think that the main goal of growing your own food in the urban environment isn't necessarily urban self-sufficiency, but more the sense of community that you can have on an allotment?

It's not a binary choice – it's both. To bring children up understanding how things are grown is very important, because that gives them a better understanding of the environment. With the best will in the world, the majority of the population are going to be living in apartments in urban areas. The idea that everyone's going to have a home with a garden in this borough is impossible. So you then have to sort of think creatively in terms of what space you've got, and what land you've got, and how you use it. But also there's the importance for mental health and well-being of being involved with the natural world and growing things. I'm really impressed that when we've done estate gardening projects, all kinds of people get together on it. I just remember like it was yesterday, this rather long-winded argument between a wizened old Cockney docker and a Somali refugee woman about how to grow tomatoes. Fascinating debate – I don't think either fully understood what the other was saying but that didn't really matter, the point was that they were doing it together: that was the important thing.

According to research by architect Russell Curtis there are 94 golf courses in London. Together they take up more land than the entire borough of Brent, which seems like an extraordinary amount of space dedicated to golf in a context where we're haggling over tiny scraps of land for community gardens or growing spaces. Do you see that as an opportunity to do something more interesting?

I think if you start trying to get rid of golf courses, you'll find them developed quite quickly into housing. So I think you've got to be quite careful about how you approach this one. What I would do is have some community-based conversations with the golf courses about access, about biodiversity, about what goes on there and whether or not they can't give over some of the land to community gardening and allotments, because golf courses tend to have vast amounts of space – that they don't actually even use for golf – around them. Personally, I don't play golf, and I have no great aspiration to take it up, but people enjoy it. Haringey, for example, has a small golf course at Alexandra Palace which is municipality-owned. It's fine by me. I don't think attacking the golfing community is the solution to our environmental difficulties.

With the climate crisis, the impacts of the pandemic and the conflict on our fragile food system, how do you envision edible spaces changing the built environment of London?

We've got to have a much stronger planning system, and local authorities have to be given far more power over building use, design, and the diversity of shopping areas. At the moment, a local authority can do precious little about the diversity of shops that are available on a particular street. The fact that Seven Sisters Road has more payday loans and bookies than anything else is something that the council has very little power to do anything about. If the council wanted to encourage the diversity of shopping there, it could do a bit but not very much.

A town centre isn't just a place to shop. It's a community. It's an interactive space. So we need to empower local authorities. That applies to buildings as well as some degree of open space and growing space for everybody. When building a new school, growing space should be built into it. The school over the road here is unique in that it has a beautiful garden, made by the school. I've got an aerial photo of that place in 1970, when it was housing. The Inner London Education Authority bought the housing and gave the school a garden. Imagine a council doing that now! The *Evening Standard* wouldn't like it. But the council had a view that children should have access to open space and gardening. It's that mentality we've got to bring back. Greening of open space is important. It can be done. It's best done by the local community rather than the council, so if people want to turn a bit of the pavement in front of the house or round a tree into a small garden, do it. It's good. It's good for them; it's good for the rest of us as well. Which is why I have an allotment!

The questions for this interview were supplied by Dee Woods. Additional questions by Phineas Harper and Jonathan Nunn.

In her book *Hungry City*, the food writer and archi-tect Carolyn Steel talks about the Ancient Greek conception of the city – made up of the *polis*, what is inside the city, and the *khôra*, what is outside of it – and how the difficulty of the expanding city was, and perhaps still is, keeping the inside fed by what surrounds it. The management of a household, or *oikonomia* – the word from which 'economy' originates – was predicated on having a house inside the polis and one outside of it, a local circular economy in which the garden of one feeds the household of the other.

This way of life is pretty much dead to anyone who doesn't have a casual holiday home they rent out in the Cotswolds, and the closest most Londoners will come to it is through the allot-ment (or, at the very least, being on a waiting list for one). But many central London restaurants are tending back towards this small, localised *oikonomia* as a vital part of what they do. This has been called 'produce-led cuisine' (a term which always leads to some wag saying, 'Well, isn't it all produce led?), although it should perhaps be called 'producer-led cuisine', where small farms across Britain act as little embassies of London, producing food which goes almost entirely to the city's best restaurants. This ties into another trend within British food, a nativism that acts as a counterpoint to an all-encompassing globalisation: Fern Verrow, a biodynamic farm in Herefordshire, exclusively supplies Spring in Somerset House with vegetables; Matt Chatfield, a farmer in Devon, sup-plies a handful of grill restaurants with cull yaw, an aged mutton made from cast ewes; NamaYasai in Sussex supplies the Japanese noodle bar Koya, plus any other restaurant in London which has an interest in serving multiple varieties of daikon. It is perhaps a small, tentative step to the next stage of true *oikonomia*, which is for the restaurant to own the farm and be almost entirely self-sufficient, like L'Arpege in Paris or L'Enclume in Cumbria.

Yet the ancient Greeks weren't talking about flooding their cities with heirloom tomatoes when they used the term *oikonomia*, rather, they were talking about wheat, the life-giver and foundation stone of most of European cuisine. In London, this process historically operated in decreasing concen-tric circles, with the wheat coming from outside the city, reaching the outskirts of London where it would be milled (at places like Three Mills by the River Lea), made into bread by bakers, and then sold in the markets in the City. Perhaps it is for this reason that most of London's great bakeries are still on the edges of London, in former or current industrial zones, supplying restaurants and cafes in the centre. The bread itself displays both global and native strands of British cooking: sourdoughs and ryes are still there, thriving, buoyed by the revolution going on in heritage grain, but now there is also focaccia, challah, pita, manakish, roti, and every type of bun known to man.

TETOTE FACTORY

On walking into Tetote Factory, you might think, 'Where should this bakery be?' It would be easy if it were in Tokyo, where it would function as a neighbourhood bakery so good that commuters from other tokubetsu-ku would divert their jour-neys for melon pan or adzuki buns. If it were in Paris, then it would be in every guidebook going, and its clientele would mainly be food tourists and cooing French chefs, who would remark that the warm custard buns were as perfect and precious as bowls in a kiln – even if the barbecue chicken bun (a bun made up of chicken nuggets, barbecue sauce and mayonnaise) exudes chaotic-evil energy. But it's not in either of those places. It's near South Ealing station, a tube stop which is mainly passed through on the way to Heathrow. It is for this reason that pretty much no one knows about the best bakery in London, except Ealingites who protect it at all costs by not talking about it to outsiders.

OREN

You could technically work your way through Oded Oren's vast menu without trying any of the bread he makes on-site; Oren is, after all, a proper restaurant, and a proper restaurant can't run on bread alone but needs showstopper protein like Barnsley lamb chops with zhoug, Tamworth pork with roasted garlic and preserved lemon, and many other things which fuse British produce with Mizrahi Jewish cookery. But equally, you kind of want Oren to throw caution to the wind and serve nothing but bread: an arayes, traditionally made with lamb but here made from hake stuffed into pita and brushed with lamb fat, the effect somehow accentuating the fish – like salt on caramel; or oblong flatbreads topped with anchovies, confit onions and sour cream; or a just-baked whole loaf of challah, glistening like a bodybuilder on Muscle Beach. There are places in Paris where you might sit through an entire tasting menu to get to the patisserie; you might do the same in Oren, just for some pita and tomato.

QUALITY WINES

Quality Wines opened in the summer of 2018 with possibly the least-needed remit a London restaurant has ever had: a small plates (STRIKE 1) wine bar (STRIKE 2) serving fresh pasta (STRIKE 3) cooked on induction hobs (how many strikes can you have?); seemingly an unoriginal way to monetise a dead section of the Quality Chop House and the deli to which it is attached. Within a few months, it appeared that, in fact, this is exactly what London needed, mainly because Nick Bramham, who cooks every plate of food that comes through the bar, understands that there is a lot of merit in picking something very simple and executing it to the highest standard possible. For a place that isn't a bakery, it is strange that the two essential things at Quality Wines both involve bread – first the obligatory focaccia (elastic, airy, and a sponge for olive oil) and then any sandwich on the menu: a tuna-melt toastie fried in butter, or a mortadella, burrata and pistachio panino – and that it is these dishes that will make you realise Quality Wines is secretly the sandwich shop London needed all along.

E5 BAKEHOUSE

E5 is perhaps the closest thing London has to a medieval-style bakery, in that it's located on the outskirts of the city (in a Hackney railway arch) and bridges the world of central London dining with farms and mills across the UK. E5 was one of the first bakeries in London to start talking about heritage grain, but unlike some of the bakeries that came after it, it is not too worthy about it. (E5 also have a mill, though they don't mill everything on-site – instead they are in the business of trying to make delicious bread, no matter what.) The best things on the menu are bakes which lie at the point between sweet and savoury; sable Breton, for instance: a salty, buttery shortbread the thickness of a Gideon Bible, with tiny shards of caramelised sourdough and buckwheat flecked throughout.

YASMINA

Back in Lebanon, Ramadan, the owner of Yasmina, used to be known by the epithet 'al Khabbaz' – simply, 'the baker'. If you find yourself around the corner from East Acton station, on an anonymous stretch of the Westway, then you will find out why: it's here, rather than Edgware Road or Park Royal, that you will taste London's best manakish, a Lebanese flatbread that is as ubiquitous and customisable as pizza. Crisp on the edges and so pneumatic that it's in danger of floating away, it can be topped with minced lamb (lahm bi ajeen) or just za'atar and cheese (the purist option), drenched in olive oil, and preferably dipped into toum and wrapped around sharp pickles.

the mosque

shaheed saleem

In 1985, Syed Sarwar Hasan moved from northern Pakistan to Harrow in north-west London and became one of the early users of the first-ever Harrow Mosque. This was not the type of mosque that non-Muslims would recognise by its appearance – there were no domes or minarets – but one that is nevertheless common all over London, where Muslim communities are less established. The mosque was formed from a pair of semi-detached houses which had been combined and adapted: the interconnecting domestic rooms were turned into prayer halls, and the bathrooms into ablution facilities. Hasan has lived through the massive growth of the Muslim community in the area, largely made up of other migrants from northern Pakistan. They have now built a landmark purpose-built mosque, the Harrow Central Mosque, which opened in the 2010s.

It was from this mosque that Hasan started Soul Kitchen in 2017, to provide a shared space and meal to those who were without. After cooking there twice a month, Hasan realised that people were not only coming because they lacked access to food, but also due to their lack of social contact and a sense of communality; the elderly and those living alone, as well as families who might not have the means to eat out, were all heavily represented. When Covid put a halt to the shared meals, Hasan and his team ran weekly food banks from which anyone could come and collect meals and everyday food items. They established five distribution points in the local area with one in a North Harrow mosque – the Salaam Centre. From here, on a Sunday, meals donated by local restaurants are distributed, along with general tinned and packaged food items, enough for around 250 meals a week.

While food does not necessarily have a specific function in religious Islamic rituals, food projects associated with mosques are an important vehicle through which values that are important to Muslims – such as sharing, providing and understanding – can be expressed; using food to create bonds and connections within, across and beyond London's Muslim communities. I say 'communities' because London probably has the most diverse Muslim population in the world, with more ethnicities, places of origin, denominations and schools of religious thought than any other single city. The majority of London's mosques have been established by Sunni Muslims from South Asia who, after post-war migrations from independent India and newly created Pakistan and Bangladesh, make up a large proportion of the city's population. But as the 20th century progressed, Muslims who had settled in London following different branches of Islam, or from other parts of the world, also established their communities, leading to the creation of a multitude of mosques across the city where a range of Islamic religious and cultural practices could be enacted.

South-west of Harrow, just off an industrial estate in Northolt, is one of these mosques: the Huseiny Masjid, London's cultural centre for the Dawoodi Bohras. I decided to visit this mosque on the outskirts of West London because I am interested in how a relatively small religious community maintains its traditions and shared identity. Dawoodi Bohras are a denomination within the Shia branch of Islam; they officially originate from the Indian state of Gujarat, but their religious roots can be traced to 12th century Egypt. Numbering approximately one million globally, they are now spread across forty countries; their population stands at around 6,500 in the UK, where they are settled mainly in the midlands and London, but despite their small size they have been highly effective in establishing a network of mosques across the country.

The social significance of food and eating has theological origins for the Bohra: their spiritual guides, the Fatimi Imams of medieval Cairo, would prepare platters filled with food known as mawaid to feed the masses on religious occasions. In 2011, drawing inspiration from these traditions, the 52nd spiritual leader of the Bohra community, Syedna Mohammed Burhanuddin, initiated a remarkable project, the Faiz al-Mawaid al-Burhaniyah (FMB). Its aim is to provide at least one wholesome meal a day to every Bohra household in the world, regardless of their socioeconomic status, with the aim of freeing up time in the household – particularly for women – to pursue other activities. Members of the community contribute financially to the project, and money that is saved on each household's food bill can be donated to the collective kitchen. Today over 135,000 community households are served in 869 cities across the world, and one of the major nodes in this global distribution network is the mosque in Northolt. The Northolt mosque grew out of the first Bohra religious centre in London in the 1970s, when a former church in Fulham was purchased and adapted for use. As the community grew and became more established, the large Northolt site was acquired and a major purpose-built mosque and community centre was opened there in 1996.

At the mosque, I meet Alefiya Shakir, a millennial born in Bradford whose grandparents migrated from northern India in the 1960s. Shakir's family used to live in Portsmouth, so they had to collect the week's evening meals on weekend visits to Northolt, but in 2019 her family moved to Chesham, and from here they were able to become more fully engaged in the life of the mosque, part of which meant being able to receive FMB meals regularly. Her's was one of over a thousand meals prepared every day and delivered by volunteers to around 400 Bohra households within a 10-mile radius. However, one of the most distinctive characteristics of the complex is the space that has been dedicated to communal eating within. The entire basement consists of a large industrial kitchen alongside an expansive hall where congregants can gather and eat together. The community shares meals here during religious events and functions, and the act of collective eating reinforces their social and religious ties. This collective function of food is further empha-sised by the way meals are eaten: not from individual plates, but rather a large dish known as a thall, from which some eight or so people will eat.

In the masjid's basement, the structure and order of the meal always stays the same. Each communal meal starts with the taking of a grain of salt, before saying 'Bismillah' aloud and offering Salawat on the Prophet; this is swiftly followed by a sweet dish, such as a halva made from ground semolina or carrots, being served. But after this, the meal is always different, reflecting the different migrationary routes of the Bohra. A small savoury dish is eaten – this might be haleem or daal chawal, acknowledging the congregation's roots in South Asia, or kuku paka or cassava curry, which traces the journey to east Africa. This is followed by a full course meal, which may well be keema, but equally spaghetti bolognese – we are still in England after all. The meal ends with some fruit and reciting Alhamdulillah, before everyone finally takes a grain of salt again.

By sharing in a collective meal which had been distributed to every Bohra family across the country, and knowing that every other member of the community was being nourished from the same source, Alefiya and her family could feel connected to, and part of, the Bohra community in London, the UK and beyond. Food as a means of tying the community together is central to the Bohras' FMB project, where this small community which is dispersed throughout the country – and indeed the world – can feel connected through networks of food distribution and meal sharing.

The idea of creating collective and shared spaces through food, as well as increasing understanding between communities, are also the founding principles of the Ramadan Tent Project (RTP), which was started in 2013 by Omar Salha and a group of fellow students at the School of Oriental and African Studies (SOAS). The group came up with the idea when they initiated an iftar – the meal for breaking the fast during the month of Ramadan – on a green space outside the school, so that international students could experience Ramadan as the communal event that they were used to. By the following year the initiative had grown, welcoming the vulnerable and those in need, and soon moving to a larger open area near SOAS, where a tent was erected to host the Open Iftars every evening for the month.

By 2019, with Open Iftars steadily growing in popularity, the RTP had become a peripatetic event, hosting iftars open to all in a series of spaces across London and other UK cities. That year the first Open Iftar was held in Trafalgar Square, alongside others at Wembley Stadium, the British Library, Southwark Cathedral and Westminster Abbey. The use of iconic spaces for Open Iftars continued as attendance increased; now, in 2022, the project estimates that it has hosted over 100,000 people in over ten cities across four continents.

RTP continuously exhorts the centrality of the collective, of sharing and understanding others, as core tenets of the Islamic faith, citing among its aims a desire to 'turn strangers into friends' and break barriers. Speakers at the events often reiterate this message, emphasising, for example, the spiritual importance of loving one another, as well as generosity and social action. By taking the iftar event from private buildings into public spaces, RTP takes places that have been built to embody institutional power structures, from which minorities can often feel excluded, and reorganises them according to Muslim cultural practices.

I speak to Atika Dawood, a born-and-bred Hackney Muslim, who first came across the Ramadan Tent Project while she was studying Arabic and linguistics at SOAS. Atika started volunteering with the RTP in 2016 and describes it as a transformative experience.

She says she was quite introverted and shy before becoming involved with the project, but being around so many people of different backgrounds – sharing the experience of fasting and organising large collective fast-breaking events – brought her out of her shell. Dawood felt emboldened by hosting iftars in such significant public spaces because she saw this as changing the narrative of being Muslim in London. Rather than feeling that she had to compromise her faith identity in public spaces, she now felt that an important aspect of her Muslim culture could be unashamedly expressed.

The aim of the RTP has always been to enable people, regardless of faith or background, to take part in breaking the fast with Muslims, although this is an organised version of what is often done spontaneously in London, without mosques or designated venues. On the day I visit Harrow Mosque, I meet Adnan, a local year 11 pupil who started helping with food distribution at the mosque five months ago. His mother Zeinab, a care worker, introduced him to the project, and now he is a regular volunteer, delivering to homes as well as assisting at the mosque. Zeinab tells me that over the previous Ramadan she set up a table outside her house with her children, giving away ice cream to anyone who would give them a smile (her idea came from the saying of the Prophet Muhammed that 'even a smile is charity'.) The event was a great success, bringing all kinds of people on her street together – people they hadn't even met before who lived amongst them.

In this way, by taking a religious ritual outside of the mosque and into a public space, these formal and informal food projects blur the line between religious and civic spaces, between Muslim and non-Muslim, while also dissolving intra-Muslim religious differences, too. Muslims can connect and engage with the city, and with each other, across ethnic and denominational boundaries that might otherwise constrain them, all within the same city. It gives visibility to Muslim religious life and invites engagement, curiosity and, through this, understanding between communities.

BEYOND BRICK LANE

Before they became destinations in their own right, London restaurants developed around other urban landmarks: Soho and Covent Garden for pre-theatre dinner; Farringdon and Spitalfields, first because of the markets, and then in the wake of their absence; Bloomsbury for hungry university students; Fitzrovia for greedy estate agents. But there is another world of London restaurants that exists in relation to less luxurious things, too: areas around hospitals with a whole ecosystem of handheld fast food for harried staff, chicken shops that are close – but not too close – to a school. Even the Bangladeshi-owned restaurants that lined Brick Lane during its heyday succeeded not because there was a local community, but because they were situated just close enough to the City to provide post-work stress relief for bankers who, being technically human, had to eat and drink sometimes.

The few restaurants on Brick Lane that don't have pictures of Harry Redknapp or fake Gordon Ramsays in their window are the ones that used to fulfil another function; from the start of the Bangladeshi independence movement, these canteens were spaces for members of political youth organisations headquartered nearby. Nooruddin Ahmed, a member of the Bangladeshi Youth League, cites Nazrul, Alauddin, Sonar Bangla and the Nirala as the four restaurants that activists would use as a 'means of getting news, as a means of organising themselves'. After independence, at the height of the skinhead presence on Brick Lane, when white customers would go into the curry houses and leave without paying, these morphed into strongholds where anti-racist action could be planned.

Today the political movements are mostly dead, but now these restaurants have a new function: as extensions of the East London Mosque on Whitechapel Road. The mosque opened in 1985 and although it has since been superseded in size by super-mosques like Morden's Baitul Futuh it is still absolutely integral to the Muslim communities in East London, chiefly Bangladeshi, Pakistani and Somali. The restaurants are male-dominated, canteen-like spaces where prayers fade into lively debate and discussion; during the month of Ramadan, in a busy iftar, they're the closest thing London has to the vibe of a turn-of-the-century Viennese grand cafe (except with far more rice).

AL KAHF

Al Kahf has something of the feel of an underground speakeasy with a prayer room; to get there, you have to go through one of those Dickensian Whitechapel alleys you thought didn't exist anymore, down some stairs and into what appears to be a social club. There is no menu, but just ask what they have on. On a stretch that is no stranger to rice (this is the London epicentre of Dhaka- and Sylheti-style biryanis, after all), Al Kahf outdoes all the competition in terms of generosity: bariis iskukaris, served with Flintstone-sized portions of lamb shoulder, only looks simple because so few places actually take care to do it well; here the lamb falls off the bone like a shrug off the shoulder, in layers of sweet fat and crispy skin, served alongside spiced rice, sweetened with currants and enriched with the lamb's own broth. It's food so good it needs no accompaniment, except a squeezy bottle of basbaas to cut through it all.

GRAAM BANGLA

Gram Bangla opened in 1997 and for two decades was the outstanding Sylheti restaurant on Brick Lane. Following a decline and a brief closure, it has now been resurrected with a differently spelled name, and is perhaps better than ever. White rice is your canvas here, which you can paint shades of scarlet, orange and yellow with everything from a soothing dal to various bhortas. You will find the whole of the Ganges in their menu: beloved river fish like rohu, hilsa and the thousand eyes of silvery keski maas, the closest thing available in London to River Severn elvers. Whatever you get, the order of shutki satni is a must – a dried, fermented fish paste that is visually unassuming but olfactorily a nuclear bomb. Just a teaspoon of it on some plain rice is enough to sate the most homesick of Bengali palates.

CAFE GRILL AND AMAR GAON

On an alternate timeline, Bangladeshis might have come to London in 2021 rather than in the 1970s. Instead of inventing the curry house, they would have arrived in a city that gets off on authenticity and chilli heat, one that was tailor-made for their cuisine: ferocious heat, pungent curries and fish ferments. White guys bored of Thai food would be making trips to Sylhet and Dhaka, and opening restaurants in Shoreditch called Shatkora. And even on this timeline, Nigella would have still dropped a recipe for a fish finger bhorta. A bhorta can come in many forms – it just needs to be a mash of something, like aubergine or potato – and veers in style between light and fresh on one end, and contains-so-much-mustard-oil-it-constitutes-a-weapon on the other. On Brick Lane, the Sylheti canteens Amar Gaon and Cafe Grill grin at one another from across the street: Amar Gaon does a brownish fish bhorta, volatile with mustard oil, whereas Cafe Grill opposite does a brighter version, white and green, that, in its balance of chilli heat, sourness and herbaceousness, is almost akin to a Thai salad.

HAJI NANNA BIRYANI

If Brick Lane is explicitly Sylheti in terms of its cuisine, all pungency and dried fish, then Whitechapel Road compresses what would be a 200 kilometres journey in Bangladesh into a stroll of 200 metres, becoming a mini Dhaka. Here, at restaurants like DHAKA BIRYANI and KOLAPATA, you can try the more gently aromatic side of Bangladeshi food, with plenty of fish fries and biryanis. The best of the lot is probably Haji Nanna Biryani, which specialises in kacchi biryani, made with short-grain kalijeera rice rather than basmati. London is a city where most people could be served a pulao rather than a biryani and not know the difference, but here it's as complex as it should be: the lamb giving each grain a slick of fat; hidden presents of egg, potato and sour plums; and the rice fragranced with just enough pandan and orange blossom water before it becomes overwhelming.

SONARGAON

For an area often characterised in the right-wing press as 'insular', you will find few culinary 'no-go zones' in Whitechapel: doner quesadillas, shatkora doners, naga wings and Ferrero Rocher naans are some of the hybrid creations you might find within a ten-metre radius of Sonargaon. The restaurant itself should be ignored; instead, you need to make a beeline for the stall outside, which serves the best samosa chaat in London. Watching samosa chaat being assembled on the street can put you into a meditative state: first, freshly deep-fried meat or veg samosas are broken apart, then they are doused in chana, then spicy chutney, then tamarind water, then yoghurt, then comes the crunch of raw onion, a drift of coriander, then more chana, more chutneys, more onion. It contains one of the best textures in food: of something hot and crispy becoming wet. The only alteration I make to the dish is a minor but vital one: add one more samosa.

My childhood memories of Southall are fragmented, characterised by the trappings of the most tired representations of South Asian communities in popular culture – 'dizzying hues' of sari fabric, the scent of samose and pani puri, the 'bustle' of the busy streets – and a sharp recollection of feeling stern disapproval on seeing South Asian men smoking cigarettes (I was a self-righteous five-year-old – today I am myself struggling to quit).

My memories of Havelock Road Gurdwara, however, are stronger: they are my earliest recollections of being in the Darbar Sahib of a Gurdwara, including on Diwali in the year 2000 when we journeyed from nearby Hounslow. Hundreds of people flanked us as we queued at the central dais to prostrate ourselves before Sri Guru Granth Sahib Ji (our living, eternal Guru) and I shyly clutched at mum's chunni. The images are still clear in my mind: the granthi with snow-white beards reciting scripture, the mesmerising sweep of the Chaur Sahib over the Guru, the shock at seeing one of the few white girls from my class queuing beside us (she had previously attempted, unsuccessfully, to convince me she was Sikh), and a childish wonder – a numinosity – that has stayed with me every time I enter the Guru's Darbar.

Alongside the serenity of the Darbar Sahib, there has always been the thrum of the langar hall. Every Gurdwara, no matter how small, has a space for the communal preparation, distribution and consumption of langar – blessed food available to all – which dates back to the establishment by Sri Guru Nanak Dev Ji of settlements where ownership of the land and its produce (in other words, *the means of production)* were held in common. Langar is arguably the most well-known aspect of Sikhi to non-Sikhs, often billed as 'free food' by the media and diasporic Sikh organisations. This limited presentation removes langar from its specific historical and spiritual context, and erases the multiple functions of the langar hall as a space. It has rendered langar vulnerable to discourses of

the gurdwara

multiculturalism focused on the utility of migrant faith groups as a prospective indicator of integration. This is evident in the media framing of Sikhs providing food to stranded truckers in Dover during the closure of the French border in 2020 (and resultant comments on social media, pitting Sikh communities against Black communities), as well as in the coverage of Havelock Road Gurdwara's 'amazing grannies' providing food to the 'vulnerable' during the pandemic (langar is for all, not just the vulnerable).

The characterisation of Sikhs as the 'right kind' of migrant – loyal in battle, servile in civil society – has a long history, going back to the annexation of Panjab by the Raj, when Sikhs quickly became an especially trusted 'loyal' force and were categorised as a 'martial race' by British eugenicists. This history has played a role in Southall's development – as Sikhs migrated to fill the demand for labour in the aftermath of the Second World War, their prominent role in the army made some employers better disposed towards them than other migrants. The R. Woolf rubber factory in nearby Hayes – whose general manager had fought alongside Sikhs in the war – recruited Sikhs in large numbers and, given its relative affordability (and its proximity to Heathrow Airport), Sikhs began to move to Southall, and the area was informally christened as 'Little Panjab'.

The real legacy of Sikhs in Southall resists such easy narratives. From the establishment of the Southall Indian Workers' Association by members of the Communist Party of India in 1956, to the Southall Uprising of 1976 following the racist murder of Gurdip Singh Chaggar, and the formation of Southall Black Sisters following the murder of Blair Peach in 1979, there has always been a strong anti-racist tradition in the area. Yet decades after these events, during the 2011 Tottenham Uprising sparked by the murder of Mark Duggan by police, Southall's Sikh community would find itself praised by David Cameron for its 'defence' of Gurdwara Sri Guru Singh Sabha,

amardeep singh dhillon

photos by mark ikaran

an event cited in broadsheets as an example of 'ordinary Britons' banding together to work with the police and unite against the 'looters'.

These distorted echoes of history are familiar to me. They remind me as much of the exhibits touring Gurdwara halls, touting the proud history of Anglo-Sikh relations ('Loyal Allies: Proud Britons') as of the Home Office-funded CCTV cameras in the Darbar Sahib of some British Gurdware. From stitched-up Gurdwara Parbandhak Committee elections to pop-up police-recruitment stalls, the Gurdwara has always been a contested political space, even as the sangat coheres a single spiritual community within its walls. It makes sense that Gurdware are sites where wider discourses around assimilation and representation can play out their contradictions, too.

In 1958, the Sikh Cultural Society began hiring Shackleton Hall for monthly prayers, and six years later it established Southall's first Gurdwara in a house at 11 Beaconsfield Road. In the same year, Guru Nanak Sat Sang Sabha – set up by Sikhs from Malaysia and Singapore – purchased the adjoining hall at St Anselm's Church. The two groups would merge in 1967 and convert a disused milk dairy on Havelock Road into a new Gurdwara under the banner Sri Guru Singh Sabha. The construction of the current Gurdwara on the site began in 1999 (during this period, the sangat relocated to the nearby Park Avenue site of the same name) and was inaugurated in 2003 by none other than the Prince of Wales. At the time of construction, it was the largest Gurdwara outside of India. It cost £17 million.

Gurdwara Sri Guru Singh Sabha is a masterclass in modern diaspora Gurdwara architecture. Designed in collaboration with non-hierarchical design firm Architects Co-Partnership, its eight chhattri (elevated dome pavilions) derive from Rajput architecture, while the large onion domes at the front and rear of the building – one gold, one cream – come from Mughal architecture. The langar hall is on the ground floor, in keeping with Sri Guru Amar Das Ji's edict, Pehle pangat, pachhe sangat – 'First eat together, then sit in congregation'. The underlying philosophy of langar is one of total equality in community, and of universal provision by the collective.

This provision often extends beyond the Gurdwara itself. Nishkam Sikh Welfare Awareness Team (SWAT) has grown from providing food to Southall's unhoused people to weekly provision at locations across the capital, from Stratford to the Strand. This provision is usually viewed as seva – a central tenet of Sikhi that animates much of the community organising done by and within our communities, loosely translated as 'selfless service'. While food provision is viewed as seva, there is disagreement within Sikh communities over whether or not that which is done outside of the langar hall can be considered langar. Unfortunately, the translation of seva as 'service', and the assignment of 'volunteer' status to those engaging in seva, decouples it from the Sikh collectivist tradition from which it originates; it becomes an individual act of charity. Activist and writer Shamsher Singh makes the point succinctly:

Our role as Sikhs isn't confined to fixing the broken people that capitalism churns out as a byproduct of its economic model. We're not neo-colonialism's personal clean-up crew. It has to go beyond 'langar is the free meal service found in every gurdwara', 'hello langar, goodbye world hunger' – these aren't Sikh ideas, they're marketing slogans.

In the langar hall of Gurdwara Sri Guru Singh Sabha hangs a portrait of Sant Jarnail Singh Bhindranwale, the controversial leader considered a Shaheed, or martyr, at the hands of the Indian state by many Sikhs: an unflinching vindication of Sikh political autonomy, emphasising the political potential of langar. As I finish my meal with an extremely sweet cup of chah, I think about the importance of langar in sustaining the year-long Kisaan Andolan (Farmers' Movement), in north-west India last year, and can't help but note that the British left lacks any comparable infrastructure which can facilitate mass resistance to state oppression for more than a few days of action. In the Gurdwara, there is a strong, active tradition of provision as a form of community construction and collective worship. Should the need arise and political context present itself – *should coalitions be effectively forged* – where better for conversations around sustained dissent to be brought into the open?

Today, Southall Station has received a shiny facelift as part of London's newest infrastructure project, the Elizabeth Line, but the platform signs remain written in both English and Gurmukhi. With Canary Wharf now 31 minutes away, many residents might wonder who exactly is being welcomed by the phrase ਜੀ ਆਇਆਂ ਨੂੰ, which is emblazoned across the entrance. A new complex of 564 new homes (50% 'affordable') and a pedestrian plaza has already been approved by Ealing Council, while the *Metro* paper this year described Southall as a 'new hotspot' for first-time buyers. Actor and writer Zainab Hasan, one of many campaigners organising as part of Ealing Independent Network to fight the assault on Southall residents by property developers, is unequivocal about what they are facing:

The excavations at Southall Gasworks by property developers build-ing unaffordable apartments has swamped nearby homes with toxic fumes – it's not an exaggeration to say that gentrification is killing us. Already in the last couple of months we've seen the closure of a community health facility and a young adult centre. Residents fought hand-to-hand in our streets with armed racist mobs to protect the people of Southall in the 1970s and 80s. Now we face rich men in suits who similarly want to force us out of our homes.

These tensions are a reminder of the limitations of gestures at inclu-sion offered by local authorities. One such gesture is the renaming of the stretch of road the Gurdwara sits on, so that the colloquially named 'Havelock Road' Gurdwara is now in fact 'Guru Nanak Road' Gurdwara. Previously named Havelock Road, after the British general who recaptured Kanpur during the Indian Uprising of 1857 – and under whose command thousands were massacred in retribution for Nana Rao's Bibighar Massacre – its renaming by Ealing Council was endorsed by one of General Havelock's descendants and many local Sikh residents. And yet, while some of the residents opposing the renaming reverted to the old dog-whistle of concerns over the erasure of colonial history, others, who were themselves members of the sangat, denounced it as an empty gesture at anti-racism – and an insensitive one at that.

For all the attempts to construct a monolithic 'Sikh community', both nationally and locally, Southall's Sikh communities continue to thwart them. My experiences of langar are of communities and spaces that resist simple narratives and binaries: heated discussions over whether or not sitting at chairs and tables rather than on the floor represents a betrayal of the anti-caste symbolism of langar; debates over scripture interjected by the cackles of aunties, on a break from preparing huge cauldrons of dahl, sharing salacious gossip; reflections on the gendered division of labour between the male-dominated Darbar Sahib and the warring matriarchies of the kitchen; arguments between preachers over whether serving chips and pizza is an effective way of attracting young people. These lively conversations have been as much a part of the langar hall as the actual provision of langar, for every hour spent serving langar as a teenager was an hour spent poring over the *Panjabi Weekly* paper, practicing reading Gurmukhi by playing trope bingo with its problematic matrimonials (WANTED: EDUCATED GIRL WITH WHEATISH COMPLEXION FOR PROFESSIONAL SON; DIVORCED GIRLS ALSO MAY APPLY). 'Free food for the vulnerable' hardly begins to encompass any of these experiences.

We moved out of Hounslow soon after that Diwali I remember so clearly, returning to West London sporadically for functions or marriage ceremonies at other Gurdware. But it was always Havelock Road that I'd associate with my early childhood. En route to Southall in 2021, for the first time in years, I said as much to mum on the phone. 'That's funny,' she muses. 'That Gurdwara was still being built in 2000.' It turns out I'd never been to that Gurdwara as a child at all. I should've seen it coming – if writing this piece has taught me anything, it's that sometimes even the narratives we tell ourselves aren't quite what they seem.

THE CHAPLI KEBAB THUCYDIDES TRAP

There's a bleak Southall joke that wonders whether Indians chose to make their home around Heathrow Airport in case they immediately had to leave again. It wasn't a joke made in jest; Southall was, from the 1960s onwards, heavily contested martial ground. On one side, a generation of Indian Punjabis making their home on the outskirts of the former imperial capital, in a country whose meddling and line-drawing had led them there in the first place; on the other, white-dominated trade unions, the National Front and the police. In truth, it was the airport that led Punjabis to Southall, the jobs there and at nearby factories that made them stay, but Southall has never forgotten the attrition it took to gain the ground, metre by metre, by the radicalism and cross-cultural solidarity of its communities. Go to Southall today and you will find a place that is tied to its history, whose sons and daughters, as documented in film-maker and photographer Harkikaran's documentary *Zimmers of Southall*, repurpose their parents' modded BMW cars and listen to the dub created by the people who had marched alongside them.

Go clockwise around the London clock, almost all the way, and you will find Hounslow, ostensibly a neighbour on the other side of Heathrow Airport, but almost another world. Hounslow and Southall are arguably the two most important South Asian neighbourhoods in London, but in many ways utterly unlike one another: Southall isolated by its lack of connectivity (until the Elizabeth Line came rolling in), Hounslow with five train stations; Southall rooted in the specificity of the Sikh Punjabi diaspora (turning London into Amritsar), Hounslow too vast for any one community to dominate; Southall a village with a united design, Hounslow a city unto itself, a cacophony of single-storey buildings, endless roads, and occasional vistas of countryside – a Kyoto if Kyoto was solely composed of retail parks, gurdwaras and airport Premier Inns. Southall and Hounslow, Sparta and Athens, tradition and modernity.

Most Southall residents will tell you the restaurants here aren't quite what they used to be: perhaps true, or perhaps nostalgia talking. Hounslow, on the other hand, is alive with the potential of unfilled space. People who grow up in houses depreciated by Heathrow's flight paths know the value of location: restaurants in semi-detached houses, kiosks in walls, a Goan restaurant in a pub basement, a quarter-sliver of a shopfront taken up by a biryani specialist, a literal museum exhibition on Islamic contributions to the world inside a fried chicken shop that also contains an upstairs prayer room. You might pass what looks like a bungalow but is actually the Shree Jalaram Seva Trust temple, where Hindus come to pray and collect vegetarian tiffin tins for the elderly. A Hounslow-ish use of space. The planes roar down so low over the temple you feel like you can touch them, all carrying new and old souls to the city. Hounslow may be where London ends, but it is where it begins, too.

TASTE OF PAKISTAN

Taste of Pakistan is something of a miracle: a restaurant actually in the middle of nowhere, on an arterial road heading towards Hanworth (no, me neither), serving some of the most direct, adrenalin-racing cooking in London, with a perpetually full dining room. You need to book and double-book here if you're coming from outside Hounslow, because somehow Taste of Pakistan has created the only booking system in London based solely on vibes – a lamb-based Berghain. But the food is worth suffering for: chapli kebabs, as big as hubcaps, pockmarked with coriander seeds; acidic charsi karahi, its name (meaning 'cannabis user') referring to its addictive qualities; Pashtun grill cooking and naans the size of torsos that sit menacingly at the head of the table, like Banquo's ghost. Don't even think of coming here without a reservation or Nas, the owner, will flame you on Google Reviews.

CHARCOAL CHICKEN

If *BuzzFeed* were to publish a *Here are 60 Things Every South Asian Millennial will TOTALLY Remember* listicle, at the top of the list, correctly, would be good seekh kebabs. Do you remember good seekh kebabs? How your mum would take you for a kebab roll and it might be the single most delicious thing you'd ever eaten? Kids these days, with their perfectly cylindrical, homogenous seekh kebabs, just don't know the pleasure of biting into a malformed kebab roll, detonating a coriander seed or a pocket of bursting hot fat. At Charcoal Chicken, a takeaway kebab shop in Hounslow themed around the colour purple, you may find the 1990s still live on in fat and pudgy seekh kebabs, dripping juice and oil into their takeaway carton. There are other things on the menu, but Charcoal is a seekh kebab specialist, so forget them: just get seekh kebabs, multiple of them, and taste your childhood again.

KHATTA MEETHA

The shopping broadway at Hounslow West tube station is one of the most idiosyncratic stretches of pavement in London, a whole South Asian boulevard plonked onto an airport approach road just before it becomes solely McDonald's and Travelodges. Here you'll find a Goan kiosk selling various chops and cutlets, a pub that sells Nepalese snacks, a Pashtun restaurant that makes chapli kebabs in the window, a Polish supermarket and at least two queues for biryani. You'll also find Khatta Meetha, a colourful takeaway that doubles up as a Lahori breakfast specialist and a paan shop. On the right, you'll find the paan and a stack of betel leaves as thick as playing cards, ready to be assembled to order, then spat out onto Hounslow's concrete. The paya is the standout here: goat feet cooked in rich and sticky sauce, finished with a tarka to make it properly decadent, like hot caramel on a sundae of fat.

CASA DE GOA

None of what is sold in Hounslow really abides by the rules of what London's food media generally consider tasty or sellable. Some of it is a strange mishmash of things designed to be economical and doesn't totally work: burnt chicken tikka burgers, halal fried breakfasts on top of waffles, a whole branch of Man vs Food. But I welcome failure, interesting failure at least, when it leaves room for a Goan restaurant called Casa De Goa in the basement of a pub, selling sorpotel in bread, beef tongue roast, homemade Goa sausage to take away, and shark ambotik, a curry of ruddy scarlet so hot and so sour that my mum would make it at my grandmother's request when her taste buds needed reawakening.

ZAM ZAM

The way biryani is being presented to Londoners has become increasingly baroque. It's now simply not a biryani without a backstory, a pastry crust, Paul Rudd (for some reason) and a hushed unveiling of steamed rice that has all the mock ceremony of a gender reveal (congratulations, it's mutton). This is literally miles away from the way most biryani is consumed in London: from aluminium foil trays in restaurants that initiate price wars with their neighbours over how little they can sell a chicken biryani for before people start questioning the economics of it (I have seen £1.99 biryani in Hounslow). The best-value biryani in London is probably the one at Zam Zam, in spitting distance of Heathrow Airport, run by a well-oiled team of Pakistani women. The biryani costs £3.50, £5 with curry, and is everything a biryani should be: a Goldilocks perfect plate of rice, not too dry and not too wet, layered, subtly spiced, steaming-hot and fresh from the degh. It's too far for most people to make the trip out, but it's possible to sleep easier just knowing it exists.

the suburbs

I like to take boys to the sports bar. The football plays on five different widescreen TVs overhead. Sometimes the boys look up at the game while they're talking to me; I look at them and dream of lingering eye contact. Sometimes they hold my hand under the table, slide along the sticky leather seat to get closer, or grip my knee while we order seven different starters and no mains. My heart always skips a beat, because I love the awkwardness of dating in the suburbs.

These bars are always in the suburbs. Gujarati sports bars are a peripheral phenomenon; they only appear where Indians live cosy, settled lives: North Circ ring road from Wembley to Southgate like lens glare, 1970s immigration wave from East Africa. Nestled in along a parade of shops, or just off a slip road roundabout, it's a blurry gradient – North Indian restaurant, old man pub, ambient lounge space, bar & grill. They're everything, anything you want them to be. I don't have favourites; I like all the sports bars. I love them all equally, unconditionally, truly.

Uncles sit at the bar on peeling leather stools, the stuffing leaking out the sides through the stitching. They're always wearing polo shirts and petrol station sunglasses. Car keys on the bar next to their pint, all collectively hiding from their wives. They're there for the football; the sizzling kebab and butter naan is just coincidental, a happy upside. Sometimes you can smell the carpets: stale beer and disinfectant. The sun never comes through the darkened windows. I close my eyes and wish for an industrial-sized bottle of hand wash in the bathroom, the shimmery pink kind.

Sometimes it feels weird to be a woman in these spaces. All the uncles perched at the bar like little birds, one eye on the footy and the other eye on the waitresses. Their voices are booming – they fill the space, leaving no room for me. But maybe that's part of their romantic charm? They either make me feel like 'one-of-the-boys', or like I'm a Precious Lady™ in contrast to my hyper-masculine backdrop. It's either that or feel like I've been caught red-handed, out of place and overexposed. But really, I don't know how to talk about sports bars without talking about men. It's a love triangle: I can't seem to find one without the other.

I think I like the comfort of dating with the shadow of my parents' generation looming over us at the bar, watching to make sure there's no funny business. Maybe this is my kink? There's something complicated and sexy about a date within earshot of the suburban immigrant dream: three-bed semi-detached house, five-door BMW, two kids – assimilation, I guess. Because I don't know if I want that for myself, yet or ever – but I'm being presented with it either way, so it's a toss-up between defiance and submission, and both those things are hot as fuck.

My worst break-up was in the sports bar round the corner from my mum's house, in Zone 4 North London. I remember shouting, crying, making a scene in the exact way I knew he hated. I could feel his embarrassment across the table. His hands were shaking and when I noticed, I felt an overwhelming pride in my capacity for spite.

The waitress handed him the bill, then she looked at me and winked. She walked away, but turned back to give me a sad, knowing smile. In that small gesture, my embarrassment about the publicness of it all just melted away. Her wink made me feel like I'd won in the court of public opinion. Like I wasn't the bad guy – I was the suffering hero, the tabloid darling. The uncles all clapped and cheered my name, waved flags with my face on. My heartbreak suddenly felt incredibly glamorous, so I leaned in to accentuate the scale of it. I wasn't there. I was outside my body. I had left the space of our sad conversation and was drifting along the dropped ceiling, past the asbestos and strip lights.

One boy was so painfully shy, every time we spoke his ears would blush. I thought it was so beautiful. How tender! To be that responsive to an environment and your place within it, to be that in tune with your own embarrassment. When he touched me, his fingers would grip me with this restrained tension. It was like he was afraid of demanding too much of me. Over the table, it was only the slightest touch of soft fingertips pressing in on my wrist. He asked before he kissed me. When our lips met I tasted the cool heat of green chillis – so despite his gentle touch, he made me wince all the same.

Another boy with different questions. I said, 'Yeah, you can come back to my mum's house to call the cab.' I thought it was so spontaneous and hot. All the lights were off and my bare kneecaps crunched against the white kitchen tiles. When he pulled a condom out of his back pocket, I laughed. I couldn't tell if he just felt lucky, or if this was premeditated and he'd spent the journey there planning all the ways he was going to fuck me. Either way, I was insanely jealous of how self-assured it made him seem.

One boy picked me up in a brand-new Mercedes. When we parked outside, he got nervous about his wing mirrors and the main road. The ick that washed over me was so powerful, I almost asked him to drive me back right then and there. I think I only stayed because I knew he'd never accept my offer to split the bill, and I love masala mogo.

One boy made me set a new rule: absolutely no SoundCloud DJs.

One boy, my favourite boy, asked me why all the uncles were looking at him. I didn't know how to answer, didn't know how to say *they're looking at you because your hand is cupping my arse cheek, and we don't really do that*. I told him it was because Indians just fucking love staring. I wasn't wrong, but it wasn't the right answer.

One boy was from Manchester. He asked if I liked it round here, and it made me laugh because I genuinely think the suburbs have bad vibes. The peripheral energy can feel like resentment sometimes, the bland emptiness of driveways and double-glazing can feel insular and lonely. It was only when he agreed with me that I felt a defensive anger. Because *he* was foreign here and, actually, maybe *he* should go back to where *he* came from. How could he ever understand the quality of this space? This periphery is a substance of its own, like a tideline, like a scum ring outlining a body of water. I realised he didn't *get* sports bars, not really and not like I did. He'd never fallen asleep across the ribbed booth seats on New Year's Eve, never ordered blackcurrant lemonade because his masi was paying, never had his cousin insist on getting crispy corn that no one touched.

I hated him a bit for that. Because I can't imagine a life without these things, can't imagine a sports bar feeling foreign or new, can't imagine a world outside of my little suburban pocket, can't really imagine leaving. I have seen it, done it, but I can't imagine it.

Oh, all these boys! I don't know how they feel in these spaces, because I never think to ask. I don't care, don't want to know, don't know how to bridge the gap between us. I should extend my hand across the table and say, 'I'm so glad you're here with me tonight', but I never do. Their interiority is a mystery to me.

You see, I know it's not the same in other places. The last time I went to Leicester, I had dinner in a sports bar called Blue Peter. We ate veg Manchurian in the dark restaurant while a drunk man sang ghazals loudly at the bar. He was wobbling on his stool while his friends gathered round, their phone flashes shining down on him in a halo. I went upstairs to find the toilets and instead found myself in the banqueting room. In there was a guy in a sequinned sherwani singing rowdy wedding songs into a wired-up karaoke mic. The mic wire was exceptionally long; it snaked across the glittery dance-floor tiles. He reached his hand out for me and I blushed. I couldn't really bring myself to look at him. I was drunk and full of my own piss, MAC Ruby Woo lipstick pressed in a greasy crescent against the dent of my chin.

London's suburban sports bars aren't as glamorous and surreal as that. They're not magical, they don't have the same poetry or intensity, but suburban crappiness is mine to share in. I love it because it belongs to me entirely. Not just the sports bars: I love the middling banality of the suburbs more than I have loved any of these boys. The skylights and scaffolding; the overpasses; the tunnels full of graffiti, crisp packets and piss. London keeps expanding outwards, spilling over itself, swallowing the territory surrounding it like a virus or a feast. I just want the city to stop!!! I can only laugh at how vain it all is. A Capital City, so important, so impossible and untrue. It can never be mine. The suburbs are the negative space, dense and opaque. My soulmate, my first: I will always love you.

If I'm being truly honest, I struggle with object permanence. The boys come and go. The new-builds grow aimlessly high along the North Circ slip road, stretching out in perfect unison across the station tracks. The city moves on and out. The sun sets over the conservatories and loft extensions, the treeless streets, tarmacked and glossy, shining like perfect gemstones. Multistorey car parks and industrial estates, gas works, pylons, rows and rows of post-war housing. I blow them all a kiss, my heart full of love and loneliness as they move past. Yeah, it's best if we just leave the image of the suburban immigrant dream on the countertop, like those uncles and their car keys. From India to East Africa to pelting down the North Circ in his brand-new Mercedes with all the windows down. Swooping over London's outline in a graceful crescent, like a shooting star. My hair flying back behind me, my hands in the air, screaming because I love the lads, love lollipop chicken, and this is my Wild Wild West.

north circular

Soho has been called London's 'dining epicentre', while Mayfair is still the best place in the world to launder money (by getting oligarchs to pay one thousand per cent mark-ups on sashimi). But between these two poles – the casual, Disneyfied 'It's a Small World' of culture-hopping restaurants in Soho, and Mayfair and St James' private clubs for adult babies – there are new pretenders to the throne, offering something the same but different. Fitzrovia is Soho for people who want five croquettes on their plate rather than three; Chelsea's dining scene is Mayfair for people too scared to leave their houses. But if you had to locate the epicentre of London's snacking culture – the place where food and its consumption are at their most conspicuous – then you would have to place the centre of gravity about nine miles north-west, somewhere on the Ealing Road. This is what London's casual dining sector could look like if it was entirely curated by Gujarati uncles.

Wembley and Harrow are maybe the only neighbourhoods in London built on the primacy of the portable bite, which can be ordered and eaten without having to divert the flow of the day, seamlessly blending in and out of life. This culture is embedded into its buildings, sometimes on street level: sit-down restaurants open up booths onto the pavement where people queue for pani puri, which they devour on the spot like Hungry Hungry Hippos. Every square metre of space is used, as stalls inch out further and further into the street, some selling more varieties of egg than you ever considered possible, others going far back, little mini-malls where you might find a Goan snack shop, a place assembling paan (destined to turn the Alperton pavement scarlet), newsagents – where, next to the tubes of Polos and Halls, you'll find a heater incubating mutton rolls – and a canteen serving infinite variations of dosa, all the same building.

Gujaratis, like the Japanese, have two food modes: serene and chaotic. Wembley–Alperton is mostly chaotic, a mini Osaka where within just a few hundred metres you will find every single vegetarian fried food possible: crispy bhajias, pani puri, pizza samosas, vada pav, Szechuan dabeli, bhindi fry, Chinese samosas (filled with chow mein), paneer bhurji pizza, egg ghotala, egg cheese bhurji, desi cheese omelette, egg Skylab (no, me neither), Australian egg fry, and every iteration of gram flour batter imaginable (and unimaginable). You couldn't have something like this in the centre – you'd have to upscale the production of dhokla to a few tons a day to keep up with rent, and chainify the pani puri stand: Pani Puri Soho, Pani Puri Fitzrovia, Pani Puri Market Halls. And therein is the paradox: chefs servicing the most open-minded, cutting-edge audience in the UK – in the world, maybe – can only produce conservative food, but it is in the conservatism of the suburbs, maybe necessarily, that chaos reigns.

DOSA EXPRESS

Previously located in the back of a mini-mall, where the entire menu of around 200 dosa variants was printed out on A4 sheets of paper and blu-tacked onto the wall in a grid, where you and a few friends could attempt a game of dosa bingo, Dosa Express has now moved to larger premises around the corner, with an outwards-facing space specifically for pani puri takeaway. If you can conceive of putting it in a dosa, then Dosa Express will most likely have it – from the traditional (masala), to the frugal and austere (just ghee), to the desi-Chinese (fried noodles with sriracha) to the !?! (chocolate with banana ice cream). Make some room for their freshly made-to-order pizza samosas – glistening parcels of melted cheese and marinara sauce which will take you back to school lunchtime tray pizzas, compressed into three hot bites.

ASHER'S AFRICANA

If Wembley resembles somewhere like Osaka, with its 'deep-fry everything' policy of small eats – Indian analogues of takoyaki and okonomiyaki, all batter and sauces – then Asher's Africana is the opposite pole that exists to balance it out, the East African-Gujarati equivalent of shojin ryori.

Asher's, a small but bright and airy space, with a semi-open kitchen where aunties stir steel pots big enough to hide in, is the closest experience available to getting invited round for rotli at your Gujarati friend's house after school. The rotli alone – so feather-light and decadent with ghee, but with a savoury wholemeal backbone that makes you feel virtuous for eating it – is worth the trip alone. Get it as part of a Gujarati thali, with two veg dishes and some pickles, and you will feel golden for the rest of the day. This would be a cult restaurant if it was anywhere else in London (give it five years, and some students, and it could be the Wembley equivalent of Silk Road).

MARU'S BHAJIA HOUSE

You can question who does the best crispy bhajias in London – those pomme soufflé-sized potato chips covered in coriander, turmeric, garlic and gram flour and deep-fried to make crispy shards; orange chips before the Black Country had even thought of battering a potato – but none of them will have the emotional resonance of Maru's, which has been frying potatoes since the mid-20th century, before and after its move from Nairobi. Writer Zarina Muhammad talks about how Maru's formed a perfect tetrahedral centre point between her mum's school, her aunt's office block, and her grandma's work at the Osram factory; this has been a meeting place for generations of Gujaratis. In some sense, the bhajia are peripheral; this is all about memories, comfort and dipping chutney.

SHREE KRISHNA VADA PAV

The best of the Dishoom menu, as all hedonists know, is somewhere in the small plates and snacks section, where you can find buttery paus, bhels, fries and cheese toasts. While Dishoom has changed the perception of Indian food in central London, Shree Krishna Vada Pav is for the ones who already knew, where the menu is this and *only* this: 70+ snacks inspired by Bombay and made for the north-west and West London Gujarati communities. The food at SKVP, like other snack shops

Shree Sai Vada Pav and Amol's Vada Pav, shares a curious affinity with the snacks from the north of England and Scotland, which is mostly unexplainable: any and all variations of fried carbohydrates – samosas, vadas, bhajias – are stuffed between soft barms/baps/buns. The ludicrously named paneer bomb, a tomato curry of curd cheese, stuffed into bread and then deep-fried, is an innovation any Glaswegian chippy would be happy to put on their menu.

JAI DURGA MAHAL

Between the curries and dosas, Chinese noodles and chaat, crispy bhajia, masala chips and south Indian uttappam, there is only one thing you need to know about this Harrow takeaway that seems to serve it all: they do chilli paneer pizza.

1   I rarely recall my dreams with any clarity, but there are spaces which
    I know turn up with some regularity. Most are not real spaces, by
    which I mean they exist in my mind and have no real analogue in the
    physical realm: a version of Beijing that looks like nothing in Beijing;
    a slow commuter train that links Paris and London; a simulation of
    New York that has condensed the city down into a fairground ride;
    a school I didn't go to. There is one space I visit in my dreams that
    does exist, and which my mind reproduces with unusual clarity:
    a bus stop at Clockhouse Junction on the North Circular Road,
    somewhere at the road's most northerly point, where I used to wait
    to get my school bus every weekday morning for seven straight years,
    and where I still wait, alone; a holding space, like the train station
    in *The Matrix Reloaded*. There is always a bus in the distance and
    I squint to see if it is a 629 or a 329, the difference between an easy
    journey and a hard one. But the bus never comes. I am still waiting.

photos by peter arkley bloxham

2   Here are some things you might find on the North Circular Road:
a kosher butchers, the vast Jehovah's Witness Assembly Hall, the
headquarters of Vitabiotics, a Romanian bakery kiosk selling cream
rolls and cherry pies, the largest independent cash and carry in
the UK, a TFC, a Spanish tapas and pizza restaurant called Volare
run by two sisters whose parents owned a pizzeria in Buenos Aires,
a dinosaur-themed adventure golf course, at least two IKEAs, at least
two Gökyüzüs, an Irish pub, an artisan gin distillery, at least twenty
builders' merchants, a mithai shop selling innumerable versions of
barfi, Brent Cross Shopping Centre, a cream limo, the worst hospital
in London (the North Mid), at least 500 mechanics shops, a Polish-
Chinese restaurant called Dom Polski, a Chinese pagoda, a Persian
sandwich shop selling tongue and brain rolls, a shop that only sells
walk-in saunas, the cursed funfair outside Brent Cross Shopping
Centre, sofa showrooms in locations that would have received a
shout-out in early-2000s DFS adverts, a retro faux-Parisian sandwich
shop called Gourmandise, a huge billboard that says 'Gorgeous
Gyros', a view of a big lake which is actually the Brent Reservoir,
Premier Inn Edmonton, a pure vegetarian Indian restaurant selling
dhokla (which on closer inspection turned out to be someone's
house), the biggest Tesco I've ever seen, my childhood newsagents,
a notorious chequered bikers' hangout called the Ace Cafe, and,
occasionally, me.

3 I also once came across a sex shop around Neasden but I cannot imagine anything more horrific than being horny on the North Circular Road.

4   I was thinking yesterday about the notion of being native to a city, or a part of a city, and what that means. I had a conversation with my friend Yvonne about the word 'native' and how often it's used defensively to put up a barrier between 'us' and 'them', particularly by the far right. 'London isn't London anymore' is a familiar refrain, declared by those whose childhood memories of London don't conform to its reality; 'We were born here' is a trump card to be played over those who weren't. I'm not convinced a born Londoner has any more ownership or right to the city than those who actively chose it. Is a baptised and lapsed Catholic worth more to the congregation than someone who has been confirmed?

   Yet there is something that gives me pause when I say to anyone that I'm a South Londoner now. Is it mine to claim? How far back do I go? Primary school? My bus route? I think home is any place you feel an immediate duty of care towards, but there is something to be said for being united by a common experience, which I don't really have. If there is a common North London experience it must be the North Circular Road: it threads through lives spent in Edmonton and Hampstead Garden Suburb, lives which would otherwise have little to do with one another. The North London experience is being shuttled round the North Circular by your mum: clockwise, anti-clockwise, through underpasses, under railed walkways, on the way to Wembley, on the way to Croydon, to IKEA, to Brent Cross, to Oriental City, to JD Sports, to the cinema, to a retail park, to the biggest shop you've ever seen in your life up until that point.

5   The South Circular means nothing to me.

6   Earlier this week I had the urge to go round the North Circular, like some demented Iain Sinclair with a Gaviscon addiction. I started at Hanger Lane and got lost in one of those tiled underpasses I used to get mugged in. I lamented that Dom Polski, the bizarre Polish-Chinese restaurant, has turned into a Polish grocery store, even though some remnant of it is still there, as a catering business within a food shop. I noticed that there is a new Chinese restaurant called Hua which has a Sichuan and Hunan menu featuring some northern specialities like yang xiezi (lamb scorpion hotpot). There is no one inside. Incongruously, a long cream limo is parked outside it. I cannot imagine who comes here, although I will make a return trip for it.

Further up is the faux-Chinoiserie of Hoo Hing, a pagoda-style building of the type that used to exist in Chinatown to signify foreignness and now only really remains in suburban shopping malls. The Park Royal industrial estate sprawls out on the right, with Bestway, a palatially huge cash and carry, sitting on top of a hill and overlooking the road like a Roman ruin on the crest of the Palatine. The next destination is Ace Cafe, a retro, 1950s-style throwback whose fate has risen and fallen with the bikers who frequent it. Today it's dead – there's an old boy reading the *Sun* and nursing a soup and a tea, and two Italian workers who seem confused by the place and only want a coffee. I think the chef is Greek, or at the very least Balkan – there is moussaka on the menu. I order a sausage-and-egg sandwich, which is pleasing. The hot butter has soaked into the white bread, which makes it stick to my teeth. I consider putting something on the jukebox but I don't have change.

I keep working my way round the North Circ clock, from 9 to 11, going clockwise through corners, roundabouts and gyratories that mark the road, like vertebrae on an arching spine. I'm not entirely sure what I'm looking for, and I'm not particularly hungry. By the time I get to East Finchley it's dark and I can no longer make out signs from across the road, so I decide to call it a day. I have a sandwich at Caspian Lounge, a Persian snack bar that also does burgers and pizza. The table next to me are discussing the merits of another sandwich shop I don't catch the name of, which the older man has decided has gone downhill. 'I was there the other day and I couldn't finish it', he says.

7   Later, I post all the pictures of my walk to Instagram without any captions. As I suspected, all the North Circular diaspora come out the woodwork with heart-eye emojis.

So much nostalgia from all of this.

I used to find this so depressing when I lived there but now that I live in another country I miss it hugely!

This is so nostalgic for me! Spent half my childhood on the North Circular.

The drive from Hounslow through North Circ on your way to an Asian wedding is rather bleak, yes.

The guy who runs Greek Pita (just around the corner) drove me and my daughter home when we came in for a quick takeaway once, because it was pissing down. Love the hospitality of the restaurants around here, not experienced it anywhere else in London.

Truly an incredibly desolate land.

North Circ is life. All of my family childhood memories were facilitated by my dad driving through this world. I hated it at the time, but I am the North Circular.

8   If purgatory exists, it would look exactly like this:

9   The houses that line the North Circular and form the city's frontier against the road are among the worst housing in London. I remember walking past condemned houses on my way to school every day, which had all been compulsorily purchased by the council in the 1970s and had simply lain empty, waiting for the road widening that didn't come. They had overgrown with snaking vines, like the city was trying to reclaim them from the road. Squatters would sometimes take them over, but I vaguely recall that after a murder in one of the houses most of them were moved out. I used to take advantage of the lack of surveillance to have a piss in their front gardens.

I'm reminded of Niloufar Haidari's description of Neasden, bisected by the North Circular, in a 2019 *Vice* article: 'The peculiar strangeness of Neasden is in its nothingness.' This road is nowhere. It does not exist in an area of London but is a singularity unto which the city is asymptotic. It is a loading screen for something else. Its transience is well captured in Ben Judah's otherwise reductive book *This Is London* (2016), where the North Circular plays host to doss houses for Romanian builders. I don't buy Judah's cynicism that everyone here hates one another, but there is no point romanticising it, either. I can't imagine a worse place to live in London.

Judah calls the North Circular our 'unwalkable city wall', but I have walked it. It is only when walking that you can see the neglect close-up. Drains clogged with algae, the fronts and sides of houses covered in a brown film of exhaust pollution, numbers scrawled on the front with graffiti. One house proudly states its address as 503 North Circular Road, which seems to me as improbable an address as 123 Fake St. The houses here have the same dead quality all border towns do. This is an inhospitable place for a walker: trying to hear yourself over the roar, dodging cyclists, left without cover from the elements. It is at its best experienced in a moving vehicle, staring through a window, with the knowledge that you will soon no longer be on it.

10 I wait 20 minutes for a 112 in the cold, eyes fixed on the horizon: there is no one else to flag it down if I miss it. It's only once I'm on the bus again that I finally feel at ease.

An alternate version of this essay was first published in Vittles.

THE UTOPIAN FOOD OF THE NORTH CIRCULAR ROAD

My dad, who is a landscape gardener, used to tell me that there was an immediate difference between doing jobs inside the North Circular Road versus outside of it. He described it almost like a threshold, a gateway into another version of London – inside, people tended to acquiesce more to quotes and advice; outside of it, people were more questioning, a little tighter. Not that they were less rich, necessarily, just that they had more interest in keeping hold of their money. It got to the point where he would generally refuse to do any gardens on the wrong side of the A406.

I suspect that this mentality amplifies the qualities of restaurants on the other side of the border. Most have the most conservative elements of the suburbs, throwbacks to something, or somewhere, or some time; Italian restaurants called Al Fresco, Cypriot tavernas by the New River covered in bougainvillaea, menus that remain untouched by decades of trends that have reformed London's dining scene further down the road. But increasingly I see restaurants ahead of the curve, images of what the casual dining sector will look like in ten years' time, when the geographic centre finally cottons on: Cypriot sandwich and soup shops, places that only serve multiple versions of vada pav, vans that sell kokorec outside dilapidated pubs, samosas and jalebi so piping hot you need to bathe your tongue in lassi to soothe third-degree burns. These places grow like unexpected weeds in the manicured garden of the suburbs, and soon they will run riot.

But what of the threshold itself? Walk around the North Circular, or take a bus, and you will find a heterogeneous jumble of things that feel like they cannot exist anywhere else in London, outcasts whose only uniting logic is that they happen to be on the same stretch of road: a neon-bathed Sri Lankan bar next to an assembly hall for a Christian sect, next to a Gujarati mithai shop. The food businesses on the North Circular are only the strangest, most boring food businesses in the city because every business on the North Circular is strange and boring, specialists which cannot find a space within the city proper. They have had to make do, and indeed thrive, with being nowhere.

JAANEMAN SWEET CENTRE

The first time I went to New York I picked up a copy of the food magazine *Lucky Peach* at random, only to see an article about Jaaneman Sweet Centre, a short walk from my house. I'd never paid that much attention to it because it was just another North Circular business, a place where I would occasionally get three-for-one samosas with green chutney for a snack. But here was someone saying it was special. It was the first time I'd seen something on the North Circular described as a destination, rather than something to pass through.

I should have paid more attention because Nalim Bapodra, owner of Jaaneman Sweet Centre, has spent the last 33 years there mastering the art of mithai. Mithai is just the umbrella name for Indian sweets, but what Jaaneman does best is dense fudge-like barfi made using a simple combination of milk, milk powder and sugar syrup. Every batch is made by Bapodra, who is always there: the store is absolutely stacked early on in the week, but as the days go on, the most popular flavours – chocolate, pistachio and almond in particular – sell out, so try to get there early. If you go and look unsure, Bapodra will encourage you to sample, sometimes forcing whole pieces on you, to the extent that by the time you've bought them you might no longer be in the mood for any more.

ACE CAFE

This bikers' cafe is the North Circular's version of a mirage, a whole American-style diner in chequered black and white, plonked on the hard edge of the Park Royal industrial estate. It seems at once entirely incongruous with its surroundings and yet utterly London: sausage sandwiches, tea and moussaka, confused Italian labourers ordering cappuccinos that would make their mothers weep, rockabilly on the jukebox. The Ace is practically a part of the road: it started life as a transport cafe for the newly built North

Circ and soon became a bikers' hang-out (apparently, in its heyday, bikers used to put songs on and try to race down to Hanger Lane and back before the track had finished). Today, it is prosaic by day, when it serves burgers, sandwiches and fry-ups, but it comes alive again with rockabilly dances, where every evening it's 1950 again.

CASPIAN LOUNGE

While London's first Persian restaurants were fairly grand places, grill and stew restaurants that marketed themselves as elevated versions of the Turkish ocakbasi, the last few years have seen more casual cafes open based around the sandwich and pizza shops of Tehran, all located in areas with big Iranian populations like Ealing and Finchley (for some reason, though they are unrelated to each other, they all have the same menu and the word 'Caspian' in the name). Caspian Lounge is located on a road perched above the roar of the North Circular and advertised as a burger joint, but you should stick to subs filled with tongue and brain, and pizzas topped with Iranian sausage and half the contents of a fridge.

GÖKYÜZÜ

A pioneer of the 'go big or go home' attitude that epitomises London's Turkish and Kurdish grill scene, Gökyüzü started off life as the most sleek of the Green Lanes restaurants and has rapidly expanded to become something of a kebab empire, its name becoming a byword for the generosity of a mixed grill simply too big for one person to finish. There are now four branches, including two on the North Circular itself, the flagship being the Chingford branch which is located in front of a Muslim cemetery and next to the Jurassic Falls dinosaur-themed adventure golf course. It is futile to describe the food: it is exactly like every ocakbaşı in London except built on a slightly larger scale.

REINDEER CAFE

Wing Yip Cricklewood is not technically on the North Circular, but it's an honorary North Circ business because of its proximity, and because of its inaccessibility except via the A406. Its layered pagoda lends it the artifice of Chinatown and houses a huge supermarket and two restaurants, one a big-occasion dim sum parlour, and the other a kind of dai pai dong cafe that might be found in the analogous interstices of Hong Kong. This is Reindeer Cafe. Most of the dishes here are better than their Chinatown equivalents (the clarity of an excellent won ton soup, the wok char on a plate of beef brisket ho fun), but it's also a chance to grab some of the more unfashionable HK dishes, like cha chaan teng-style macaroni breakfasts with ham or sausage, or the simple textural pleasure of a bowl of curry soup filled with fish balls, pork rinds and turnip.

Anything to declare? No. Of course not! The trick is to pretend you aren't life-threateningly out of breath from lugging 30 kilos of buried food on the brisk trek from aeroplane seat to passport control. You bless God and catch your breath on the travelators when they show up, paddling furiously like a duck while racing other passengers to passport control. You set your face like cold pap because this hopefully retains the dregs of your dignity while you skate precariously between legality and illegality. By the time you stand an hour in Heathrow's snaking queue to the immigration booth, where sweat is slithering down under your clothes, your legs are trembling with exhaustion and stress. You tell yourself you have an hour or two before you defrost and fall to pieces. You are almost at the other side, where everything will be tipped into the freezer and you can exhale and fall into a bed, any bed. There are all kinds of stories you recount to yourself as the hand-luggage strap finally gives way and you see an immigration officer swearing under his breath at the numbers coming through to be processed. You think of how the price of an economy ticket has earned you a not-so-warm welcome, has earned your bags and your buried Nigerian comestibles diplomatic immunity. You've learnt not to smile because defiance works, convincing customs officers you have nothing to hide.

On your way out, one officer asks you to step aside and open your bags for a search. You don't care at this stage because you know the guys at this last point are not committed diggers. They are too distracted. Plantains are at the bottom of the Bermuda Triangle, wrapped in three different cellophane bags. None of the stories you tell yourself to justify smuggling in food care about things like dignity and posture. This is how you carry home with you. The end justifies the means and you are already at your destination *in your mind*, frying up your plantains and loading them on a plate alongside steamed Basmati rice and stew. If you are caught and all your precious food is seized, binned, burned ... and you are thoroughly humiliated, you know you will break down and cry in the car, because it is never just about the food you tried to smuggle in via Heathrow.

yemisi aribisala

Two foods in particular – mangoes and plantains – are smuggled into London every day, for reasons of discrepancy in taste after these products have travelled two thousand kilometres: I have never tasted a mango, anywhere in the world, that compares to a Nigerian mango. My hand is on my heart as I say this. When you park your car under the Falomo bridge on Lagos Island to buy a bunch of plantains from any of the women who are setting up night stalls, the first impression you get of the plantains offered for sale is their weightiness, the tautness of plantain flesh pressing against skin, the reddish sunburn that suggests the plantains ripened on the tree. Plantains displayed on the pavement in front of Bekem's Food Store in North London, or delivered by our Ghanaian middle-woman from Luton (who retails 'African food' alongside Ivorian attiéké, habaneros, okros and yams), or bought for a pound per plantain on amazon.co.uk, don't taste the same as those bought in Lagos. They just don't.

This isn't about having a patriotic palate. Before anything else, plantains have a universal allure. I have never met one person in all my life who dislikes plantains. I am sure I know one or two people who don't like bananas. But plantains harvested at the perfect time, fried, steamed, and added to a pot of black-eyed beans near the end of cooking, or profligately sunk into ogbono soup, or fried and dipped into melted chocolate? Never.

Plantains, in their starchy, sweet, hot softness, can be intoxicating. My father's dinner when I lived at home, almost every single night, was fried plantains eaten with some stewed beef or chicken. The plantains were deep-fried in groundnut oil until brown in parts, golden in others, then kept in a food flask so that by his arrival home they were perspiring, moist and slouched seductively in the flask's stainless-steel interior, oozing the distinct fragrance of treacly enticement counterbalanced by aromatics of peppery red stew. I'm not sure who had the temerity to begin stealing, with filthy fingers, pieces of plantain from the flask of food. The stealing quickly became contagious, each child daily taking out one or two pieces of fried plantain from the flask, until one day he came back and there were perhaps three or four pieces of fried plantain left. He roared at us in our beds while we pretended to be groggy with sleep, warning us of all kinds of torture if he ever returned and found his food flask tampered with again.

A Nigerian journalist who used to edit my food writing at the Nigerian newspaper *234Next* once annotated my submitted article with the words:

I love fried plantains, dodo. My late father used to call it 'the food of the gods'. It is one of the major deficiencies of South Africa and to my mind, of South Africans, that they do not know what plantain is and they have made no efforts to improve on their ignorance. When I come to Lagos as I do every month for work, I have to make an effort to control my dodo intake in my own self interest.

There is no doubt a fried-plantain itch that stretches from the African continent to the Caribbean islands. The itch that counts is the national one – the Nigerian one. We have friends in the Western Cape in South Africa who smuggle plantains from Nigeria through Johannesburg airport customs by pretending they need wheelchairs. They sit gingerly on the plantains till customs are cleared. At departure in Nigeria, a tip to the customs officers makes carrying plantains, fermented locust beans or human heads on board painless. In Joburg's OR Tambo Airport, you can tip the officers off by dropping 20 South African rand into a designated dustbin after the customs checkpoint. And sometimes those same friends (of plantain and wheelchair fame) carry bursting bags of Western Cape pomo the other way, to Nigeria. Yes, there is definitely plenty of pomo in Nigeria, but when a cow hasn't been led from one end of Nigeria to another for grazing by gun-toting herdsmen, it is amazing how thick and luscious its hide is. The taste of long treks and stress is absent from South African meat and, for migrants with the taste of exodus still under their tongues, South African pomo is gourmet pomo.

Around Christmas 2021, I am having a conversation by email with the American author John Birdsall, about his piece on Julián Garcia, an asylum seeker from Mexico who endured inhumane abuse and food deprivation at a facility for hopeful immigrants to the US:

My goodness, this is something so emotionally high-strung, people weep tears over it. And this is what I mean when I tell you that superiority or regard is not distinguished by gilded, air-conditioned rooms where you are presented with theatrically arranged plates of food. In my opinion, you know true regard, by indignities that people are willing to endure over the subject matter. Over the food is what I mean. Obviously there is an appropriate way that people will behave in public in the context of food...or perhaps there isn't when we are talking about fire on your tail migration and food...

I can barely keep my mind on the subject matter, my thinking hijacked by psychogenic gathering of food into shopping baskets. It is force of habit, this daily tabulation of what's eaten and what's left, that can never be shut down for inordinate fear of not getting my children what they need (they are far from malnourished). Migrant anxiety about ferrying food through ports of entry feels like life and death, no matter how many times I reassure myself I can now buy plantains and yams at Golders Green.

Heathrow is the default port of entry for soft bootlegging of gourmet Nigerian food. (My use of the word 'gourmet' is deliberate because there are so many Nigerian foods that you can buy in London.) Yet as I pointed out before, buying them here creates an emotional crisis that you are ashamed to talk about, because they-don't-taste-like-the-real-thing. It isn't bluster, it is pain. *We are safe, fed, warm*, SAFE ... until something about Julián Garcia triggers memories of landing after a ten-hour flight, legs cramped from giving up room for a massive fruitcake dripping rum that I baked and couldn't leave behind in the Western Cape. This sits alongside a few thousand rands' worth of biltong and dried boerewors, my Ijebu fufu, which has no strong aroma of fermenting cassava and is therefore priceless, and my precious dried Cameroonian peppers.

How do you weigh the personal crisis of nostalgic hunger against a pragmatic obligation to protect the ecosystem of the country you are travelling to? Do the right thing where it concerns emotions versus compliance with food importation policies. I mean, how does the Nigerian man on a London street convince himself that the moral thing to do is *not* put five kilos of fermented locust beans in his underwear bag? I'm talking about morality because you can't illegally carry food across borders unless you are aware the particular food is banned, and if you *are* aware, then all of the tipping and corrupting officials at both ends of the journey require more than a bit of extra cash, something that migrants don't typically have a lot of. I want to say that the access to certain food that we force by any means possible is a panacea to the stress of transition. We aren't allowed to complain – those of us who know our privilege in buying plane tickets willingly push the head of trauma down. It is contemptible to whine when people are hanging on to aeroplane wings to gain a new life. What you do is eat, and insist on eating, and panic over the integrity of plantains.

It might be that the thwarting of systems gives many migrants a yearned-for sense of power in a place where they have to work incredibly hard at fashioning a new life. The corollary to needing to leave a place and go to another – leaving everything you've known all your life and wholeheartedly selling the past, with the possibility of never again seeing friends and family members, burning many bridges with the petrol of bitter tears – might be the phenomenon of smuggling seeds (ogbono, ose Nsukka, grains of paradise, selim peppers, little alligators), which is essential to this process of migration and symbolic of hope. If you can make something grow when you land, then you've claimed a plot of *terra firma*. Pepper seeds in a pot of soil on a windowsill facing France will quickly sprout heat and soothe heartache.

Heathrow Airport has a way of enhancing lostness. You know this
isn't intentional. The building means to say welcome, but ceilings
fly above, the floors move under your feet, advertisement boards
flash past, indiscernible words boom and scramble out of the airport
announcement system, and you are reduced to a disquieting clutch-
ing of bags. You feel like the British barn swallow that has migrated
thousands of miles, overwintering in South Africa, after stopping to
fatten up in Ebbaken, Cross River State Nigeria ... traveling 200 miles
a day over deserts and oceans, facing death by storms and hunger,
with no guarantee of making its destination, only to be chased off
by bird scarers at Heathrow.

A friend is returning from Nigeria after a few days. When I ask
casually over WhatsApp what he is bringing back, the list is long:
snails, pomo, kilishi, asun. That's how important food from home
is. And fried plantains will always be at the top of the list of Nigerian
immigrant food pining. 'Dodo', cut in long, tapering, chip-like strips
because my fried plantains need to have both soft and crunchy parts
to them, which means they have to be fat in some parts and thin in
others. They are fried in coconut oil, sprinkled with cinnamon, not
salt. Served scalding hot, eaten scalding hot.
    I preferably eat as I fry.

THE END(S)

Every city looks the same when entering by train. It could be Tokyo, Rome, or London, but no matter what, you will enter along a line that contains the city's detritus: warehouses, light industry, graffiti. It's a truthful way of coming into a city because you get to experience its ugliest, most unvarnished spaces first – Rome's Trevi fountain comes as an even more pleasant surprise when you've experienced a trip through eight miles of Plutonian Lazio hinterland.

Entering via the airport, however, is always a well-manicured lie. Often you don't even enter the city; in the case of London, you will most likely be dumped somewhere close to a Home Counties industrial estate and greeted by a 'Welcome to London' banner featuring one of the Queen's Guard looking solemn. But from the airport, going in by car, by train, by bus, you get – even just for a brief second – to experience the London known by Londoners themselves, before tourist London kicks in: vast retail parks, car dealerships, concrete stretches of A-road, faceless offices, new-builds under construction. And while 99% of people will wait until the buildings get taller, the horizon disappears, and the Shard turns from a distant beacon into a Mordorian monolith, there is a 1% who might want to get out and eat.

If you come in via Heathrow, the choices are obvious: the entirety of Hounslow; Southall; the Tetote custard bun. But if you come in from Gatwick, you will have the opportunity to experience South London's isolated dead zones, areas which are harder to reach from central London than Paris, and are often perceived as blank spaces on the map by Londoners for whom Eltham or Erith are just names they see on the front of buses. But this is London: there is always life here. In south-South London, you may be able to find the city's most extraordinary jerk cooking, an isolated Nigerian community vaster than Peckham's, or the biggest concentration of Koreans in Europe, amid the most bureaucratic architecture the city has to offer: places which always seem to be an hour from anywhere and therefore get to keep all their secrets in peace, untroubled by the rest of London. Sometimes it's worth getting off.

If you come in via Stansted, however, God help you.

CHICK & BEERS

The way many Londoners speak of New Malden is similar to the patronising way the British talk about Ireland: they know it's close, and they constantly chide themselves for not visiting, but they never actually go. This means things which might get a rave broadsheet review, a visit from ten of London's most insufferable influencers, and then become a citywide chain, just … get left alone, being excellent. Chick & Beers does this with the subgenre of Korean fried chicken, now a mainstay on central London menus and food halls (Korean or otherwise) despite no version being anywhere near to the one you get here, tucked away under a slab of anonymous office block. It's the ganjang (soy) version that is worth the journey, the batter tasting like the honey cornflake cakes that every primary school child has attempted to make, yet saved from overwhelming sugariness by the pungency of garlic and crisped onion, the batter pitched somewhere between craggy and Jeff Koons' hyper-gloss.

TASTY JERK

The most suspense-filled walk in the city is the one along Whitehorse Road, in Selhurst Park's shadow, where the smoke from Tasty Jerk's extraction starts to become unignorable. Bite into a piece of jerk pork and you can taste the long, careful cooking of the meat, the complexity of the marinade, the sting of Scotch bonnets, the breakdown of connective tissue, the fat rendering and crisping – soft as chicharron and sweeter and more delicious than any siu yuk. You can taste decades' worth of seasoning on those three blackened drums; notes of char, soot, black bile and petroleum in the smoke that rushes your nose and throat at first bite. You're not just tasting cooking but craftsmanship – heritage that should be protected by UNESCO –

tracing a lineage running back to the First Men, who decided that, with enough wood and space, they could cook a whole pig on a spit. And that's just the pork. Eating the chicken, with diabolically hot pepper sauce seeping into every bone and crevice, on a bench somewhere in Thornton Heath, is one of the top three things you're allowed to legally do in public in London.

LALE RESTAURANT

It's just about common knowledge that much of the best Greek (in fact, Cypriot) cooking can be found in Palmers Green, and is funnelled across North London in a Zone 4 arc of spit, fire and souvlaki. But what is less well-known is that there is another community of Cypriots around Bexley, Eltham and Welling, possibly due to the presence of Christ the Saviour Orthodox Church in Welling (although it's unclear which came first, the church or the people). Either way, here suburban Italian restaurants are interspersed with genuine tavernas and takeaways – like Lale, run by two brothers who have been serving Turkish-Cypriot food to the citizens of Eltham for over 30 years. The thing to get here is the doner, Cypriot-style – dense and lean, hand-cut into thick shards – along with the adana, and the seftali, a caul fat-wrapped kebab roughly the size and structure of a sausage in batter. Oh, and garlic sauce. Lots of garlic sauce.

N'FES

At some point in the mid-2010s London developed a grits obsession, possibly sparked by the opening of The Lockhart in Marylebone. But without the context, without any soul, the dish was replicated and watered down, served as a facsimile of the original to people who'd never eaten it before. There *is* one community in London that eats something like grits, and that is the Turkish one, where kuymak – a rich breakfast dish of cornmeal, water, butter and cheese – is still eaten by those who come from Turkey's northern Black Sea coast. Still, given most Turkish people in London are either from the south or from Istanbul, it's rare –

except, inexplicably, in Welling, at a cafe next to a TFC called N'fes, where you can find it, stretching in great reams like dense taffy in an infinite cheese pull, alongside homely dishes of the day and tantuni. It comes with bread in a little skillet, and you will need a long cycle around South London's many hills to sweat it all out.

KOREDE'S AFRICOAL

Mention Erith to a Londoner and you will get a few stock responses. 'Where?' might be one. 'Isn't that in Gondor?' is another. Just as Lena Dunham falls asleep and wakes up on Brighton Beach in *Girls*, a Londoner might, in a drunken stupor, mistakenly take the night bus all the way to Erith, where the buildings melt away and the mighty Thames looks like a sea separating Kent and Essex. Sometimes it's worth riding buses to their termini – Erith feels spiritually like Kent, but it also has one of the biggest Nigerian communities in the UK, and an unlikely restaurant scene. At K'S SPICE, you'll find uncles and aunties expertly moulding glossy balls of pounded yam, the colour of unhewn marble, into improvised scoops for Yoruba soups with more sprezzatura than any Italian. At Korede's Africoal, a short walk away, you can find great suya – the great Hausa contribution to barbecue culture, where the creamy, lanolin-tinged fat cap on a perfectly grilled rack of lamb ribs mixes deliriously with homemade yaji. Perhaps Erith is too far away and not concentrated enough to be a restaurant destination (*yet*), but it is a reminder that London is still London right up until the ends, and the ends of the ends.

CONTRIBUTORS

NABIL AL-KINANI, by day, is a built-environment professional with a keen interest in urbanism, cultural place-making, sustainable development and community cohesion. By night, he is a cultural producer that uses creative practice to deliver change-making projects that draw focus on the relationship between space and stories. His areas of expertise lie in people and places, through an anthropological lens.

YEMISI ARIBISALA is a Nigerian-born writer and visual artist best known for her thematic use of food writing as an entry point to understanding Nigerian culture and society. She lives and paints in London.

PETER ARKLEY BLOXHAM is a writer and photographer from London. He completed an MA in creative writing from the University of East Anglia in 2015 and is currently working on an untitled project that combines flash fiction with photography. He enjoys capturing scenes in everyday environments that suggest stories about ordinary people and their lives.

SAMEH ASAMI is the owner of Levant Book Cafe.

SANA BADRI is a British-Tunisian artist born in Tunis. Raised and living in London, she is an educator first, teaching at a high school in Inner London. Sana borrows from social practices to explore the communities she is embedded in through photography. Her motivation to create images is primarily to build and maintain meaningful connections with her subjects, and foster a visual dialogue that speaks to those inside those communities.

BARCLAY BRAM is an anthropologist in London. His Dad is Polish.

STEPHEN BURANYI is a writer on politics and the history of science whose work appears in the *Guardian* and *The New York Times*. He lives in London.

ZOË CAVE has a background in public sociology, is currently chief curator of the Open House Festival and a consultant at Frame Projects. She's a die-hard Portra 400 fan and snaps bodies, buildings, and other bits.

ADITYA CHAKRABORTTY is senior economics commentator for the *Guardian*, where he writes a regular column and reports from around Britain and the world. In December 2017, he won the British Journalism Award for Comment Journalist of the year. His work has also won a Social Policy Association award, a Harold Wincott prize for Business Journalism and he has also been on numerous years a finalist for an Orwell Prize for journalism. Aditya is now working on his first book, which is about Edmonton and London, and is to be published by Allen Lane / Penguin.

JEREMY CORBYN is the MP for Islington North.

LEAH COWAN is an editor and writer; her first book *Border Nation: A Story of Migration* was published in 2021 by Pluto Press. She writes and speaks on race, gender, and state violence. She works at Project 17, an advice centre that supports families with No Recourse to Public Funds (NRPF) who are facing homelessness. Her newsletter *The Sipping News*, a journey into cocktail-making and drinking with a focus on queer and trans people of colour's history and ingredient provenance, is forthcoming.

ZAIN DADA is a writer and cultural producer. He is the co-founder of Khidr Collective Zine – a zine platforming the work of British Muslims.

Zain's directing credits include 2019 Outspoken Prize-winning short visual poem, *The Moon Is A Meme* and 2020 Outspoken Prize-nominated animation short, *Otherstani*. Zain is a Winston Churchill Fellow after publishing his research on the future of community arts. Zain wrote his first play, *Blue Mist*, as part of Soho Theatre Writers Lab 19/20 and Royal Court's Introduction to Playwriting 19/20. His first writing credit, *Emily (GLITCHED) In Paris* was for The Royal Court Theatre's *Living Newspaper* series in March 2021.

ELAINEA EMMOTT is a portrait, food photographer, food writer and chef/home cook. She cooked for Heston Blumenthal on TV show *Crazy Delicious* and now cooks food from her heritage, inventively making ingredients shine on the plate, feasting with the eyes and feeding the bellies using staple ingredients via supper clubs and online workshops in London with her son.

MELEK ERDAL is an Istanbul-born Kurdish chef and writer who grew up in North and East London. She opened her own cafe in 2013, inspired by the food of her roots and upbringing, and has since moved onto teaching and writing about food, culture and identity, running masterclasses, pop-ups and telling food stories through her documentary videos, essays and community-focused food activism. She is an advocate for food as a resilient form of connection and preserving identity and history and her most recent work has been with food sustainability charities Made in Hackney and the Felix Project, along with regular appearances on BBC Radio 4's *The Kitchen Cabinet*.

JESS FAGIN is an anthropologist from London who researches themes of identity and belonging in the production of British meat. She is completing a PhD at the University of Exeter on the narrative constructions of nationhood and racialisation in British sheep slaughterhouses, and has an MA in the Anthropology of Food from SOAS, London. She has had work published in *Food and Landscape* (2017), *Offal: Rejected and Reclaimed Food* (2016), and *Vittles*.

MALCOLM GLOVER'S work is primarily driven by a documentary sensibility. He is interested in how individuals interact with their environment and with each other. He loves quirks of human nature and this is reflected in the images he takes which are a celebration of shared experience and community. He is an established photographic artist, whose work has been published and exhibited both internationally and throughout the UK. His work has been purchased for public and private collections.

HARK1KARAN is a community photographer hailing from South London. He captures the Punjabi and Sikh communities to which he belongs, as well as various aspects of London culture. 'For me, photography is an extension of seva, a Sikh practice of selfless service. My process is about giving back and storytelling.'

PHINEAS HARPER is an architecture critic. They are chief executive of Open City and make mobiles.

VIRGINIA HARTLEY is writing a novel.

OWEN HATHERLEY writes on culture and politics for various publications. He is the author of many books, including *Militant Modernism* (Zero, 2009) *Landscapes of Communism* (Penguin, 2015) and *Red Metropolis* (Repeater, 2020). His most recent books are a collection of essays, *Clean Living Under Difficult Circumstances* (Verso, 2021), and *Modern Buildings in Britain* (Penguin, 2022).

He is a commissioning editor at Jacobin, the editor of *The Alternative Guide to the London Boroughs* (Open City, 2020), and the culture editor of *Tribune*.

ANNA HODGSON and HARRY DARBY collaborate across the fields of illustration, design, pottery and filmmaking.

JENNY LAU is a British Chinese writer and community organiser operating in ESEA spaces. Her platform *Celestial Peach* tells stories about Chinese food and the people and culture behind it. She is currently slowly releasing her self-published essay series *An A–Z Of Chinese Food*.

SIRUI MA is a photographer based in London. Born in Beijing and raised between there, New York City and London, Ma's work often explores multicultural identities, seeing the world around her through the lens of her own experience.

YVONNE MAXWELL is a Saint Lucian-Nigerian documentary photographer and writer whose work covers stories on migration, social justice, culture, food and identity of the Black communities within the UK and across the wider Black diaspora. Her work has been published in *Vittles*, *Resy*, *Belly Full: Caribbean Food in the UK* and *Plantain Papers*, among others.

REBECCA MAY JOHNSON is a writer. Her first book, *Small Fires, An Epic in the Kitchen*, was published by Pushkin Press in August 2022. She earned a PhD in Contemporary German Literature from UCL for her study of Barbara Köhler's reworking of the *Odyssey*, *Niemands Frau*. She likes dancing, cooking, and staring at the ground on her allotment. She dreams of canteens.

MAX MIECHOWSKI is a British photographer based in London. His projects, which centre on themes of community and connection, have been exhibited widely in places such as Paris Photo Fair, Photo London, Peckham 24 and The Taylor Wessing Photographic Portrait Prize at the National Portrait Gallery.

CARLA MONTEMAYOR has been a Londoner for nearly 15 years. She was born and raised in Manila, Philippines and is a first-generation immigrant. She works as a communications specialist in the migration sector and writes creative non-fiction around the themes of migration, belonging and erased histories. She received a London Writers Award in 2021 and was shortlisted for the Specimen Prize (2021) and the Life Writing Prize (2020). She was nominated for a Pushcart Prize in 2022 by *Hinterland Magazine* for *The Shapeshifters*, a piece about the storytelling tradition among women in her family. She is working on a memoir about love, grief and home.

ZARINA MUHAMMAD (b.1994, London) is a writer and an art critic at *The White Pube*. She writes about exhibitions, institutions, food and other little bits in between. Cancer sun/aries moon/sagittarius ascendant. 'Intellectual charlatan', 'sociopathic pseudo-critic', leading proponent of 'The Philosophy of the Warm Tummy' and cowboy in the art world. *thewhitepube.com* / *@thewhitepube*

JONATHAN NUNN is a food and city writer. He is also the founder and co-editor of *Vittles*, an online newsletter dedicated to food culture. *London Feeds Itself* is his first book as editor and writer.

ROSA NUSSBAUM is the founder of Studio Christopher Victor, a graphic design practice specialising in book design and production.

SANTIAGO PELUFFO SONEYRA is a London-based Latin American journalist, writer and activist. His professional experience spans over 15 years, after a career as a reporter and editor for several print and online media and international news agencies in Latin America, Europe and the UK. He is the co-author of two anthologies of short stories by Latin American writers in London, *Visitantes* (2019), as well as playwright for *Point of No Return* (2022), as well as the co-director at Latin Elephant charity. Twitter/Instagram: @santuli23

CLAUDIA RODEN is a food writer. Born in Egypt and drawn to the subject of food through a desire to evoke her own lost heritage, she has written about the cuisines of the Middle East, North Africa, the Mediterranean, Italy and Spain, and about Jewish food.

SHAHED SALEEM is the founder of East End architecture practice Makespace. His research and practice interests are in the architecture of migrant communities, and their relationship to heritage, belonging and nationhood. His book, *The British Mosque*, was published by Historic England in 2018, and he co-curated the V&A Pavilion at the Venice Biennale 2021.

AMARDEEP SINGH DHILLON is a queer writer, bartender and organiser. He's a co-editor at *Red Pepper* magazine, programme coordinator at political festival The World Transformed and founding member of South London Bartenders Network. He tweets @amardeepsinghd

RUBY TANDOH is a writer who has contributed to the *New Yorker*, *Vittles*, *Taste*, *Eater* and *Elle*. She's the author of *Eat Up!* and *Cook As You Are*.

CIARAN THAPAR is an educator and author based in South London. He runs storytelling workshops for young people, and organisations that work with them, to tackle social exclusion in schools and communities. He writes stories about London, British multiculturalism and the arts, especially UK rap music. His debut book, *Cut Short*, was published by Penguin UK in 2021.

MIKE WILSON is Executive Director of Pembroke House in Walworth. Founded in 1885 in response to growing inner-city inequality, Pembroke House is one of London's original 'settlement houses' – part of a movement that inspired the architects of the modern welfare state. Today, Mike is working with partners to explore a new settlement model fit for the challenges of the 21st century.

DEE WOODS is a Fellow of the Royal Society of Arts, an award-winning food system leader and the co-founder of Granville Kitchen. A passionate knowledge broker, pollinator and weaver who advocates for good food for all and a just food system, her work meets at the nexus of human rights, food sovereignty, agroecology, community, policy, decolonial research, culture, climate and social justice.

ACKNOWLEDGEMENTS

For decades Londoners have been fed a lie – that the chronic cost of land in the capital is due to an ever-growing number who want to live and trade here. The London affordability crisis, most acute in the city centre, is (we have been told) the inevitable consequence of so many people wanting in. Average rents now high enough to gobble 80% of the city's post-tax median salary are (we have been told) our fault for wanting to live here in the first place.

The 2021 census has finally debunked this cynical myth. It turns out the population of central London, including the boroughs of Westminster, and Kensington and Chelsea, has been falling even as their property prices climb higher than ever. This scandal illustrates how far the London land market has degenerated from any common-sense idea of supply-and-demand and offers the best proof yet that the post-2008 property rush has been anti-urban, hollowing out London's core.

But Open City has never been interested in London as a grand centre surrounded by concentric bands of unaffordability. We believe in interrogating the whole city – in our Open House Festival, our education programmes and our publishing. This book, in its poignant and sassy chapters, celebrates that bigger London – way beyond the overheated core – a London that is anything but hollow. *London Feeds Itself* is gusty, vivacious and important: the perfect evidence that land prices are the worst measure imaginable for what makes a good place to live, work – and eat.

I am enormously grateful to the many brilliant photographers, writers and illustrators whose sumptuous contributions form the main courses of this book. In particular to Rosa Nussbaum whose design makes it a feast for the eyes and to Jonathan Nunn whose wit, commissions and editing are as delicious and as nourishing as the food – and the London – he describes.

Phineas Harper, Open City

CREDITS

SUPPORTERS

STAFF

Hafsa Adan, Hilary Ip-Bowen, Adrianna Carroll-Battaglino, Alistair Cartwright, Zoë Cave, Sahiba Chadha, Rachel Copel, Marcela Escobar, Siân Evey-Arli, Chris Fisher, Merlin Fulcher, Karl Gent, Nadine Hammad, Phineas Harper, Rhea Martin, Siraaj Mitha, Elliot Nash, Sarah Phillips, Simon Vickery, Elis Shin, Matea Vlaskalic, Poppy Waring

TOUR GUIDES

Mike Althorpe, Lachlan Anderson-Frank, Maggie Baddeley, Cameron Bray, Nick Edwards, David Garrard, Aidan Hall, Marianna Janowicz, Paul Lincoln, Eleanor Marshall, Benedict O'Looney, Rosalind Peebles, Grant Smith, Jon Wright, Billy Reading, Jessica Barker-Wren, Francis Pugh, Martin Scholar, Alison Rae, Jack Chesher, Sarah Jackson, Joseph Granata, Áine Grace, Rosamund Lily West, Siufan Adey, Noel Wright

SPECIAL THANKS

Tim Craft, Caz Facey, Rob Fiehn, Paul Gorman, Brian Hand, Lauren Healey, Ben James, Madeleine Kessler, Leo Pollak, Catherine Slessor, Manijeh Verghese, Ellis Woodman, Museum of London, Ramadan Tent Project, Sonny Malhotra

OPEN HOUSE FESTIVAL HEADLINE SPONSOR

Rightmove

OPEN CITY PRINCIPAL PARTNERS

Allford Hall Monaghan Morris
Derwent
London Property Alliance (WPA and CPA)
Rocket Properties
Clarion Housing Association
Foster + Partners
Hawkins\Brown
Trowers and Hamlins

OPEN CITY MEMBERS

Almacantar
Baylight Properties
Haworth Tompkins
Peter Barber Architects

PATRONS AND BEST FRIENDS

Ruth Allen, Christopher Attwood, Peter Barber, Patrick Bellew, Francis Botham, Patricia Brotherston, Paul Carpenter, Paul Carter, Martin Collins, John Curran, Claire Curtice, Anne-Marie Duchet, Peter Ellement, Maria Fitzgerald, Sara Habanananda, Meg Harper, Michael Johns, Crispin Kelly, Faaiza Lali, Alan Leibowitz, Chai Hong Lim, Janet Lowe, Andrew McManus, Michael Melnick, Farshid Moussavi, David Neilson, Rosa Nussbaum, Susanne Rauprich, Ludwig Ray, Jane Raybould, Helen Sanders, Maria Smith, Tom Smith, Mark Stadler, Paul Steeples, John Story, Jonathan Thompson, Gerrie van Noord, Carolyn Wagstaff, Yi Wen, Kevin Whale

COLOPHON

EDITOR
Jonathan Nunn

COPY EDITOR
Sophie Whitehead

EDITORIAL ASSISTANT
Rachel Copel

ILLUSTRATIONS
Anna Hodgson and Harry Darby

GRAPHIC DESIGN
Studio Christopher Victor

TYPOGRAPHY
Arnhem (Fred Smeijers / TYPE BY, 2002)
and Forme Grotesque (Jeremy Johnson /
Colophon, 2022)

PRINTING
Printed in the UK by &Printed

First published in 2022 by Open City

Open City is a registered charity dedicated
to making cities more open, accessible
and equitable. Charity number 1072104.

www.open-city.org.uk

London feeds itself
Open City, Jonathan Nunn and authors 2022

ISBN 978-1-9160169-3-4

COVER
The photograph inserted into the cover is by either
Malcolm Glover, Hark1karan or Max Miechowski.
Images on the first and last pages are by Hark1karan.